European Monetary Integration: 1958–2002

This book describes the monetary integration of Europe from 1958 to 2002. The Community progression from the coordination of economic and monetary policies between Member States to the convergence of these policies is described and analysed.

European Monetary Integration: 1958–2002 discusses the technical operating procedures and institutional features of:

(1) The European Monetary Agreement of 1958 which introduced a European specificity to the Bretton Woods fixed, but adjustable, parity system of exchange rates;

(2) the first stage, 1971–73, of the modified Barre/Werner Plan to implement the Community commitment of 1969 to reach an economic and monetary union within a ten-year period;

(3) the joint European float of 1973–78 in the context of the collapse of the gold–dollar standard of the Bretton Woods international and monetary system;

(4) the European Monetary System of multiple exchange rate bands which for the first time, are based upon on numéraire totally unrelated to the US dollar or gold;

(5) the Maastricht road to reach an economic and monetary union with a single currency by 1999 with the introduction of Euro banknotes and coins by 2002. The monetary, budgetary and exchange rate regimes which are to be established at Stage III are explained in detail. A separate chapter analyses efforts to fulfil the original community goals of free movement of goods, services, capital and labour

European Monetary Integration: 1958–2002 is an excellent overview of the historical background and economic framework of European monetary integration.

Emmanuel Apel is Associate Professor of Economics at the University of Ottawa, Canada. He has extensive experience in teaching economics and has published widely on international finance and related subjects.

European Monetary Integration: 1958–2002

Emmanuel Apel

London and New York

First published 1998
by Routledge
11 New Fetter Lane, London EC4P 4EE

Simultaneously published in the USA and Canada
by Routledge
29 West 35th Street, New York, NY 10001

Typeset in Times by Florencetype Ltd, Stoodleigh, Devon
Printed and bound in Great Britain by Creative Print and
Design (Wales), Ebbw Vale

British Library Cataloguing in Publication Data
A catalogue record for this book is available from the British
Library

Library of Congress Cataloguing in Publication Data
Apel, Emmanuel
European monetary integration 1958–2002 / Emmanuel Apel.
Includes biographical references and index.
1. Monetary policy– European Economic Community
countries. 2. Monetary unions–European Economic
Community countries. 3. European Economic Community.
4. Monetary policy–European Union countries. 5. Monetary
unions–European Union countries. 6. European Monetary
System (Organisation) 7. European Union
countries–Economic integration. I. Title.
HG930.5.A86 1998
332. 4'94–dc21

ISBN 0–415–11432–2 (hbk)
ISBN 0–415–11433–0 (pbk)

To A.L. for her patience and encouragement, and F.F. for her quiet presence

Contents

Tables

Boxes

Preface

'L'Europe sera monétaire ou ne sera pas.' – Jean Monnet

'If monetary union goes ahead, the European Union will be divided.' – Malcolm Rifkind

This book essentially deals with the post-Second World War road travelled by Europe to reach an economic and monetary union, which – it seems – will be initially launched in 1999. Although that date is inscribed in the Maastricht Treaty, a postponement is possible within the legal framework of the Treaty. In the event that either France or Germany, or both, have not fulfilled the necessary conditions for participating in the monetary union, the European Union will not launch a monetary union without the participation of the two Member States that have been the motor of European integration in the post-war period.

To the North American observer, the European pursuit of a large, liberalized single market (a component of an economic union) with a population of 370 million persons (40 percent more than the US population) and a gross domestic product (GDP) almost equivalent to that of the US (1994 figures using purchasing power exchange rates) is 'optimizing' economic behaviour on the part of Europeans. To that same observer, the simultaneous pursuit of a monetary union (single currency with a single monetary policy) is not necessarily 'optimal' and is sometimes viewed as sheer economic folly, driven more by political arguments than by clear and convincing economic arguments. Each European country may have a different political agenda to fill by pushing for a monetary union. The putative French agenda is two-fold. First, a single currency with a single European central bank will dilute, once and for all, the Bundesbank's predominant influence on European monetary policy. Secondly, the Euro will be able ultimately to rival the US dollar as an international reserve asset, and by extension, Europe – with France at the centre! – will be able to rival the asymmetric influence of the US in international forums. The putative German agenda is that a single currency with a single European central bank will pave the way towards greater political integration, culminating in a 'federal' Europe, which will end, once and for all, any threat or perceived threat that Germany may pose to its neighbours.

This book is addressed to undergraduates who may have casually read or heard about some of the issues, events, institutions and monetary systems described in this text, but were never given the 'threads' to understand that there is some historical continuity to all this sound and fury in the construction of Europe over the past forty years. The European idea of a monetary union was not invented in 1989 by some energetic President of the European Commission named Jacques Delors. It has a long history and perhaps even some economic justification. The Introduction provides an overview of European political and economic integration since the post-war period. The other chapters are self-explanatory and follow, for the most part, a chronological order from 1958 to 2002. The reader should be warned that some parts of Chapters 4 and 5 deal with the future and are therefore tentative. Chapter 3 deals with the creation of a single European market, or what most people know as 'Europe 1992'. It is included in this book because the single market goal included provisions for financial integration and provided the impetus in the late 1980s to reconsider – after a long pause – the goal of a monetary union. Although the reader will soon notice the absence of the typical equations in economic textbooks, a few courses in undergraduate economic theory are prerequisites to fully appreciate – or to question – some of the details presented in this book.

The author is grateful and indebted to Michel Lelart of the CNRS (Paris and Orléans) for his valuable comments on the manuscript and for the many hours spent discussing the finer points of European economic and monetary integration. The author wishes to thank the Ministère de la Recherche et de l'Enseignement Supérieur (France) for its financial support – which allowed him to travel to Frankfurt, Brussels, Luxembourg and Paris – and Carmen Enseñat de Villalonga for her translations of Swedish texts. He is also grateful to the students at HEC (Jouy-en-Josas, France) who provided useful feedback on the manuscript. The author appreciates the help provided by the Delegations of the Commission of the European Communities in Ottawa and Paris to obtain official documents on short notice.

Ottawa, February 1997

Notice to reader

Although the term 'European Union' was officially introduced as of 1 November 1993, the term 'European Community(ies)' is still valid. In this text, no particular significance should be attributed to the interchangeable use of these two terms. In mid-1997, ECU1 $\cong$ US$1.15.

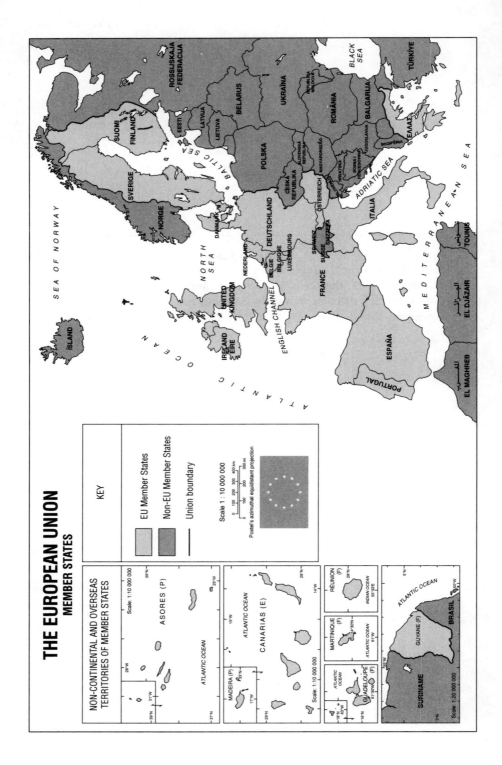

THE EUROPEAN UNION
MEMBER STATES

NON-CONTINENTAL AND OVERSEAS
TERRITORIES OF MEMBER STATES

Scale: 1:10 000 000

ASORES (P)

ATLANTIC OCEAN

28°W   25°W

39°N

31°W
39°N

MADEIRA (P)   17°W

37°N

Scale: 1:10 000 000

CANARIAS (E)

ATLANTIC OCEAN

15°W   14°W

28°N

29°N

RÉUNION (F)

INDIAN OCEAN   55°33'E   28°N

MARTINIQUE (F)

ATLANTIC OCEAN   61°W   14°30'N

GUADELOUPE (F)

ATLANTIC OCEAN   61°30'W   16°N

18°N
63°W

Scale: 1:20 000 000

SURINAME

GUYANE (F)

ATLANTIC OCEAN

55°W   55°W

5°N

BRASIL

60°W

KEY

EU Member States

Non-EU Member States

Union boundary

Scale 1 : 10 000 000

0   100   200   300   400 km
0   100   200   300 mi

Poster's azimuthal equidistant projection

SEA OF NORWAY

ISLAND

ATLANTIC OCEAN

NORTH SEA

ENGLISH CHANNEL

IRELAND EIRE

UNITED KINGDOM

NEDERLAND

BELGIQUE BELGIE

LUXEMBOURG

FRANCE

ESPAÑA

PORTUGAL

EL MAGHREB

EL DJÁZAIR

TOUNIS

MEDITERRANEAN SEA

ITALIA

SVIZZERA SUISSE SCHWEIZ

DEUTSCHLAND

DANMARK

SVERIGE

NORGE

SUOMI FINLAND

EESTI

LATVIJA

LIETUVA

BALTIC SEA

POLSKA

ČESKÁ REPUBLIKA

SLOVENSKÁ REPUBLIKA

ÖSTERREICH

MAGYARORSZÁG

SLOVENIJA

HRVATSKA

BOSNA HERCEGOVINA

JUGOSLAVIJA

SHQIPËRIA

ROMÂNIA

Republika Moldova

UKRAÏNA

BELARUS

ROSSIJSKAJA FEDERÁCIJA

BALGARIJA

ΕΛΛΑΣ

ADRIATIC SEA

BLACK SEA

TÜRKIYE

BASIC STATISTICS OF THE EUROPEAN UNION AND ITS 15 MEMBER STATES: COMPARISON BETWEEN THE EUROPEAN UNION (EUR15), THE UNITED STATES AND JAPAN

(1994 figures)

	AREA 1 000 km²	POPULATION million	POPULATION DENSITY inhabitants per km²	GROSS DOMESTIC PRODUCT AT MARKET PRICES* 1 000 million PPS[1]	PER CAPITA GROSS DOMETICS PRODUCT* PPS[1]
B	31	10.1	332	187.7	18 540
DK	43	5.2	121	97.5	18 810
D	357	81.4	228	1 459.3	17 890
EL	132	10.4	79	105.8	10 160
E	505	39.1	78	501.6	12 790
F	544	57.6	106	1 044.3	18 120
IRL	70	39.1	51	49.2	13 790
I	301	57.2	190	974.2	16 770
L	3	0.4	155	10.5	26 140
NL	41	15.4	373	260.5	16 900
A	84	8.0	96	148.2	18 480
P	92	9.9	107	111.0	11 220
FIN	337	5.1	15	77.5	15 210
S	450	8.8	20	141.7	16 140
UK	244	58.4	239	970.2	16 660
EUR 15	3 234	370.9	115	6 139.6	16 520
USA	9 373	260.8	28	6 232.5	23 890
JAPAN	378	124.7	330	2 409.6	19 278

[1] PPS = Purchasing power standard – a common unit representing an identical volume of goods and services for each country

[1] PPS = BFR 41.99; DM 2.31; DKR 9.89; PTA 129.76; FF 6.98; UKL 0.68; DRA 223.77; LIT 1 648.04; IRL 0.71; LFR 41.90; HFL 2.31; ESC 136.52; OS 15.67; SKR 10.76; FMK 6.95; USD 1.03; YEN 193.17

*Estimates

Source: European Commission services

Introduction: '... An ever closer union'[1]

EUROPE AND CHARLEMAGNE

When treating any serious topic dealing with Europe, it is customary for Continental writers to invoke the historical 'idea of Europe'. Invariably, reference is made to Paul Valéry who, in the aftermath of the First World War, reflected on the cultural roots and future of Europe. In a speech at the University of Zurich in November 1922, he formulated the three essential historical roots that constitute the 'idea of Europe', namely Greece, Rome and Christianity:

> Je considérerai comme européens tous les peuples qui ont subi au cours de l'Histoire les trois influences que je vais dire. La première est celle de Rome ... modèle éternel de la puissance organisée et stable. La seconde est celle du christianisme qui vise et atteint progressivement le profond de la conscience ... [et la troisième] est ce qu'il y a de plus distinctif dans notre civilisation. Nous lui [la Grèce] devons la discipline de l'Esprit [d'où devait sortir notre science]. Nous lui devons une méthode de penser qui tend à rapporter toutes choses à l'homme, à l'homme complet.
>
> (Valéry [Collected Works] 1957)

The 'modern' history of Europe is usually delineated by the Carolingian period when 'Europa' is well established with Charlemagne as its 'Pater'. By 800, this Western Empire, based on the three essential elements evoked by Valéry and composed of an area approximately marked by present-day France, West Germany, Austria, Belgium, Luxembourg, the Netherlands, and northern Italy (ex-Venice), will form, some 1,150 years later and after innumerable fratricidal wars, the core of the nation-states engaged in the post-Second World War (re)-integration of Europe. The peace, order, justice and even the monetary union[2] that Charlemagne had imposed on his Empire was not to last long. By 843, his grandsons were dividing up the 'imperium francorum' into three kingdoms, a move that will allow much later the emergence in Europe of the modern nation-state, which will be the source of so many wars. In 842, in the city of

Strasbourg – the present-day parliamentary capital of Europe – Charles II (the Bald) and his half-brother, Louis the German, in an alliance against their eldest brother, Lothaire, the putative inheritor of the Empire, pronounce in two languages, the *romana lingua* (Old French or Vulgar Latin) and *teudisca lingua* (Old High German spoken by the Franks), the Oaths of Strasbourg,[3] which lead to a conciliation in the form of the Treaty of Verdun (843). Lothaire chooses the central Kingdom and rules over a long, narrow strip of land, the Lotharingie, which will be at the origin of numerous conflicts between France and Germany over the next eleven centuries. Charles II rules over Francia occidentalis while Louis the German receives Francia orientalis, a large part of present-day Germany. Some claim that the 'Oaths' of the Treaty of Paris and the Treaty of Rome establishing the European Coal and Steel Community in 1951 and the European Economic Community in 1957, respectively, as well as the more recent 'Oath of Maastricht' establishing in 1992 the framework for the future monetary union, are an attempt by France and Germany, the motor of the post-Second World War movement towards European integration, to reintegrate Europe on the old foundations of a 'Europe of Charlemagne' that his grandsons had been unable to keep together. Apart from the economic benefits derived from the integration of many relatively small economic spaces in Europe, it is usually argued that the end-goal of this reintegration exercise is to avoid a repetition of, *inter alia*, what happened in 1916 at Verdun where 340,000 French and German soldiers perished, some 1,000 years after the Treaty of Verdun.

The end of the Second World War was a watershed for the descendants of Charlemagne. Extreme nationalism had destroyed Europe for the second time in as many generations during the twentieth century. The destructive forces of nationalism, which had degenerated into genocide, created a climate of reflection on how Europe – home of Western Civilization – could have descended into Dante's Inferno. Europe would need to find a new model of political organization.

NATIONALISM AND FEDERALISM IN EUROPE

For a short period of time at the turn of nineteenth century, 'La Grande Nation', under Napoleon, rules over a 'Grand Empire' which, by 1811, includes one-half of Europe: Italy, Germany, Poland and Spain. After the defeat of Napoleon, the Congress of Vienna (1815) was to 'restore' a new European order, based on a 'European concert' between the victorious powers, Austria, Britain, Prussia, Russia and, later, France. But the principles of the French Revolution clashed with the new order imposed by the Congress of Vienna, giving rise to an upsurge of liberating nationalism against the Europe of Vienna. It is around this time, in the mid-nineteenth century, that intellectuals like Victor Hugo draft a new model for the organization of Europe. The new model is called federalism. Inspired by earlier writers like Immanuel Kant (1795) and Claude Henri de Saint-Simon (1814), the new intellectual projects to integrate the nations and peoples of Europe range from purely cooperative plans to the idea of establishing supranational institutions in order to curtail effectively the sovereignty of each nation-state. In Saint-Simon's proposal of 1814, France and England are to form an alliance and establish a Parliament which will form the basis of a European representative institution as the other European nations, like Germany, accede to a parliamentary form of government. In the 1830s, Mazzini, who promoted the movement for the unification of Italy as a republic, believed that the nation-state should only be the precursor of a large European federation to unite the 'old world'. In 1849, Victor Hugo, at the Congress for Peace held in Paris, proposes a 'United States of Europe' based on universal suffrage. He states:

> Un jour viendra où, vous France, vous Russie, vous Italie, vous Angleterre, vous Allemagne, vous toutes nations du continent, sans perdre vos qualités distinctes et votre glorieuse individualité, vous vous fondrez dans une unité supérieure et vous constituerez la fraternité européenne. . . . Un jour viendra où les boulets seront remplacés par les votes, par le suffrage universel des peuples, par le véritable arbitrage d'un sénat souverain qui sera à l'Europe ce que le Parlement est à l'Angleterre, ce que la Diète est à l'Allemagne et ce que l'Assemblée législative est à la France.
>
> (Bossuat 1994: 12)

The Franco-Prussian War of 1870 and the First World War were to derail these intellectual projects. After the First World War, individuals such as the Count R. Coudenhove-Kalergi established in 1923 in Vienna a 'Pan-European' organization, formulating in 1926 a detailed federalist plan that included a single currency (Bossuat 1994: 27). A few years after France, Germany and five other European nations signed in 1925 the Locarno Pact, which became the symbol of a Franco-German reconciliation and the establishment of an era of peace in Europe, Aristide Briand, the then French foreign affairs minister, proposed in an address to the League of Nations on 8 September 1929 the establishment of a 'federal link' among the people of Europe. These efforts were pushed aside with the economic depression and the rise of Hitler in the 1930s.

The contemporary history of European integration begins out of the ashes of the Second World War. Soon after the end of the war, Winston Churchill, in a speech pronounced on 19 September 1946 at the University of Zurich, called for a United States of Europe, singling out the essential need for Franco-German cooperation:

> I am now going to say something that will astonish you. The first step in re-creation of the European family must be a partnership between France and Germany. In this way only can France recover the moral

leadership of Europe. There can be no revival of Europe without a spiritually great France and a spiritually great Germany. This structure of the United States of Europe, if well and truly built, will be such as to make the material strength of a single state less important. Small nations will count as much as large ones and gain their honour by their contribution to the common cause.

(Churchill 1946: 7381)

According to Churchill, the United Kingdom should be a promoter of this project rather than an active participant; the primary British obligation was to the Commonwealth and the Atlantic link. As he told de Gaulle during the Second World War: 'Between the mainland and the high seas, we shall always choose the high seas'.

INITIAL STEPS TOWARDS ECONOMIC INTEGRATION

The key date and event for the economic integration of the post-Second World War Europe is 9 May 1950, with the declaration of the then French foreign affairs minister Robert Schuman proposing, on the initiative of Jean Monnet, to place the coal and steel resources of France and Germany under a common authority, open to any other European country wishing to participate in such an endeavour:

> L'Europe ne se fera pas d'un coup, ni dans une construction d'ensemble: elle se fera par des réalisations concrètes créant d'abord une solidarité de fait. Le rassemblement des nations européennes exige que l'opposition séculaire de la France et de l'Allemagne soit éliminée; l'action entreprise doit toucher au premier chef la France et l'Allemagne ... le Gouvernement français propose de placer l'ensemble de la production franco-allemande de charbon et d'acier, sous une Haute Autorité commune, dans une organisation ouverte à la participation des autres pays d'Europe. ... Par la mise en commun de productions de base et l'institution d'une Haute Autorité nouvelle, dont les décisions lieront la France, l'Allemagne et les pays qui y adhéreront, cette proposition réalisera les premières assises concrètes d'une fédération européenne indispensable à la préservation de la paix.

The founding fathers of modern-day Europe – Jean Monnet, Robert Schuman, Konrad Adenauer, Alcide de Gasperi[4] and others – understood that in order to overcome their deep-rooted hostilities, superiority complexes and warring tendencies, the nation-states of Europe – and in particular France and Germany – must join forces and work towards 'a destiny henceforward shared'.[5] However, in contrast to the grandiose schemes proposed in the nineteenth and early twentieth centuries, they also understood that European integration could only be accomplished by small steps starting with concrete economic and political issues, which would have spill-over effects in the creation of supranational institutions. This is known as the 'functional' approach towards integration, or what Margaret Thatcher derisively called the 'conveyor belt towards federalism'.

In the economic sphere, this approach began in 1950 with the launching of an intergovernmental conference, which brought together France, West Germany, Italy and the Benelux countries, to place coal, iron ore and steel, a source of Franco-German conflict, under the control of a common High Authority which was made answerable to an Assembly with powers to dismiss it. The actions of the High Authority could be legally challenged by a European Court of Justice. The institutional model of the European Coal and Steel Community (ECSC) was to be adopted, with a few modifications, for the European Economic Community (EEC) and the European Atomic Energy Community (Euratom). The establishment of these latter two Communities was negotiated at the Second Intergovernmental Conference launched in 1955 at Messina (Sicily) and ended with the signature of the Treaties of Rome in 1957. The EEC provided: (i) for the progressive establishment of a customs union with a common external tariff; (ii) for the gradual implementation of the free movement of workers, goods, services and capital, and of common policies in the area of competition, agriculture, transport and state aid; (iii) for the harmonization ('approximation' in Treaty terminology) of tax laws and labour laws ('social policy' in Treaty terminology); and (iv) for the coordination of fiscal, monetary and exchange rate policies. From the outset, the EEC and Euratom shared the same Parliamentary Assembly and Court of Justice with the ECSC, but its High Authority, the Commission, had less authority over Member governments. The institutions of the EEC–Euratom were merged with those of the ECSC in 1967.

Initial British approach towards European integration

The supranationalism and 'dirigisme' of price and production decisions inherent in the High Authority of the ECSC, as proposed and implemented by the Schuman plan, had the effect of ensuring that the United Kingdom did not participate in the negotiations leading up to the Treaty of Paris. The ECSC, proposed by the Franco-German scheme and supported by Italy and the Benelux countries, was contrary to British national interest. The United Kingdom was interested in limited arrangements of European intergovernmental cooperation, not in integration that implied a loss of sovereignty. At the inaugural meeting of the intergovernmental conference held in Messina on 2 June 1955, the United Kingdom was invited by the Six to participate in the negotiations that led to the Treaties of Rome. The position of the United Kingdom may be summarized by the declaration of the British observer, Russell Bretherton, at Messina:

I leave Messina happy because even if you continue meeting you will not agree; even if you agree, nothing will result; and even if something results, it will be a disaster.

After the Spaak Committee, which was set up to draft recommendations, proposed the formation of a customs union and the establishment of *common* European economic policies, the United Kingdom withdrew in 1956 from the Intergovernmental Conference and expressed a preference for negotiations towards a European free-trade area. The United Kingdom was more interested in the creation of a post-war Europe in which free trade and cooperation between the countries would flourish. As the negotiations of the Six drew to a close in February 1957, the Council of the Organization for European Economic Cooperation (OEEC) – an organization established in 1948 to allocate US aid provided for the reconstruction of Europe under the Marshall Plan – began negotiations, under the leadership of the United Kingdom, with a view to create an all-embracing European free-trade area spanning the Six and the other OEEC countries. When those negotiations finally broke down in late 1958, the United Kingdom, Sweden, Norway, Denmark, Austria, Switzerland and Portugal joined together to establish in 1960 a smaller European Free-Trade Area (EFTA). Such an arrangement was more in keeping with the British philosophy of economic integration, which would only involve an intergovernmental forum for economic cooperation and eschew all federalist structures of the EEC and Euratom. The EFTA would also allow the UK to set its own external tariffs so as to maintain its special relationship with the Commonwealth countries and to avoid participating in the common agricultural programme of the EEC, which would increase the price of imported foodstuff.

Soon after the first phase of the implementation of a common external tariff by the six Member States of the Community in 1961, the United Kingdom, under the Conservative government of Harold Macmillan, reconsidered the merits of membership in the EEC for the following reasons: (i) at the beginnning of the 1960s many of the member states of the British Commonwealth were opting for membership in the non-aligned group of states; (ii) as the special Anglo-American political relationship was becoming less important, the United Kingdom risked political isolation by remaining outside the European Economic Community; (iii) with the rapidly growing EEC market combined with the lack of a free-trade agreement between the EEC and EFTA, British businessmen believed that non-membership did not make economic sense. In other words, the very creation of the EEC had economic centripetal forces on the countries that chose to remain outside.[6] However, Britain had 'missed the boat' (cf. Denman 1995). Suspicious of British motives to accede to the European Communities and desirous to maintain the special Franco-German axis intact, de Gaulle, as President of France, will veto twice – once in 1963 and again in 1967 – British requests for membership in the EEC. It is only with the departure of de Gaulle from the political scene that the United Kingdom, along with Ireland and Denmark, will be allowed to join the EEC in 1973 when his successor, Georges Pompidou, saw Britain as a counterweight to what he feared was Germany's inevitable future political and economic domination in the Community.

RELAUNCHING OF EUROPE IN THE MID-1980s AFTER A LONG INTERLUDE

Although by the end of 1960s the free movement of goods through the establishment of a customs union had been achieved, the free movement of workers, services and capital within the twelve-year timetable set by the Treaty of Rome had not been achieved. No substantial progress was made in these areas except in a few isolated instances. The goal of achieving coordinated national macroeconomic policies was also unfulfilled. After the departure of de Gaulle, attempts were made in the early 1970s to set the Community on a path towards a monetary union (see Chapter 1). However, the international economic shocks of the 1970s derailed these efforts. Instead, the Community was reacting to the collapse of the international monetary system established in the post-war period.

Single market

After temporarily abandoning in the mid-1970s the goal of achieving a monetary union, and establishing in the late 1970s a European system of fixed exchange rates based on the ECU after the collapse of the Bretton Woods international system of fixed exchange rates based on the US dollar (see Chapter 1), the Community in the early 1980s began an intense debate on how to revitalize European integration. The debate, under the leadership of Altiero Spinelli, a member of the European Parliament, produced a 'draft Treaty establishing the European Union', adopted by the European Parliament in 1984. Although this federalist proposal had no chance of being adopted by the Council, it presented a major challenge to the Member States to consider changes to the European Community. In 1984, two *ad hoc* committees – the Dooge Committee, chaired by the Irish Senator James Dooge, and the Adonnino Committee – were established to study, respectively, institutional reforms and areas of progress to create 'a people's Europe' that would respond to the concerns and interest of the ordinary citizen. The reports of these two committees formed the background to the initiative undertaken by the new Commission president, Jacques Delors, who, on 12 March 1985, outlined to the European Parliament a programme to achieve the completion of a large, single market by the end of 1992. The Heads of State or Government at the European Council meeting of June 1985 in Milan approved the

Commission's (1985) *White Paper* (also known as the Cockfield White Paper, after the then Commissioner Cockfield), entitled 'Completing the Internal Market', which sets out a detailed timetable for enacting nearly 300 measures to remove non-tariff barriers by the end of 1992. In order to increase the chances of achieving such a goal within seven years, the declarations would have to be translated into a Treaty with a revised Community decision-making process that would include more majority voting within the Council so as to preclude the use of the national veto on measures dealing with the implementation of the single market. Accordingly, a third intergovernmental conference was launched to recommend a package of reforms which would guarantee fulfilment of the 1992 programme. The result was the Single European Act (SEA) (1986), a series of amendments to the Treaties establishing the Communities. The SEA, which came into force on 1 July 1987, laid down the detailed legal framework for establishing a single market by the end of 1992 and closer policy cooperation on the environment, research and technology. In line with the Dooge and Adonnino reports, the SEA also enhanced the role of the European Parliament by introducing the 'cooperation procedure' with Council in the adoption of Community legislation (see Box I.1).

Box I.1 Institutions of the European Union

I. The European *Commission* is composed of 20 Members, appointed for a period of five years by common agreement between the Member governments. There are two nationals each from France, Germany, Italy, Spain and the United Kingdom and one from each of the other ten Member States. One member is appointed as President of the Commission. The President and the other members of the Commission nominated are subject as a body to a vote of approval by the European Parliament. In broad terms the Commission's role is to act as the guardian of the Treaties (e.g. it may bring a case before the Court of Justice to ensure that Community law is enforced), to serve as the executive arm of the Communities (e.g. to implement the Common Agricultural Policy, the Common Competition Policy, etc.) to initiate Community policy, and to facilitate agreement within the Council or between the Council and Parliament. The Commission can be forced to resign *en bloc* by a vote of censure in Parliament supported by a two-thirds majority, but this has yet to happen. As Commissioners are not allowed to receive instructions from their governments, the Commission is truly a supranational institution.

The Commission is backed by a civil service, mainly located in Brussels. It comprises 23 departments, called Directorates-General, each responsible for implementation of common policies and general administration.

II. The *Council* is made up of one representative from each of the governments of the 15 Member States. Each government normally sends one of its ministers. Its membership thus varies with the subjects discussed. For example, the Council, composed of the Ministers of Economics and Finance, is known as 'Ecofin'. The Council is the main decision-making institution and is thus part of the legislative arm of the Community, which it shares in *certain areas* with the European Parliament. The Council, which represents the Member States, enacts Union legislation, in the form of regulations, directives or decisions. *Regulations* are directly applied without the need for national measures to implement them; *directives* bind Member States as to the objectives to be achieved while leaving the national authorities the power to choose the form and the means to be used; *decisions* are binding in all their aspects upon those to whom they are addressed. A decision may be addressed to any or all Member States, to undertakings or to individuals. Article 148 of the Union Treaty distinguishes between decisions adopted by unanimity, by a simple majority, by a qualified majority, and by a double qualified majority. A simple majority is eight Member States in favour out of 15. When decisions are taken in the Council by a qualified majority vote, France, Germany, Italy and the United Kingdom have ten votes each; Spain has eight; Belgium, Greece, the Netherlands and Portugal five each; Austria and Sweden, four each; Denmark, Finland and Ireland three each, and Luxembourg two. A qualified majority means 62 votes out of a total of 87. Most decisions are taken by qualified majority. In rare cases whenever the Council may take decisions on an issue not requiring a Commission proposal, the Council needs 62 votes in favour representing at least 10 Member States, i.e. a double qualified majority. Unanimity is only required on issues of fundamental importance such as the accession of a new Member State, amendments to the Treaties or the launching of a new common policy.

The Presidency of the Council rotates between the Member States at six-monthly intervals. The rotation cycle, which until 1998 follows a modified alphabetical order according to the country's name in the language of that country, is determined, as of 1998, so that each 'troika' (the past, current and future Presidency) includes one large Member State. The ground for the Council's discussion is prepared by 'Coreper' [a French acronym], a committee of Member States' permanent representatives to the Union in Brussels.

The *European Council* is composed of the Heads of State or Government *and* of the President of the Commission, who usually meet at least twice a year (the 'European Summits') to provide the necessary impetus and the general guidelines to the European Union. The European Council evolved from the practice, started in 1974, of organizing regular meetings of the Heads of State or Government. The arrangement was formalized by the Single European Act in 1987. As a launch pad for major political initiatives and a forum for settling controversial issues blocked at ministerial level, the European Council has no legal legislative powers. It does, however, define the principles of and general guidelines for the common foreign and security policy.

The Member State holding the Presidency of the European Council coincides with the Member State holding the Presidency of the Council.

III. The *European Parliament*, composed of 626 members, is elected every five years by direct universal suffrage since 1979. Germany has 99 seats, France, Italy and the United Kingdom 87 seats each, Spain 64, The Netherlands 31, Belgium, Greece and Portugal 25 each, Sweden 22, Austria 21, Denmark and Finland 16 each, Ireland 15 and Luxembourg 6. Prior to 1987, Parliament essentially had a consultative role: the Commission proposed and the Council decided after consulting Parliament. The Single European Act (1986) increased Parliament's powers with regard to single market legislation by introducing a 'cooperation procedure' which called for two readings in Parliament and two in the Council. The 1992 Treaty on European Union takes a further step towards recognition of the legislative powers of Parliament. It introduces a new 'co-decision procedure' in a number of important areas which gives Parliament, in conjunction with the Council, the power to adopt regulations and directives on an equal footing. In fact, Parliament may now veto the Council's position provided that an absolute majority (314) of the Members of the European Parliament are in favour and the conciliation procedure between Parliament and Council has failed. This procedure applies to the single market, research and the new areas covered by the Treaty on European Union, namely trans-European networks, consumer protection, education, culture and health. By contrast Parliament only has a consultative role in relation to agricultural prices and matters relating to the creation of a monetary union. Finally, for certain decisions of major importance such as international agreements and accession of new member states, the Council can act only with Parliament's assent.

In the Treaty on European Union, the 'co-decision procedure' is found in 14 cases; the 'cooperation procedure' is found in 15 cases; the 'consultation procedure' is found in 19 cases. There are 16 cases, of which nine deal with the Economic and Monetary Union section of the Treaty, where Parliament is not even consulted prior to a Council decision.

The European Parliament is composed of political groups organized at the Community level, not national level. To organize an
official political group in Parliament a minimum of either 29 members
from the same Member State, or 23 members from two different
Member States, or 18 members from three different Member States,
or 14 members from four different Member States is necessary.

IV. The *Court of Justice*, composed of 15 judges appointed for six
years by agreement among the governments, ensures that implementation of the Treaties is in accordance with the rule of law. The judges
are assisted by nine advocates-general. An additional *Court of First
Instance* was set up in 1987. The Court, whose independence is guaranteed, passes judgment, at the request of a Community institution,
a Member State or an individual directly concerned, on any legal
instrument enacted by European or national institutions, which is
alleged to be incompatible with Community law. Judgments of the
Court overrule those of national courts; furthermore, the Court is
now empowered to fine a Member State which does not comply with
its judgments.

V. The *Court of Auditors*, set up in 1975, has 15 members appointed
for a six-year term by agreement between the Member States. Its role
is to check that revenue is received and expenditure incurred 'in a
lawful and regular manner' and that the Community's financial affairs
are properly managed.

Towards the economic and monetary union

In the late 1980s, as it became clear that Member States had the political
will and, with the SEA, the procedural flexibility needed to achieve the
single market, attention swiftly returned to the single currency, which had
been debated in the early 1970s. The then President of the Commission,
Jacques Delors, among others,[7] shared the view that the free movement
of capital, goods and services was not compatible with nationally determined monetary policies and the fixed but adjustable exchange rate target
bands of the European Monetary System (EMS) established in 1979. He
believed that the EMS would be too fragile to survive in that new environment and that it could be severely damaged if common economic and
monetary policies were not put in place. In academic circles, this argument was known as the 'inconsistent quartet' (Padoa-Schioppa 1988: 373),
which referred to the incompatibility of free trade, full capital mobility,
fixed exchange rates and national autonomy in the conduct of monetary
policy. In June 1988, the European Council set up a committee, chaired
by Delors, to draft proposals for an economic and monetary union. The

Delors Committee reported in April 1989 recommending a three-stage approach towards economic and monetary union, with a discussion of the necessary institutional changes and transfer of powers to Community institutions that such an approach would require. At the Madrid European Council meeting of June 1989, the Heads of State or Government could only agree to launch the first stage of the Delors proposal, which dealt with the complete liberalization of capital flows between the twelve Member States of the Community, and to reaffirm the general commitment to reach an economic and monetary union by a process to be laid down at a future intergovernmental conference. But events in Central and Eastern Europe quickly overtook the Community. With the fall of the Berlin Wall in late 1989, the then President of France, François Mitterrand, pushed for the economic and monetary union goal with a single currency as a means of deepening German integration in Europe. Accordingly, at the Strasbourg European Council meeting of December 1989 the Heads of State or Government agreed to call an intergovernmental conference by the end of 1990 to prepare the necessary Treaty revisions for a complete economic and monetary union. The collapse of the Soviet empire in Central and Eastern Europe and the all but inevitable reunification of Germany led both France and Germany to seek closer political integration of the Community. Germany argued that with the negotiations to establish an economic and monetary union, a parallel effort should be undertaken with respect to a common European foreign and security policy so as to reassure Germany's neighbours – especially the Eastern ones – of her unequivocal commitment to a cooperative approach in these areas. Thus, the Dublin European Council of June 1990 adopted the proposal of Chancellor Kohl and President Mitterrand that an intergovernmental conference on political union be held in parallel with the one established for EMU. The result of these two intergovernmental conferences was the Treaty on European Union or the Maastricht Treaty (1992). The goal and the step-by-step approach to achieve an economic and monetary union with a single currency was entrenched for the first time in a Community treaty.

Towards the free movement of people

The Treaty of Rome establishing the EEC did not provide for the removal of internal frontiers with respect to the movement of people. Although residents of the Community were guaranteed the right to work where they wished, the removal of border controls for people travelling across the internal frontiers required an agreement that included provisions extending beyond the powers available in the Treaty of Rome. Removal of internal borders requires common visa and asylum policies between the Member States of the Community vis-à-vis third countries and cooperation between the Home and Justice departments of the Member States to

Box I.2 Forms of economic and monetary integration

Free-trade area: elimination of all tariffs and quotas on goods between the member states of the area, but no common trade policy, i.e. no common external tariffs and quotas with respect to third parties. An example is the European Free Trade Association (EFTA) of 1960 composed of the United Kingdom, Sweden, Norway, Denmark, Austria, Switzerland and Portugal and which still exists today with a membership composed of only Iceland, Norway, Switzerland and Liechtenstein.

Customs union: same as above but with a common trade policy with respect to third parties. An example is provided by provisions in the Treaty of Rome and implemented from 1958 to 1968 between the six Community Member States.

Common market: a higher degree of integration than the customs union since a common market includes *common* policies between Member States in areas such as agriculture, transport, competition law, tax laws and regional policies. An example is again provided by some of the provisions of the Treaty of Rome.

Economic union: a higher degree of integration than the common market since it also includes the free movement of labour and capital, no cross-border restrictions on the provisions of services, the effective coordination of macroeconomic policies (budgetary, monetary and exchange rates) and, possibly, provisions for mutual assistance between Member States. An example is the Treaty of Rome with the Single European Act of 1986. According to the Werner Report (1970) and the Delors Report (1989), the principal features of an economic union are:

- a single market within which labour, goods, services and capital can move freely;
- common competition policies, common structural and regional policies;
- effectively coordinated macroeconomic policies, including binding rules for national budgetary policies.

Monetary union: usually considered as the ultimate stage of economic integration composed of the following conditions: the guarantee of a complete and irreversible convertibility of the currencies, the full liberalization of capital flows between Member States, the complete integration of the banking and financial markets between Member States, the irrevocable fixing of exchange rates without any margin of fluctuation and a single monetary policy managed by a single central bank. The national currencies may eventually disappear to be replaced by a single currency. An example is the monetary union outlined in the Maastricht Treaty of 1992.

combat terrorism, smuggling of illegal merchandise (drugs), and organized crime. To that extent, the free movement of persons required a legal framework that transcended the Community treaty. In their desire to remove the Rhine as a Community internal frontier, France and Germany, joined by the Benelux countries, signed in 1985 an intergovernmental agreement, known as the Schengen Agreement, to lay the foundations for an area of free circulation of people, regardless of nationality, within the Community without passport checks at internal land, sea and airport frontiers. This Agreement was followed by a Convention composed of 142 articles. In 1990, Italy signed the Convention, followed by Spain and Portugal (1991), by Greece (1992)[8], by Austria (1995) and by Denmark, Finland and Sweden (1996). The latter three Member States signed the Convention, after resolving the collateral problem of how to integrate into the Schengen space the long-standing Nordic passport-free zone by allowing Norway and Iceland, who are not members of the European Union, observer status. Hence, all the Member States, except the United Kingdom and Ireland, have signed the Convention.

Effective March 1995, the provisions of the Schengen Convention were provisionally applied between France, Germany, the Benelux countries, Spain and Portugal. Once a person enters the external borders of this limited Schengen space, he/she may freely cross any *internal* land, air or sea border without being subjected to any further identity check. Since then, and as of March 1996, the Convention has been permanently implemented between the seven countries, except that France has re-established an internal frontier with the Benelux countries because the Netherlands is not in compliance with Article 71.2 of the Convention, which stipulates that the contracting parties must take all necessary administrative and legal measures to prevent the export of illegal drugs, including cannabis (France 1996: 66). Austria and Italy are expected to join the Schengen space in April 1998. If the parliaments of the five Nordic countries ratify the Convention, they are expected to implement the provisions of the Convention in early 1999.

Since the original signature of the Schengen Agreement in 1985, a Community commitment to respect the principle of the free movement of *persons* has been introduced into the Single European Act (Article 8A) and re-introduced in the Treaty on European Union (Article 7A). The United Kingdom has always argued that these articles refer only to nationals of the Member States and therefore internal border controls must be maintained to prevent illegal immigration. More recently, some Member States at the Sixth Intergovernmental Conference recommend that the Schengen Convention be incorporated into the third pillar of the Maastricht Treaty, which deals with the provisions on cooperation in the fields of justice and home affairs. This would 'communitarize' the procedures, which would eventually involve the Commission, the Council and the European Parliament.

POLITICAL INTEGRATION

The Community's efforts to give economic integration a political dimension, with an ultimate objective of preventing renewed military conflict between the Member States of the European Community, date back to the early years of its existence. In fact, even before the signing of the Treaty of Paris in 1951, establishing the European Coal and Steel Community, the Pleven Plan of 1950, named after the then French prime minister, proposed to apply the functional approach of European integration to the area of a European common defence policy. In the face of an increasing threat from the Soviet Union, the establishment of the European Defence Community (EDC) of 1952 was to allow the rearmament of West Germany under a common European command. The rejection of the EDC by the French National Assembly in 1954 was a clear setback in the political integration of Europe in the area of a common defence and foreign policy. In the early 1960s, President de Gaulle of France tried to establish a 'Political Union' in the area of foreign policy, defence and culture along traditional lines of intergovernmental cooperation. His Fouchet Plan (1961/62) was defeated for three reasons. First, the other five Member States of the Community felt that his model of political integration was a clear departure from the supranational principles of integration set out in the Treaties of Paris and Rome and would lead to a Community institutional structure based on a looser, more intergovernmental organization. Secondly, the role of the United Kingdom in the Fouchet Plan was unclear. Thirdly, a European defence policy that was to be independent from NATO raised serious reservations among the other Member States. The Davignon Report of 1970, requested by the 1969 Hague Summit of Community Heads of State or Government, heralded the start of European Political Cooperation (EPC) which never went beyond consultations of Community foreign ministers. Further moves in 1975 (Tindemans Report) to transform all relations between Member States into a 'European Union' were not put into effect. Title III of the Single European Act gave formal recognition to the EPC, which gave the European Council, composed of the Heads of State or Government and of the President of the Commission, and the Council of Foreign Ministers the responsibility to coordinate the foreign policy of the Member States.

The interdependence between economic and political integration became more evident in the aftermath to the fall of the Berlin Wall in 1989. The President of France, François Mitterrand, pushed for the Economic and Monetary Union (EMU) goal with a single currency as a means of deepening German economic integration in Europe. Germany, on the other hand, was willing to accept a *well-defined* process towards EMU *provided* that a parallel effort was undertaken with respect to a common European foreign and security policy so as to reassure Germany's neighbours of its unequivocal commitment to a cooperative approach in these areas (see Guilhaudis 1993: 62–69). Accordingly, provisions for a common foreign and security policy were included in the Treaty on European Union, which stipulates that the longer-term perspective of a common defence policy of the European Union is to be developed with the Western European Union (WEU) as the military arm of the European Union or, alternatively, as the 'European pillar' of the Atlantic Alliance. The WEU is an organization whose origins date back to 1948 when Belgium, France, Luxembourg, the Netherlands and the United Kingdom established the Western Union, also known as the Brussels Pact, for purposes of collective self-defence. After the French National Assembly failed to ratify the EDC in 1954, the Federal Republic of Germany and Italy were invited to join the other five states in a new organization called the WEU, which by then had no military autonomy from NATO, which had been established in 1949. More recently, Spain, Portugal and Greece joined the WEU. Currently, only Denmark and the four 'neutral' Member States – Austria, Finland, Ireland and Sweden – are not fully-fledged members of the WEU.[9]

While the main thrust of the common foreign and security policy is still predominantly in the area of intergovernmental cooperation, Germany, supported by the Commission, would like to place the common foreign and security pillar of the Maastricht Treaty into the regular decision-making process of the Community, namely the procedure which involves the Commission with its right of initiative and Parliament with its co-decision powers shared with the Council acting by a qualified majority or a double majority, which is defined as a majority of the Member States representing a majority of the population. Decisions that involve military operations should be made in such a fashion that a minority must not prevent the majority from taking joint military actions. Moreover, the non-participating minority should financially support such actions (Deutschland 1995a). In mid-1996, with the reintegration of France into the military arm of NATO, the latter granted its European allies political control and strategic direction of certain military missions. Under the agreement, NATO may supply military forces, equipment and logistical infrastructure to the Western European Union under the Combined Joint Task Forces (CJTF) for missions defined in the WEU Petersberg Declaration of 1992, namely humanitarian, peace-keeping and crisis-management (e.g. the re-establishment of peace) missions that require combat forces. Any Member State not actively participating in these missions would be expected to support them financially and not to prevent the other Member States from participating ('constructive veto'). The four 'neutral' Member States who are not NATO members have signalled their willingness to participate in such an arrangement on defence and security in the post-cold war Europe. Other military forces and equipment made available to the WEU could be provided by 'Eurocorps', a joint force composed of 50,000 men from Germany, France, Belgium, Spain and Luxembourg. Eurocorps is a Franco-German idea launched at the fifty-ninth Franco-German summit in May 1992 to develop an embryonic European military force. Following US reactions, Eurocorps may, under certain conditions, be integrated into the European military command of NATO.

SIXTH INTERGOVERNMENTAL CONFERENCE OF 1996–97

In March 1996, the European Union launched the Sixth Intergovernmental Conference with a view to revise the Treaty on European Union. A Reflection Group, chaired by Carlos Westendorp (1995) and composed of representatives from each Member State, from the Commission and from the European Parliament, had a mandate to 'reflect' on all the major issues that have to be addressed in the context of the planned revision of the Maastricht Treaty. On the basis of the report of this Reflection Group, the Intergovernmental Conference is to come up with major proposals on the reform of European Union institutions, which is necessary not only to incorporate within the next decade some twelve new Member States but also to have a coherent and functional common foreign and security policy.

Enlargement

The future enlargement of the Union from the present fifteen states to some twenty-seven states raises issues of the need to reform the decision mechanism of the EU institutions, to reform the common agricultural and regional aid policies to avert a significant increase in the expenditures of the European Union budget, and to define the objectives and the instruments of the future common European defence policy.

In addition to the original Six Member States and the United Kingdom, Ireland and Denmark, the European Union is composed of Greece, which joined in 1981, Spain and Portugal (1986), and Austria, Finland and Sweden (1995). Negotiations for the enlargement of the European Union are scheduled to begin in 1998, some six months after the end of the Intergovernmental Conference. Germany, concerned about potential political instability on or close to its eastern borders, would like the EU to give priority to the Czech Republic, Poland and Hungary so that these countries could join the EU by 2000. On the other hand, Bonn has reservations about the Baltic States (Estonia, Latvia, Lithuania) joining the first wave of new members because it might encourage their desire for a defence guarantee, either through NATO membership or through the Western European Union. This could provoke a nationalist backlash in Russia. At the Madrid European Council meeting of December 1995, the Heads of State or Government decided that the Commission will prepare opinions on the countries which have applied for EU membership. In light of these reports, the European Council will take the necessary decisions for launching accession negotiations. In short, all applicants will be treated equally, but it is left open whether all negotiations will start at the same time. This compromise position satisfies both Germany and France, which is determined not to allow any differentiation between applicants early in the process. By the beginning of 1996, the following countries had already applied for membership: Cyprus, Malta,[10] Estonia, Hungary, Poland, Romania, Slovakia, Latvia, Czech Republic, Bulgaria and Lithuania. Slovenia applied for membership in mid-1996 after having resolved the bilateral problem with Italy over the property rights of the Italians who were forced to leave Istria at the end of the Second World War. By mid-1996, a consensus between Brussels (the Commission), Bonn and Paris is that enlargement should proceed in phases, in line with the economic strength and political maturity of the candidates, with an advance guard admitted in 2002. The fact is that it may take a long time to harmonize social, agricultural and industrial policies before admitting some of these countries into the first pillar of the Maastricht Treaty, which deals with the provisions of the Single Market and the Economic and Monetary Union. The countries facing a delay beyond 2002 could be granted partial membership by inviting them to join the common foreign and security pillar of the Maastricht Treaty.

A multi-speed Europe

The Intergovernmental Conference is the scene of a debate between two old and conflicting ideas with regard to the construction of Europe, namely, whether Europe should continue to be integrated along federalist lines with the dilution of old-style national sovereignty, or whether Europe should continue to be integrated along the lines of a 'Europe of Nations' ('Europe des patries'), based primarily on intergovernmental cooperation, which eschews all supranational institutions like the Commission and the European Court of Justice, or decision-making in the Council by majority voting. For each vision, there exists many strands, but currently Germany and the right wing of the British Conservative Party best represent the former vision and the latter vision, respectively.

The German view is encapsulated by two position papers written by Lamers and Schäuble, who are members of the ruling Christian-Democratic Union of the Bundestag. In their first position paper (Deutschland 1994), released in September 1994, they explain that in order to accelerate the construction of Europe on the basis of a federalist model, there must be a 'hard core' in the Union, consisting of the founding members minus Italy, with Germany and France forming the 'core' of the 'hard core'. The hard core may move more rapidly towards integration than the outer core. The European Union must not be forever bound to advance at the speed of its slowest members. However, eventually all Member States must participate in the same European institutions and adopt the same common policies. The metaphor usually given by Germany is: 'Some of the ships in the convoy may lag behind, but they all eventually dock at the same port.' This vision of European integration gives rise to a process known as a 'multi-speed' Europe. The Union has long practised certain forms of a multi-speed Europe. Exceptions and exemptions, normally of a limited and temporary nature, have been provided in Community law, such as in the transition provisions provided to new Member States or to the Member States to join the Economic and Monetary Union, which is described in Chapter 4. As the EU is enlarged, all the new central European countries will not be able immediately to participate fully in all the common policies. In the German view of a multi-speed Europe, all Member States are ultimately fully and equally integrated in a federalist framework. The 'hard core' has the responsibility to lead the others towards this form of integration.

In their second position paper, composed of two parts (Deutschland 1995a, 1995b) and released in Berlin on 13 June 1995, Lamers and Schäuble recommend future institutional changes at the European Union level. While avoiding the express use of the 'hard core' notion as they did in their first controversial paper, this later position paper has a 'federalist' tone and forms the basis of the German government's proposals presented at the Intergovernmental Conference. It calls for the introduction of majority voting on foreign policy issues in the European Union and the scrapping of the present consensus system. With respect to military operations, it argues that a minority of Member States could agree not to take part in a particular action but should not be allowed to prevent the majority from carrying out common defence actions. In other areas, it proposes to extend the application of qualified majority voting in regular EU decision-making, accompanied by a revision of the weighting of votes of governments in the Council of Ministers. This marks the wish of Germany, supported by France, to have voting power that reflects economic and demographic strength. For some decisions, it proposes a system of double majority: a simple majority of the Member States representing a majority of the Union population. In order to improve the operating efficiency of the Commission of an enlarged European Union, it calls for a review of the present system whereby each EU Member State has at least one Commissioner in Brussels.

Europe à la carte

The views of the former Prime Minister Margaret Thatcher and the current Tory MP John Redwood are typical of the right-wing British Conservative Party. Although they grudgingly accept the fact that national interest demands a place for Britain at the European table, they believe that most of the measures taken over the past thirty years towards European integration along federalist lines, with the ever-increasing intrusiveness of European institutions such as the Commission and the European Court of Justice, have been a mistake. Removal of all internal trade barriers to achieve the free movement of goods, services, capital and workers is a desirable objective for the Community; trying to impose a common employment, social or agricultural policy at the European level is a mistake. Further deepening of European integration symbolized by the single currency, the social policy protocol of the Maastricht Treaty, more majority voting in the Council instead of the present unanimity requirement, and a common foreign and defence policy decided by majority voting, represents a loss of the inherent British right to self-government with the supremacy of Parliament. Britain must regain control of its national destiny, a form of 'British Gaullism'. Britain should work towards an 'à la carte' Europe, which is a series of relations, involving different combinations of Member States and based on intergovernmental cooperation rather than outright federal integration. According to this vision of Europe, a Member State chooses its partners depending on the issue or circumstance. For instance, most single market measures could be legislated and enforced within the present institutional framework (Commission, Council, the European Parliament and the European Court of Justice) while social and employment policies, foreign and defence policies, and justice and home affairs should be the subject of intergovernmental cooperation between those Member States that can agree. This type of 'à la carte' integration leads to a Europe of 'variable geometry', a term coined by the former UK foreign secretary Douglas Hurd. Parallel institutional structures and procedures would be established to deal with various issues and policies. On some policy matters, all Member States would participate within the framework of one set of institutions; on other policy matters, only a subset of Member States would participate within the framework of another set of institutions or procedures. Thus, the term 'variable geometry' refers to the various combinations of policy, Member State, and institutional procedure defining the European map. Current examples of a Europe 'à la carte' are provided by the British opt-outs of the single currency and of the Social Policy protocol, which deals with the promotion of employment, social protection, and working conditions. In her Bruges speech of 20 September 1988, Margaret Thatcher emphasized Britain's intergovernmental vision of the Community's future:

> Britain does not dream of some cosy, isolated existence on the fringes of the Community. Britain's destiny is in Europe, as part of the Community. . . . [Member States should work] more closely together on the things we can do better together than alone . . . whether it be in trade, in defence, or in our relations with the rest of the world. . . . Europe will be stronger precisely because it has France in as France,

Spain in as Spain, Britain in as Britain, each with its own customs, traditions and identity.

Parts of that speech echoed what De Gaulle – in a verbal assault against the Community institutions after the defeat of his Fouchet Plan – declared in his famous press conference of 15 May 1962 that

> . . . il n'y a que les États qui soient à cet égard valables, légitimes et capables de réaliser. J'ai déjà dit, et je répète, qu'à l'heure qu'il est, il ne peut pas y avoir d'autre Europe que celle des États, en dehors naturellement des mythes, des fictions, des parades.

The problem of constructing the integration of Europe on the basis of an 'à la carte' principle is highlighted by the UK opt-out on European social legislation. Competition in the single market could be distorted if the harmonization of minimum social standards, such as regulations relating to social security, the protection of workers on the termination of an employment contract, or the establishment of European Works Councils, is applied in all Member States except the UK. In a single market, firms may very well displace their production from Member States with high levels of non-wage labour costs to Member States where the non-wage labour costs are lower, as in the UK. In a single market environment, this is known as 'social dumping'. Another example of a problem created by a Europe 'à la carte' is provided by the UK opt-out of the single currency. Let us suppose that the major EU countries participate in a monetary union with a single currency while the UK, a Member State participating in the single market, refuses either to join the monetary union or to tie its national currency to the single currency. Then, Britain could engage in a monetary policy or fiscal policy that could lead to a transitory real depreciation of its national currency against the single currency. The UK would have obtained a temporary competitive advantage over its trading partners in the single market.

In a document entitled *A Partnership of Nations* (United Kingdom 1996), a thirty-eight-page booklet setting out the British government's approach to the Intergovernmental Conference, the main areas in need of reform are identified. The essential message is that the benefits of EU membership greatly outweigh the disadvantages as long as the nation-state, rather than any supranational institution, remains the dominant structure in the integration of Europe. The highlights of this document are as follows:

• Legislative process: the UK government will seek further means of entrenching subsidiarity into decision-making. Subsidiarity is the principle that decisions should always be taken at the lowest level, i.e. the national or regional government of a Member State, unless the stated objective cannot be achieved by the Member State acting alone, in which case the decision should be taken by Community institutions.

- The Council: there must neither be a weakening of qualified majority voting in the Council nor a further erosion of the principle of unanimity, which is a national safeguard; moreover, the government believes that the present four large Member States are under-represented in the present voting system; the government suggests that the smaller states would share their six-month presidencies with one of the six larger states – Germany, France, Italy, the United Kingdom, Spain and the Netherlands; the government also wishes to maintain the current Maastricht provision that policies with respect to foreign and security matters and justice and home affairs be taken by a unanimous vote in the Council.
- Commission: the government suggests a sunset clause which would ensure that Commission proposals for legislation would lapse after three years unless they had by then become law; the government also suggests a two-tier Commission following enlargement of the EU, with larger states having voting members and smaller states non-voting ones.
- European Parliament: the government believes that the EP does not need new powers and that the EP must not displace the primary role of national parliaments.
- Social policy (employment policies): the United Kingdom will not relinquish its opt-out on the Social Policy Protocol attached to the Maastricht Treaty.

The 'flexibility clause'

The current French government under Chirac/Juppé believes, like the German government, in a multi-speed Europe but, unlike Germany, believes that the political centre of gravity should not rest in the Commission and the European Parliament, but rather in the Council of Ministers and in national parliaments. In order to eschew the controversy over the various models envisaged in the further integration of Europe, France and Germany raised in December 1995 the banner of the 'flexibility clause'. In the context of the revision of the Maastricht Treaty, the leaders of these two Member States, in an attempt to prevent any single Member State (read the UK) from holding up the integration process, presented the idea that, whenever the keenest members of the European family agreed on areas of further integration, they should race ahead of the laggards, provided that this process does not compromise the institutional framework of the Union or distort competition. The reference to a 'single institutional framework' in the negotiations of the 'flexibility clause' reflects the fear that a wild proliferation of *ad hoc* arrangements between varying numbers of Member States would lead to a collapse of the European Union.

The Commission (1996c: 22), in support of the 'flexibility clause', suggested that the implementation of such a principle will have to be guided by the following conditions:

- compatibility with the objectives of the Union;
- consistency with the institutional framework of the Union;
- opportunity for other Member States which are willing and able to join at any time;
- safeguarding the single market and the policies accompanying it.

Britain is adding another condition: whenever a subset of Member States decides to forge ahead in further integration, all Member States of the EU would have to agree on the details, as well as the principle, of such further integration. In other words, a single Member State would have the right to block such a move.

1 European economic and monetary cooperation: 1958–78

INTRODUCTION

This chapter examines, in a chronological order, the main measures of macroeconomic and monetary policy cooperation between the Member States to implement the objectives of the Treaty of Rome. It also examines the first serious attempt by the Community to go beyond the provisions of the Treaty of Rome to establish a monetary union. A short review of the Bretton Woods international monetary system, with its fixed but adjustable exchange rate regime, is also presented.

BRETTON WOODS AND THE EUROPEAN MONETARY AGREEMENT

The post-war Bretton Woods international monetary system was based on a system of fixed but adjustable parities with the US dollar. The system required each International Monetary Fund (IMF) member country to maintain its currency within a band of ±1 percent around the defined bilateral parities. Since Western European countries imposed restrictions on currency convertibility between their own currencies during the period 1946 to 1958, an IMF member was considered to have effectively fulfilled its obligation if it only maintained the ±1 percent margins of fluctuation around the US dollar parity. This *de facto* Bretton Woods rule had, of course, the consequence of creating a currency band twice as wide between two European currencies. The maximum *instantaneous* fluctuation of any non-US dollar currency against another non-US dollar currency was 2 percent on either side of its bilateral parity. For example, if the Deutsche mark appreciated by 1 percent against its US dollar parity and, at the same time, the French franc depreciated by 1 percent against its US dollar parity, the instantaneous depreciation of the French franc against the Deutsche mark was 2 percent from the FF/DM bilateral parity.[1] Moreover, the rule of ±1 percent margins around the parity value with the US dollar implied a possible maximum *temporal* movement of 4 percent between two non-US dollar currencies. For example, assuming that initially the

French franc was resting on its strong margin against the US dollar and the Deutsche mark was resting on its weak margin against the US dollar, a later reversal of these positions for the French franc and Deutsche mark implied a 4 percent depreciation of the French franc against the Deutsche mark, i.e. the sum of a 2 percent depreciation of the French franc against the US dollar and of a 2 percent appreciation of the Deutsche mark against the US dollar (see Box 1.1).

As Western European countries lifted in 1958 the restrictions on currency convertibility for transactions related to the current account, the implied maximum allowable fluctuation between any two European currencies under the *de facto* Bretton Woods rules became unacceptable. Accordingly, in December 1958, some seventeen European countries, which included the original signatories of the Treaty of Rome as well as the United Kingdom, Ireland and Sweden, agreed to narrow the margins of fluctuations around the parity value with the US dollar from ±1 percent to ±0.75 percent,[2] consequently reducing, on the basis of the above argument, (i) the maximum *instantaneous* fluctuation around the bilateral parity of any two European currencies from 2 percent to 1.5 percent and (ii) the maximum *temporal* movement between any two European currencies from 4 percent to 3 percent. This measure constituted a part of an agreement known as the European Monetary Agreement (EMA). The EMA served as a framework for cooperation between the monetary authorities of the contracting parties, with the broad objective of encouraging multilateralism in international trade and currency convertibility. Its two principal operational aspects were: the European Fund, from which members could receive short or medium-term balance-of-payments assistance, and the Multilateral System of Settlements, under which each member country's central bank was assured of obtaining settlement in US dollars of its holdings of other members' currencies.

Continental European aversion for flexible exchange rates

The decision, taken at Bretton Woods in 1944, to establish an international monetary system based on fixed exchange rates was in line with Continental European's general dislike for flexible exchange rates. In the post-war period, three reasons are usually advanced to explain this European attitude towards flexible exchange rates (see Giavazzi and Giovannini 1989: 1):

- the European experience with the flexible exchange rate regime during the period 1919 to 1926;
- the presumed negative impact of flexible exchange rates on trade and direct investment flows and their welfare implications for relatively open European economies;
- the difficulties to administer the Common Agricultural Policy of the European Community under a flexible exchange regime.

Box 1.1 Bretton Woods exchange rate terminology

Gold parity: the gold content of each currency, as agreed at the Bretton Woods Conference of 1944. For example, the US dollar originally contained 0.88867088 grams of fine gold (=$35 per fine ounce of gold). All references to the gold content of a currency were formally abolished by the International Monetary Fund in 1978.

French franc–US dollar parity: the bilateral parity of the French franc against the US dollar. It was equal to the ratio of the French franc gold parity and the US dollar gold parity. Under the original terms of the Bretton Woods Agreement, US dollar gold parity could not be modified. Therefore, a change in the French franc–dollar parity could only be made by changing the French franc gold parity.

Bilateral parity of two non-US dollar currencies: the ratio of each of the two US dollar parities of the two non-dollar currencies. For example, the FF/DM bilateral parity is equal to the ratio the FF/US$ parity and the DM/US$ parity.

Maximum instantaneous fluctuation or spread of a currency around its US dollar parity: the maximum allowable movement of a currency against the US dollar, at any given moment, calculated from its dollar parity. For example, under the Bretton Woods rules, the French franc had a maximum instantaneous spread of 1 percent (absolute value) on *either side* of its US dollar parity. This is sometimes indicated in the literature as ±1 percent.

Maximum temporal fluctuation or spread of a currency against the US dollar: the maximum allowable movement of a currency over time, which is equal to the sum of the maximum instantaneous spread (absolute value) around its US dollar parity. For example, under the Bretton Woods rules, the French franc had a maximum temporal spread of 2 percent against the US dollar. This is equal to the sum of the maximum instantaneous spread of 1 percent (absolute value) around its US dollar parity.

If each currency has a maximum instantaneous spread defined only against its US dollar parity, as was the *de facto* case under Bretton Woods, then the implied (or derived) bilateral maximum instantaneous spread of the two non-US dollar currencies around their bilateral parity is equal to twice their maximum instantaneous spread around their US dollar parities. For example, the implied maximum instantaneous spread of the French franc on either side of its FF/DM bilateral parity is, under the rules of Bretton Woods, 2 percent (absolute value). Analogously, the maximum temporal spread of the French franc against the DM is 4 percent.

The first reason is related to the belief that foreign exchange speculation makes a system of freely fluctuating exchange rates unstable. Once an exchange rate begins to depreciate, speculators who expect further depreciation immediately sell the currency causing further depreciation, which in turn feeds further speculation. When this vicious depreciation cycle is terminated, the exchange rate is significantly misaligned creating a serious misallocation of resources between the trading partners. Nurske (1944: 117) concluded that 'the dangers of cumulative and self-aggravating movements under a regime of freely fluctuating exchange rates are clearly demonstrated by the French experience of 1922–26.' In short, a flexible exchange rate regime is inherently unstable because of destabilizing speculation. Friedman (1953), in his classic defence of flexible exchange rates, argued that there is no empirical foundation for this claim and that exchange rate instability reflects instability in the economy.

The second reason is explained by the increased price uncertainty under the flexible exchange rate regime. Price uncertainty is created by the exchange rate variation between the time when a commitment to accept delivery of, or to make payment in, foreign currency is made and when the actual transaction takes place. To reduce or eliminate the exchange rate uncertainty under the flexible exchange rate regime, most international traders engage in forward foreign exchange contracts. The cost of these contracts increases the effective price of internationally traded goods and thus tends to reduce the level of trade. If external trade constitutes an important share of GDP – as is the case for most European countries – the limitations on the opportunity to gain from trade lowers the country's welfare. A similar argument is made about the impact of a flexible exchange rate regime on long-term international capital movements. Flexible exchange rates reduce long-term direct investment because they result in greater uncertainty about the value and real rate of return of foreign investments. Consequently, long-term direct investment is inefficiently distributed between countries, resulting in a welfare loss.

It is difficult to verify empirically the hypothesis that increased exchange rate volatility – presumably the case with flexible exchange rates – has a negative impact on international trade (see International Monetary Fund 1984). Moreover, the negative impact of flexible exchange rates on capital flows is empirically not clear when contrasted with the fixed exchange rate regime wherein countries frequently set up barriers to the free movement of private long-term capital for purposes of achieving balance-of-payments equilibrium.

The third reason advanced to explain the European dislike for flexible exchange rates is related to the difficulties of implementing the Community's Common Agricultural Programme (CAP) under a flexible exchange rate regime. The Treaty of Rome establishing the European Economic Community contained provisions for the implementation of a CAP. The first CAP market regulations were adopted in 1962 with the final phase adopted in 1968. These regulations included the principle of a guaranteed price – denominated in a common numéraire such as the US dollar and later the ECU – for agricultural products with their free movement throughout the Community. The difficulties created by a variation in the exchange rates is highlighted by the 1969 devaluation of the French franc against the Deutsche mark. On the basis of the single guaranteed price denominated in US dollars, the price of French agricultural products, calculated in French francs, should have increased while the price of German agricultural products, calculated in Deutsche marks, should have decreased. In order to shelter the farmers in each Member State from such domestic price variations caused by the exchange rate variation, the Community was forced to introduce for the first time a 'representative' exchange rate (later called 'green' rate) to set the domestic agricultural price in each country. The difference between the 'green' exchange rate and the market exchange rate, combined with the free movement of agricultural products between Member States, required the establishment of a complex system of subsidies and taxes to avert disruptive trade flows as the agricultural products crossed internal frontiers of Member States whose exchange rates had been realigned (Rosenblatt 1978; Rosenblatt *et al.* 1988). These taxes and subsidies were called 'Monetary Compensatory Amounts' (MCAs). The MCAs took the form of import subsidies (taxes) and export levies (subsidies) on the agricultural trade of the Member State whose currency had been devalued (revalued). The system of establishing MCAs to close the gap between the 'green' rates and the market exchange rate would have been almost impossible to administer under flexible exchange rates.

ECONOMIC AND MONETARY POLICY COORDINATION BY COMMITTEES

Up until the end of the 1960s, economic and monetary policy coordination, which according to the Treaty of Rome (EEC) was the responsibility of the Ecofin Council (Article 145), was unnecessary. The balance-of-payments disequilibria which existed initially in the Community had been corrected at the end of 1958 by a devaluation of the French franc, and then in 1961 by a revaluation of the Deutsche mark and Dutch guilder. The Community countries as a whole enjoyed vigorous economic expansion of approximately 6 percent per year. This expansion was encouraged by the rapid progress of intra-Community trade resulting from the elimination of tariff barriers and by the continuous growth of external trade under the stimulus of international liberalization. In fact, during the first half of the 1960s, the Ecofin Council was, for the most part, just engaged in the formal exercise of setting up the machinery to achieve the macroeconomic goals stipulated by the Treaty. The macroeconomic goals '. . .

[of] ensur[ing] equilibrium of [each Member State's] overall balance of payments and [of] maintain[ing] confidence in its currency, while ensuring a high level of employment and the stability of the level of prices' (Article 104), were to be achieved by a coordination of economic policies (Article 3.g), by each Member State considering its short-term [conjunctural] macroeconomic policies as policies of *common* interest (Article 103), and by each Member State considering its exchange rate as a matter of *common* interest (Article 107). Accordingly, the Council established various committees: the Short-Term Economic Policy Committee (1960), the Medium-Term Economic Policy Committee (1964), the Committee of Governors of the Central Banks (1964) and the Budget Policy Committee (1965). Moreover, in keeping with Article 105.2, a Monetary Committee, with consultative status, had been established in 1958 to keep under review the monetary and financial situation of Member States and to report its recommendations to the Council.

Barre Plan of 1969

The problems of compatibility between the national economic trends began to appear in the late 1960s. The overheated German economy caused the monetary authorities of that country to apply a restrictive monetary policy which was the source of the recession in the first half of 1967. The sharp drop in German imports had an adverse effect on the economic trend in most of the other Member States. The German trade balance registered massive surpluses. From 1968 onwards, the economic recovery was accompanied by divergences in price trends and in external balances between Member States, notably between France and Germany. There was also a diversity of attitudes in the Member States with regard to medium-term domestic economic policy priorities which threatened the external equilibrium of the Member States. These problems came to a head with the intense speculation against the French franc in favour of the Deutsche mark during the 'May crisis' of 1968, which created severe tensions on the bilateral parities of Community currencies. The potential problems posed by the Community currency tensions to the development of the common market and notably to the Common Agricultural Policy based on the free movement of, and a single price for, Community agricultural products, led a discussion on the necessity for the coordination of economic and monetary policies between Member States and to establish monetary facilities for mutual balance-of-payments assistance between Member States as stipulated in Article 108 of the Treaty of Rome.

On 12 February 1969, the Commission submitted to the Council an important Memorandum on the coordination of economic policies between Member States. This Memorandum is known as the Barre Plan (Commission of the European Communities 1969) and named after the then Vice-president of the Commission responsible for economic affairs. It contained three major recommendations based on the principle that the coordination of economic policies between Member States must be combined with Community facilities for monetary support:

- *Coordination of the national medium-term economic policies of Member States.* First, it would be necessary to take concerted action to define the basic goals of the Member States concerning the rates of growth of production and employment, the price trend, the current account of the balance of payments and the overall balance of payments. Secondly, in order to attain these economic goals, a coordination of *medium-term economic policies* should be undertaken to guarantee the compatibility of policies among Member States.
- *Closer coordination of short-term economic policies.* The need to better coordinate *short-term* economic policies between Member States to prevent the various economies from departing from the medium-term guidelines laid down. To this end, the Commission recommends that more than just an exchange of views be done in the Monetary Committee or the Budget Policy Committee. More effective use of the consultation procedures is to be applied before Member States adopt changes in economic policies. For instance, proposed national budgets should be debated in the Budget Committee before their adoption by Member States.
- *Establishment of Community machinery for monetary cooperation.* In keeping with Article 108 of the Treaty of Rome dealing with mutual assistance in case of balance-of-payments difficulties (current or capital account), the Commission recommends the establishment of a short-term monetary facility and of a medium-term facility. The rationale of such a recommendation is that coordination between Member States of their economic and monetary policies will require at times mutual support for temporary balance-of-payments difficulties. The short-term monetary facility is envisaged as follows:

(i)   an undertaking by each participating country to place funds not exceeding a given ceiling at the disposal of the other countries;

(ii) activation of the system through a mere request by a participating country to its partners with the indebtedness of any participant not to exceed a certain ceiling;

(iii) a loan period of three months with the possibility of renewal provided that the Community receives from the borrowing country a satisfactory plan to eliminate the deficit.

The medium-term financial assistance could be granted only on a recommendation from the Commission to the Council after a determination that the balance-of-payments problems required a medium-term loan.

for the first time that a plan with a view to the creation of an economic and monetary union should be drafted: the unilateral devaluation of the French franc in August 1969, the unilateral decision first to float the Deutsche mark in September of the same year, then to revalue it in October 1969 with the accompanying problems created for the Common Agricultural Policy that was based on fixed exchange rates, and finally the departure of General de Gaulle from the political scene. In keeping with this resolution emanating from the highest political level, the Commission submitted in March 1970 to the Ecofin Council a report, entitled 'A Plan for the Phases [*sic*] Establishment of an Economic and Monetary Union' (Commission of the European Communities 1970), which proposed a three-stage approach to an economic and monetary union, starting in 1971 and ending approximately ten years later. In the last stage, the report proposed the elimination, in two steps, of the margins of fluctuation of the member countries' currencies, and the irrevocable fixing of the parities. It did not explicitly mention the single currency as the final objective.

On the basis of this Commission report, the Council requested that a committee of experts chaired by Pierre Werner, the then Prime Minister and Minister of Finance of Luxembourg, further study the question of the realization by stages of an economic and monetary union. The Werner Report (1970), entitled 'A Report to the Council and the Commission on the Realisation by Stages of Economic and Monetary Union in the Community (definitive text)', was released in October 1970. The definitive text of the Werner Report advocated a multi-stage approach towards an economic and monetary union, with the first stage beginning in January 1971 and with the final stage ending some ten years later. The Werner Report proposed a package of concrete measures for the first stage. This approach provided for the progressive elimination of exchange rate fluctuations between Community currencies with, in the final stage, the elimination of margins of fluctuation in rates of exchange, the irrevocable fixing of parity ratios, and the total liberalization of movements of capital. The Report also proposed the establishment of a European Fund for monetary cooperation in the first stage as a precursor to the Community system of European central banks for the final stage. From the very start, the budget policy of the Member States should be conducted in accordance with Community objectives. Throughout the process towards a monetary union, *parallel* progress should be made towards the harmonization of economic policies and towards the achievement of the goal of the free movement of goods, services, capital and workers. The institutional framework to achieve this monetary union would require the transfer of powers from national to Community institutions in both the monetary and fiscal areas, with a more powerful European Parliament.

The Werner Report also included in Annex 5 an important technical report known as the Ansiaux Committee Report, named after Baron Ansiaux, the then Chairman of the Committee of Governors of the

Central Banks of the Member States. This annex explained in some detail how to operate an exchange rate system with two different bands: one, with respect to the US dollar parities and the other, with respect to the bilateral parities of Community currencies. The Ansiaux Committee explained how to maintain the diameter of the first band constant while at the same time reducing the diameter of the second band. This proposal clearly went beyond the EMA which simply narrowed the margins of fluctuation of the Community currencies around their US dollar parities.

The 'monetarists' vs the 'economists'

The definitive text of the Werner Report was a compromise between two opposing schools called the 'monetarists', represented by the French and the Belgians/Luxembourgeois, and the 'economists', represented by the Germans and the Dutch. The 'monetarists' school (no relation to the North American homonym) believed that an essential prerequisite to an economic union was a strong monetary institutional framework with totally fixed and irrevocable parities (and in the extreme, a single currency) which, in turn, would promote the convergence of economic policies. The 'economists' believed that an essential prerequisite to major progress towards institutionalized forms of monetary integration, involving irrevocably fixed exchange rates and leading ultimately to a single currency and a single monetary policy, was a high degree of coordination and convergence of economic policies. According to this school, a monetary union could only be the crowning achievement of a gradual process that would harmonize economic policies between the Member States. In a spirit of compromise, the definitive text of the Werner Report refers to the 'parallel progress' that must be undertaken towards the *economic and monetary* union.

Follow-up to the Werner Report

Certain aspects of the Werner Report had a 'federalist' tone which raised some concerns among some Member States, like France. The Report contained many references to the creation of supranational institutions:

> On the institutional plane, in the final stage, two Community organs are indispensable: a centre for decision for economic policy and a Community system for the central banks. . . . The centre of economic decision will be politically responsible to a European Parliament.
> (Part VII, para. D of Werner Report 1970)

Economic and monetary union means that the principal decisions of economic policy will be taken at Community level and therefore that the necessary powers will be transferred from the national plane to the Community plane. These transfers of responsibility and the creation of the corresponding Community institutions represent a process of fundamental political significance which entails the progressive development of political cooperation.

(Part VII, para. B of Werner Report 1970)

On the basis of the Werner Report and the recommendations of the Commission, the Council adopted on 22 March 1971, a Resolution of intent regarding the political will of Member States to establish progressively an economic and monetary union and three Decisions to strengthen economic and monetary policy coordination. Furthermore, in conformity with the said Resolution and as a first step towards a monetary union, the Community Central Banks agreed to narrow the margins of fluctuations between Community currencies. These points are now amplified.

The Resolution, which has no legal force, resolves to begin in 1971 the process to attain in stages the goal of an economic and monetary union with the realization, at the end of a ten-year period, of:

- rigidly fixed and irrevocable parities between the currencies of the Member States and the adoption of a single currency with a Community system of central banks;
- an economic area in which all goods, services, capital and labour are allowed to move freely.

The Council stipulates that the measures to achieve a monetary union must be taken in parallel with measures to increase coordination of macroeconomic policies between Member States. These measures taken to achieve, in parallel, an economic and monetary union may require some transfer of powers and responsibilities from national institutions to Community institutions. Those transfers must be implemented only insofar as they are absolutely necessary for attaining the Community goals. The Council commitment to achieve an economic and monetary union will formally be retained until 1974 when the Council is unable to adopt a resolution to move to stage two of the step-by-step approach towards the economic and monetary union.

Then, having regard to the objectives of the above Resolution, the Council adopts three Decisions to implement the first stage of the process towards the economic and monetary union:

A Decision (71/141/EEC) on strengthening the coordination of short-term economic policies of the Member States. This Decision stipulates, for the first time, that the Council shall hold three meetings yearly for the purpose of examining the economic situation in the Community. The Council shall adopt guidelines on short-term economic policy which the Community and each Member State are to follow in order to achieve 'harmonious economic development'. These guidelines include fixing public budget estimates for each Member State and the adoption of an annual report on the economic situation of the Community. This annual report is then brought to the attention of each national parliament so that it may be taken into account when each government debates its public budget.

A Decision (71/142/EEC) on strengthening the cooperation between the central banks of the Member States to coordinate their monetary and credit matter policies within the Committee of Governors of Central Banks.

A Decision (71/143/EEC) to set up the machinery for medium-term financial assistance (MTFA), as originally proposed in the Barre Plan of 1969. Under this facility, which is to become operational as of 1 January 1972, the Member States shall make available to each other loans in case of balance-of-payments difficulties. This mutual assistance shall be in the form of conditional credits, with ceilings and with a term of two to five years. The commitment ceilings are as follows:

Germany: 600 million units of account
Belgium–Luxembourg: 200 million u.a.
France: 600 million u.a.
Italy: 400 million u.a.
The Netherlands: 200 million u.a.

Finally, the Governors of the Central Banks of the Member States of the EEC agree in April 1971 to narrow the margins of fluctuation between Community currencies, effective 1 June 1971, by maintaining the ±0.75 percent EMA margins against the US dollar parity, while at the same time reducing the maximum instantaneous fluctuation from 1.5 percent to 1.2 percent around any bilateral parity of two Community currencies (Banque nationale de Belgique 1972: XXII). This agreement between Central Banks is similar to the Community exchange rate mechanism described in the Ansiaux Committee Report (Annex 5 of the Werner Report 1970) and in an article by Ansiaux (1972). This mechanism proposes to maintain the margins of fluctuation with respect to the US dollar while reducing the margins of fluctuation between Community currencies so as not always to provide, as under the EMA, a smaller band of fluctuation to the US dollar than to any two Community currencies. The upper and lower margins of fluctuation of a Community currency around its US dollar parity define what is called the 'tunnel'. The diameter of the tunnel is equal to the maximum temporal spread of a Community currency against the US dollar. Inside the tunnel is what is referred to as the 'snake', with a diameter equal to the maximum instantaneous spread allowed between any two Community currencies. The diameter of the snake is smaller than the diameter of the tunnel.[3] The system also provides for possible interventions in dollars and in the Community currencies which will require intra-Community credit facilities between Community central banks.

The snake in the tunnel

The international events that occurred as of May 1971 effectively scuttled the above agreement between the Community Central Banks. In the face of intense speculation against the dollar, Germany was forced to announce in May 1971 that the Deutsche mark would temporarily float against the dollar. The Dutch guilder followed. France maintained its parity with the US dollar but established a dual foreign exchange market. Moreover, the Bretton Woods international monetary system definitely collapsed with the announcement, on 15 August 1971, that the United States Treasury would no longer convert the dollar into gold[4] – a cornerstone of the post-war international monetary system. In an attempt to salvage the fixed but adjustable Bretton Woods system of parities, the Group of Ten (paradoxically composed of eleven countries, i.e. G7 plus Belgium, the Netherlands, Sweden and Switzerland) agreed in late 1971 to change the parity values (or central rates) against the US dollar and to widen the margins of fluctuation around these new US dollar parities from ±1 percent to ±2.25 percent.[5] This decision, known as the Smithsonian or Washington Agreement, was ratified by the IMF on 18 December 1971. These widened margins of fluctuation vis-à-vis the US dollar were unacceptable to the Community as they implied a possible maximum bilateral *temporal* spread of 9 percent between two Community currencies,[6] which was three times as wide as the maximum temporal spread allowed under the EMA provisions. In response, the Council adopted a Resolution on 21 March 1972 allowing the Community Central banks to make full use of the larger Smithsonian margins of fluctuation vis-à-vis the US dollar while, at the same time, maintaining between any two given Community currencies – apart from the Benelux currencies – a maximum instantaneous spread of 2.25 percent on either side of their bilateral parity. Accordingly, the market fluctuations of any two European Community currencies *over time* and the distance between two currencies at any *point in time* could not exceed those allowed between any one of these currencies and the US dollar, i.e. 4.5 and 2.25 percent, respectively. As for the Benelux currencies, the maximum instantaneous spread from their bilateral parity was maintained at 1.5 percent, as the Benelux countries had agreed in August 1971.

European common margins arrangement (Basle Agreement)

The Central Banks of the then six Member States of the Community and of the three prospective Member States (Denmark, Ireland and the United Kingdom) signed an Agreement (Central banks of the Member States of the European Economic Community 1972) on 10 April 1972, to implement, effective 24 April 1972, the Council Resolution. This agreement, also known as the 1972 Basle Agreement, is sometimes referred to as the 'snake in the tunnel'.[7] The axis of the tunnel is represented by the parity of any given Community currency against the US dollar, and its two outer extremes are formed by the fluctuation limits of +2.25 percent and –2.25 percent against the dollar parity. Within the tunnel – which therefore has a diameter of 4.50 percent – is the snake, that is the Community band in which the European currencies participating in the Basle Agreement move. The snake or Community band is necessarily narrower than the tunnel since the maximum instantaneous spread of rates which any two Community currencies can show in relation to their bilateral parity is limited to 2.25 percent – the maximum diameter of the 'snake'.

The Community Central banks also decided that the Smithsonian ('tunnel') marginal interventions would be carried out in dollars and that the Basle ('snake') marginal interventions would be carried out in Community currencies.[8] Accordingly, *bilateral* lines of credit between Community Central banks, known as the 'very short-term financing' (VSTF) facility, were established to finance the 'snake' marginal interventions. Three examples illustrate this system.

Example 1

Assumptions: The French franc/US$ rate is +2.25 percent from its Smithsonian parity and the Deutsche mark/US$ rate is on its Smithsonian parity.

Thus, the French franc is resting on its weak edge relative to the dollar and relative to the DM, i.e. the French franc is resting on the ceiling of the tunnel and on the upper flank of the snake. Therefore, the Banque de France is expected, under the terms of the Smithsonian and Basle Agreements, to intervene with US dollars, i.e. sell US dollars and buy its own currency on the foreign exchange market, in order to prevent the French franc from crossing its tunnel margin. This dollar intervention also prevents the French franc from crossing its snake margin against the Deutsche mark.

Example 2

Assumptions: The FF/US$ rate is +1.26 percent from its Smithsonian parity (a depreciation of the French franc relative to its US dollar parity). The DM/US$ rate is –0.99 percent from its Smithsonian parity (an appreciation of the DM relative to its US dollar parity).

Since neither the French franc nor the Deutsche mark is on the margins of the tunnel, no dollar intervention is necessary on the part of either the Deutsche Bundesbank or the Banque de France. However, the FF/DM rate is +2.25 percent from its bilateral parity (=1.26 percent +0.99 percent), with the French franc on its weak edge relative to the DM. Therefore, under the Basle Agreement, the Banque de France must sell DMs and buy its own currency on the Paris foreign exchange market in order to prevent the French franc from crossing its snake margin vis-à-vis the DM. Under the Basle Agreement, the Banque de France may borrow DMs – in principle, in unlimited amounts – from the Bundesbank to carry out this intervention.

Example 3

Assumptions: The FF/US$ rate is –0.99 percent from its Smithsonian parity. The DM/US$ rate is +1.26 percent from its Smithsonian parity.

Again, since neither the French franc nor the Deutsche mark is on the margins of the tunnel, no dollar intervention is necessary. However, the FF/DM rate is –2.25 percent from its bilateral parity, with the French franc on its strong edge relative to the DM, i.e. on the lower flank of the snake. Therefore, under the Basle Agreement, the Bundesbank must sell French francs and buy its own currency on the Frankfurt foreign exchange market in order to prevent the DM from crossing its snake margin vis-à-vis the French franc. Under the VSTF facility, the Bundesbank may borrow French francs from the Banque de France to carry out this intervention.

These three examples illustrate that the 'snake' may undulate through the tunnel, and that, at any point in time, one Community currency cannot be on the ceiling of the tunnel while the other is on the floor of the tunnel. It should also be understood that the diameter of the snake is not necessarily constant over time (for more details, see Banque nationale de Belgique 1972).

Shortly after the inception of the 'snake in the tunnel' on 24 April 1972, four prospective EEC Member States joined it – the United Kingdom, Ireland and Denmark on 1 May 1972 and Norway on 23 May 1972. When a run on sterling began in mid-June, sparked off by an imminent prospect of a national dock strike and more general fears about industrial strife and its implications for successful policies to contain inflation, sterling began to float against the US dollar on 23 June 1972 and at the same time withdrew from the snake. The Irish pound, with its fixed peg to the British pound since 1929, followed suit. In the period leading up to the Danish referendum on joining the EEC, Denmark also withdrew from the snake on 27 June 1972. Then, on 10 October 1972, after the positive results of the referendum, Denmark rejoined the snake. At the end of 1972, the dispensation, permitting the Italian authorities to support the lira within the snake by way of exclusive dollar intervention, expired. The dollar's acute weakness early in February 1973 sent all the snake currencies, except the lira, close to their strong edge with the dollar. Instead of continuing the intervention against the snake currencies, Italy decided on 13 February 1973 to withdraw from the scheme.

Very short-term financing (VSTF) facility

Under the VSTF facility established pursuant to the terms of the Agreement of 10 April 1972, the debtor central bank must settle the debt with the creditor central bank within thirty days from the end of the month in which the debt is incurred, with the possibility of a three-month renewal by mutual consent of the creditor and debtor central bank. When a financing operation falls due for settlement, the debtor central bank may liquidate its debt by means of assets in the currency of the creditor, in gold, in dollars, in other foreign currencies, or in Special Drawing Rights, in a proportion based on the composition of its own reserves held in these categories as at the end of the month preceding settlement. The interest rate applied on the outstanding debt of the debtor central bank is equal to the arithmetic mean of the official discount rates of the participating central banks.

With the demonetization of gold by the IMF, the option to reimburse the debt with gold was withdrawn with the amendments of 8 July 1975 introduced in the Agreement between Community central banks with respect to the VSTF facility. These amendments also allowed for an *automatic* three-month renewal of the debt at the request of the debtor central bank, provided that its *total* amount of debt outstanding vis-à-vis all the Community central banks at no time exceeded a ceiling equal to the debtor quota of the central bank concerned under the Short-Term Monetary Support facility. Moreover, any debt renewed automatically for three months could be renewed a second time for a further three months, subject to the agreement of the creditor or creditors. Under the terms of this amendment, the Community central banks also agreed that the STMS facility could be used as an additional financing mechanism to the VSTF facility available for intervention purposes to maintain a currency within its narrow snake band.

European Monetary Cooperation Fund (EMCF)

With a view to promote the progressive establishment of economic and monetary union, the Member States of the Community decided to establish a European Monetary Cooperation Fund on 6 April 1973, pursuant to a Council Decision of 12 September 1972. The idea of a Fund was first put forward by the Heads of State or Government at The Hague Summit of 1–2 December 1969: 'They have agreed that the possibility should be examined of setting up a European reserve fund, to which a common economic and monetary policy would lead' (Final Communiqué, point 8.3). It was then proposed in the Werner Report (1970) and its function and role as a precursor of a European central bank were described in the accompanying Ansiaux Committee Report (Werner Report 1970: Annex 5). It was also evoked in the Council Resolution of 22 March 1971, taken with respect to the Community commitment to progressively achieve an economic and monetary union.

However, the EMCF is ultimately given more limited tasks than was originally envisioned. In the first stage of its operation, this new body is to be responsible for the following matters:

1   the cooperation necessary to facilitate the gradual narrowing of the margins of fluctuation of the Community currencies against each other;
2   the administration of the Short-Term Monetary Support facility established as an agreement between Community central banks in February 1970, already described above;
3   the multilateralization of positions in the VSTF facility resulting from intervention carried out by the central banks in Community currencies.

With the establishment of the EMCF, all bilateral debts and credits held by Community central banks in connection with the VSTF facility of the snake arrangement were administered by that Fund. Typically, intervention to maintain a Community currency within the band defined by the snake arrangement is as follows: the central bank of the Member State with the weak currency borrows the currency of the central bank with the strong currency so that the former may buy its own currency on the foreign exchange market. This gives rise to a *bilateral* relation between the two central banks when the debts and credits are settled. By contrast, multilateralization of debts and credits means that the obligations and claims are settled vis-à-vis the Fund. Multilateralization allows the implementation of automatic and uniform rules for the availability and settlement of claims and debts and allows the payment of debts in a currency or asset different from the one borrowed.

The snake without the tunnel

At the beginning of 1973, it was becoming clear that the general realignment of parities against the US dollar and the widening of the margins of fluctuation of the Smithsonian Agreement were not sufficient to maintain stability of the international monetary system. In February 1973, the speculation against the US dollar and in favour of the German mark and the Japanese yen increased. On 12 February 1973, the dollar was devalued for the second time. Despite the dollar devaluation of 10 percent against the official price of gold, which increased from $38 to $42.22 per ounce, the foreign exchange markets remained unsettled and had to be closed at the beginning of March 1973. When they re-opened, the central parities against the US dollar were no longer defended and the major currencies floated against the US dollar. In view of these circumstances, the Community Finance Ministers decided to retain the maximum allowable instantaneous spread of 2.25 percent on either side of the bilateral parity

of any two currencies that participated in the Basle Agreement (1.5 percent in the case of the relation between the Dutch guilder and the Belgian
franc) and to cease their systematic intervention at the maximum fluctuation margins of the US dollar. The Community exchange rate regime was
now a joint float, i.e. the new regime did away with the 'tunnel' and maintained the 'snake'.

By the time the tunnel disappeared on 12 March 1973, seven currencies were participating in the joint float: six Community currencies – the
Danish krone, the Dutch guilder, the French franc, the Belgian and
Luxembourg francs, and the Deutsche mark – and one non-Community
currency, the Norwegian krone. Another non-Community currency, the
Swedish krona, entered the joint float on 19 March 1973. By the beginning of 1979, only a mini-snake was left, containing five Community
currencies: the Danish krone, which had maintained its participation in
the joint float at the cost of several devaluations, and four stronger currencies: the Dutch guilder, the Belgian and Luxembourg francs and the
Deutsche mark.

In general, two major factors can explain the difficulties faced by the
European joint float during the period 1973–78, during which time eight
realignments took place and one major currency, the French franc, left,
re-joined, and left again the snake arrangement (see Table 1.1). The first
factor is the destabilizing influence that the US dollar weakness had on
the exchange rates between Community currencies. As financial assets
were moving out of the US dollar and into strong European currencies,
the divergence between weak and strong European currencies was accen-
tuated, requiring massive interventions – and ultimately a realignment –
to maintain the European currencies within the snake margins. The 3
percent revaluation of the DM against participating currencies on 12
March 1973 is such an example. The second factor is the first round of
oil price shocks of 1973–74. It affected European countries to differing
degrees and elicited different policy responses from the monetary authorities. The results were divergences in Member States' monetary policies
and economic performances. Between 1973 and 1979, for instance, the
average annual rate of inflation was 11 percent in France but only 4.7
percent in Germany.

TEMPORARY SUSPENSION OF THE GOAL TO ACHIEVE
AN ECONOMIC AND MONETARY UNION

The final quarter of 1973 witnessed a spectacular increase in oil prices. In
view of this economic shock of unprecedented magnitude, combined with
the different policy responses of the Member States, the Council was
unable to adopt a resolution in December 1973 on the transition to
Stage II of the Economic and Monetary Union, pursuant to the previous
resolutions regarding the ten-year timetable mentioned in the Council

Table 1.1 Key dates and events of the 'snake' and the 'tunnel' arrangement

24 Apr. 1972	Belgium, France, Federal Republic of Germany, Italy, Luxembourg and the Netherlands agree to maintain their currencies within 2.25% of either side of their bilateral parity ('snake') while maintaining margins of ±2.25% around the US dollar parity ('tunnel').
1 May 1972	The British pound, the Irish pound and the Danish krone join the snake.
23 May 1972	The Norwegian krone is associated with the snake.
23 June 1972	The British pound and the Irish pound leave the snake.
27 June 1972	The Danish krone leaves the snake.
10 Oct. 1972	The Danish krone rejoins the snake.
13 Feb. 1973	The Italian lira leaves the snake.
12 Mar. 1973	The 'tunnel' disappears. A 'snake' realignment. 3% revaluation of the Deutsche mark against the EMUA*.
19 Mar. 1973	The Swedish krona is associated with the snake.
29 June 1973	5.5% revaluation of the Deutsche mark against the EMUA.
17 Sept. 1973	5% revaluation of the Dutch guilder against the EMUA.
16 Nov. 1973	5% revaluation of the Norwegian krone against the EMUA.
19 Jan. 1974	The French franc leaves the snake.
10 July 1975	The French franc rejoins the snake.
15 Mar. 1976	The French franc again leaves the snake.
17 Oct. 1976	2% revaluation of the Deutsche mark against the EMUA; 4% devaluation of the Danish krone against the EMUA; 1% devaluation of the Norwegian krone and Swedish krona against the EMUA.
1 Apr. 1977	6% devaluation of the Swedish krona and 3% devaluation of both the Danish and Norwegian kroner against the EMUA.
28 Aug. 1977	The Swedish krona leaves the snake; 5% devaluation of both the Danish and Norwegian kroner against the EMUA.
13 Feb. 1978	8% devaluation of the Norwegian krone against the EMUA.
17 Oct. 1978	4% revaluation of the Deutsche mark and 2% revaluation of both the Dutch guilder and Belgian–Luxembourg franc against the EMUA.
12 Dec. 1978	The Norwegian krone leaves the snake.

*The European Monetary Unit of Account is defined as 0.88867088 gram of fine gold (the gold parity of the US dollar from 1934 to 1971). This is one of the Community's new units of account to replace the US dollar from 3 April 1973 to 31 December 1978.

Source: Commission of the European Communities 1982: 69.

Resolution of 22 March 1971 and in the statement of the Heads of State or Government at their Paris Summit Conference of October 1972. By the beginning of 1974, serious economic disequilibria existed in the Member States of the Community. The most serious disequilibria affected the trends in prices and balance-of-payments, both of which varied considerably from one country to another. The increase in oil prices gave a vigorous boost to inflation and turned some of the traditional current account surpluses into deficits. By the end of 1974, the year-to-year increases of consumer prices were 24 percent in Italy, 17–18 percent in the United Kingdom and Ireland, 15 percent in France, 16 percent in Belgium and Denmark, 11 percent in the Netherlands and Luxembourg, but only 5 percent in Germany where a tight monetary policy was maintained. Germany maintained its current account surplus, while the external deficits of France, Denmark and in particular the United Kingdom and Italy worsened considerably. The impact of inflation and the oil crisis meant, in particular, that the Community exchange rate system could not be restored so as to include all Member States. In fact, in January 1974, the French government informed the Community authorities of its decision to suspend its intervention on foreign exchange markets. In view of the deteriorating economic situation and of the risks inherent in the lack of coordination of economic policies between Member States to implement the macroeconomic objectives set out in Article 104 of the Treaty of Rome, namely to maintain equilibrium in the balance of payments and to ensure stable prices, the Ecofin Council, on 18 February 1974, adopted additional measures to reinforce economic policy coordination between Member States. They were as follows.

A Decision (74/120/EEC) to achieve a high degree of convergence of economic policies between Member States. This Decision adds the following significant provisions to the coordination Decision of March 1971:

- It introduces for the first time the objective of achieving the 'convergence' of economic policies, not just the 'coordination' of economic policies.
- It introduces for the first time the legal requirement to hold a meeting of the Council once a month to discuss economic problems.
- It introduces for the first time the legal requirement on a Member State to hold prior consultations with Community institutions before changing an exchange rate parity.
- It introduces for the first time the right of the Commission to address a recommendation to a Member State whose economic policies diverge from the guidelines fixed by the Council. Moreover, the Member State must provide a response to the Commission's recommendations.

A Decision (74/122/EEC) to reinforce policy convergence by merging the three existing economic committees, namely the Short-Term Economic Policy Committee, the Budget Policy Committee and the Medium-Term

Economic Policy Committee, into one Economic Policy Committee composed of four representatives from the Commission and four representatives from each Member State. This committee is responsible for the elaboration of both short-term and medium-term economic policies;

A Resolution to strengthen the Short-Term Monetary Support facility. Accordingly, in February 1974, the Central Banks of the nine Member States agreed to increase the quotas available under the STMS facility and to differentiate between the size of debtor quotas and creditor quotas, the latter being twice as high as the former to safeguard the viability of the system under varying distributions of payment imbalances among Member States. The total debtor quotas and debtor *rallonge* were increased to EMUA2,725 million and EMUA1,500 million, respectively (1 EMUA = gold parity of the 1934–71 US dollar). Italy drew on this facility in 1974.

The first oil price shock also created unsustainable current account imbalances for some Member States. Accordingly, the Community designed (Council Decision of 17 February 1975) a new mechanism, known as the Community Loan Mechanism (CLM), to assist Member States with medium-term current account problems due to the oil price shock. Under this mechanism, the Community is allowed to borrow up to 3,000 million dollars, or its equivalent amount, from non-Member States, financial institutions, or on international markets to lend in turn the funds to the Member States. This mechanism is different from the MTFA facility in that it 'recycles' funds from outside the Community to Community Member States. Both Italy and Ireland used the CLM soon after its establishment. In the 1980s, the terms and ceilings of this facility were amended several times (Chapter 2).

CONCLUSION

The period 1958–78 was characterized by the establishment of committees and procedures to coordinate economic and monetary policies of the Member States, in keeping with the provisions of the Treaty of Rome establishing the EEC. This period was also characterized by the first proposal and formal analysis of a process by which the Member States could achieve a monetary union within the framework of the Bretton Woods international monetary system of fixed but adjustable exchange rates against the US dollar. As of 1969, the political will to reach a monetary union was clearly expressed. From that date, the Community will never permanently abandon this goal. With the first oil price shock and the definitive collapse of the fixed exchange rate regime based on the US dollar as the anchor of the international monetary system, the formal process to implement the monetary union is derailed. In 1974, the Community suspends *sine die* the Werner Plan to achieve a monetary union by 1980, and instead stresses the need to achieve the convergence of macroeconomic policies between Member States. The procedures are established in the February 1974 Decision to attain a high degree of convergence of the economic policies of the Member States. By the end of the 1970s, there is very little convergence of policies between the Member States. The fixed exchange rate system of the Community (the snake) is reduced to little more than a system in which the Benelux currencies and the Danish krone are attached to the Deutsche mark. The Community is in need of a new regional exchange rate system that will pave the way to strengthen the convergence of economic and monetary policies.

2   European Monetary System (EMS): 1979–90

INTRODUCTION

The proposed new European Monetary System (EMS), shepherded by President Valéry Giscard d'Estaing of France and Chancellor Helmut Schmidt of Germany, was intended to replace the European fixed exchange rate system known as the 'snake' by establishing a new institutional framework for maintaining stability between Community currencies while allowing them to float vis-à-vis the other currencies. The first phase of the EMS also was to lay the *initial* foundations 'for the creation of closer monetary cooperation leading to a zone of monetary stability in Europe' (Resolution of the Brussels European Council, 5 December 1978). The effective implementation of the EMS on 13 March 1979 – originally planned for 1 January 1979 but delayed because of a dispute over a related technical issue dealing with the impact of the new numéraire, the ECU, on the Common Agricultural Policy – was accompanied by a new Agreement between the Central Banks (Central banks of the Member States of the European Economic Community 1979). All the then nine Member States of the Community joined the EMS. However, at the outset one Member State, the United Kingdom, under pressure from the trade unions and the Parliamentary Labour Party who were afraid that the UK would be prevented from devaluing the pound in order to maintain competitiveness and employment, opted out of the Exchange Rate Mechanism (ERM) of the EMS (see Johnson 1994).

There are three main features to the European Monetary System: (1) the European Currency Unit (ECU), (2) the Exchange Rate Mechanism (ERM), and (3) the credit mechanisms. As described below, the EMS is in part a reinforcement and/or an extension of features that were established and implemented in the joint European exchange rate mechanism of the 1970s, known as the 'snake'. However, the new system has some fundamental differences. The new numéraire, the ECU, is much more than just a mere unit of account, as was the case for the EMUA, the numéraire of the 'snake' arrangement. From gold and US dollars, the ECU is created into an official reserve asset, held by the EMCF. The ECU is also used, as part of the Exchange Rate Mechanism of the EMS, to provide an early warning signal to participating Member States that their macroeconomic policies are inconsistent with the established ECU parities, averting the need to engage in significant bilateral marginal intervention between currencies. And, if marginal intervention is required, the provisions of the EMS provide the central bank with the weak currency with enhanced means to defend the weak edge of the band around each bilateral parity. The Exchange Rate Mechanism is designed, in theory, to assign more evenly the obligations between Member States with strong currencies and Member States with weak currencies. Also, under the EMS the total amount of credit available under the the the Short-Term Monetary Support (STMS) facility and the Medium-Term Financial Assistance (MTFA) facility – both established in the early 1970s – is increased. Finally, after a two-year transitional period, the EMCF is envisaged to be replaced with a European Monetary Fund, which would create *ex nihilo* official ECU reserve assets. Because of German reluctance to create a new monetary asset without an independent European central bank to control its supply, this provision of the EMS was never implemented.

From the French perspective, this new Community monetary system is created in the spirit of a continuation, after a pause and numerous setbacks during the 1970s, of the efforts to ultimately attain an economic and monetary union, as stipulated in the Resolutions of The Hague Summit of December 1969 and the Paris Summit of October 1972. From the German perspective, the creation of the EMS is an attempt to link the Deutsche mark to the other Community currencies to prevent the excessive appreciation of the DM against those currencies that had withdrawn from the snake (Gros and Thygesen 1992).

THE ECU

Just as the US dollar was at the centre of the Bretton Woods international monetary system and was its *de facto* numéraire and reserve asset (the dollar is 'as good as gold'), the ECU is designed to be the unit of account and the reserve asset at the centre of the EMS. However, unlike the US dollar in the Bretton Woods system, the ECU is not a numéraire based on a single currency but is defined as a weighted average, or basket, of the currencies of the Member States.

At the outset, the composition and value of the ECU are equal to the composition and value of the European Unit of Account (EUA), a numéraire which was introduced and defined on 21 April 1975 (see Box 2.1) for accounting purposes under the Lomé Convention governing economic and financial relations between the Community and the associated countries in Africa and in the Caribbean and Pacific areas. In addition to its function under the Lomé Convention, the EUA is mainly used for accounting operations of the European Investment Bank, established in

Box 2.1 A few European units of account

Unit of Account (UA): equal to one US dollar

European Monetary Unit of Account (EMUA): equal to 0.88867088 grams of fine gold, which was equal to one US dollar before the first devaluation of the US dollar with respect to gold announced in 1971 and ratified by the US Congress in February 1972. This unit of account was used as a numéraire by:

- the EMCF from 1973 to 1978;
- the European central banks participating in the 'snake' exchange rate system to define the bilateral central rates.

European Unit of Account (EUA): equal to a weighted basket of nine currencies of the Member States of the European Community. The EUA was defined in April 1975 under the Lomé Convention and used as a numéraire by:

- the European Development Fund (EDF), as of 1975;
- the European Investment Bank (EIB), as of 1975;
- the European Coal and Steel Community, as of 1976;
- the European Community for its general budget and customs matters, as of 1978.

ECU [not officially considered an acronym; a generic name]: initially defined to be equal to an EUA, and originally designed to be an open basket of currencies whose composition could be – and has been – changed. Created in 1979 and soon adopted by all Community institutions as the numéraire for bookkeeping purposes, the ECU is defined since 1 November 1993 as a closed basket of twelve currencies. On 1 January 1999, the ECU, whose name will be changed to Euro, is scheduled to become a currency in its own right created by the European Central Bank and to legally replace the national units of account of those Member States designated to form the single currency zone. The new Euro banknotes and Eurocent coins are to be introduced as of 1 January 2002.

Representative or 'green' rates: agri-monetary exchange rates to convert common agricultural prices, which were set by Council in terms of the EMUA or the ECU (after March 1979), into national currencies. Variations in exchange rates created price variations in agricultural products. This was incompatible with the requirement of agricultural price stability stipulated in the Common Agricultural Programme (CAP) of the Treaty of Rome. From 1969, an agri-monetary system was devised to shelter this sector from variations in exchange rates by converting CAP prices into national currencies at rates different from market exchange rates. These conversion rates were called 'representative' or, after March 1979, 'green' rates. The gap between the 'representative rate' or 'green rate' and the market exchange rate gave rise to the Monetary Compensatory Amounts (MCAs), which were taxes or subsidies placed on Member States' trade in agricultural products to prevent any exploitation of the difference between market rates and representative/green rates (see Rosenblatt *et al.* 1988).

1958 under the Treaty of Rome, and, as of December 1977, for accounting operations of the general budget of the Community.

The idea of creating a Community unit of account appeared necessary in the wake of the two major devaluations of the US dollar against gold of December 1971 and of February 1973 and the collapse in March 1973 of the fixed but adjustable exchange rate system of Bretton Woods. The European Community had heretofore used the US dollar as the unit of account for all bookkeeping activities. In 1973, with the establishment of the European Monetary Cooperation Fund (EMCF), it created a new unit of account called the European Monetary Unit of Account (EMUA) defined in terms of a given quantity of gold equal to the gold content of the 1934–71 US dollar, namely 0.88867088 gram of fine gold.[1] By the mid-1970s with the demonetization of gold and the clear desire of the IMF to entirely eliminate any link of a currency to gold, the Community once again needed a new unit of account: the European Unit of Account (EUA), defined on 21 April 1975.

The European Unit of Account (EUA) and the ECU

A brief description of the recipe to define the EUA is in order since this unit of account will become four years later the foundation of the definition of the ECU.

First, it is decided that the EUA must be composed of all the currencies of the Member States of the Community, which in 1975 is composed of nine Member States. Secondly, it is agreed that this basket of currencies is to be a weighted average of its constituent parts, with the percentage weights determined by the relative importance of each Member State's gross domestic product and intra-community trade – both of which are calculated over a five-year period – and by the relative contribution of each Central Bank to the Short-Term Monetary Support facility. The percentage weights are shown in column 1 of Table 2.1.

The percentage weight of each currency in the EUA basket is not sufficient to determine the *quantities* of each currency in the basket. To solve this unknown, it is agreed – and this is the third part of the recipe – that the *value* of the basket of currencies, as of a particular day (or over a

Table 2.1 Composition and value of the EUA/ECU basket

Currency	Weight agreed upon for the EUA basket (%)	Quantity of each currency	Value of EUA/ECU on 12.03.1979 = ECU central rate on 13.03.1979	Weight on 13.03.1979 (ECU) (%)
	(1)	(2)	(3)	(4)
Deutsche mark (DM)	27.3	0.828	2.51064	32.98
French franc (FF)	19.5	1.15	5.79831	19.83
Pound sterling (UKL)	17.5	0.0885	0.663247	13.34
Italian lira (LIT)	14.0	109.0	1148.15	9.5
Dutch guilder (HFL)	9.0	0.286	2.72077	10.51
Belgian franc (BFR)	7.9	3.66	39.4582	9.28
Danish krone (DKR)	3.0	0.217	7.08592	3.06
Irish punt (IRL)	1.5	0.00759	0.662638	1.15
Luxembourg franc (LFR)	0.3	0.14	39.4582	0.35

Notes:
(1) The criteria for assigning these weights in 1975 are indicated in the text.
(2) Based on the weight given in column (1) and the average exchange rate of the ith currency against the SDR prevailing over the three-month period 28 March to 27 June 1974.
(3) Communicated by the Governors of the Central Banks of the Member States of the EEC and based on the currency composition of the EUA basket shown in column (2) and each currency's bilateral market US dollar rate observed on 12 March 1979. For details, see text below and *Communication* published by the Commission on 28 December 1978 (reproduced in Monetary Committee of the European Community 1989: 129–130).
(4) The weight of the ith currency $w(i) = x(i)/z(i)$ where $x(i)$ is the quantity (column 2) of the ith currency in the ECU basket and $z(i)$ is the value of the ECU in terms of the ith currency. It is to be noted that by 1979 the weight of each currency had changed from the weights that had been agreed upon in 1975 at the time the EUA was defined since the denominator (ECU value) had changed during that period of time.

particular three-month period, as was actually decided), should be equal to one Special Drawing Right (SDR).[2] On that day the EUA has the same value as an SDR, but the EUA can thereafter evolve on its own. The quantities of each currency shown in column 2 of Table 2.1 are determined, in principle,[3] by taking the average value of each currency against the SDR over the period 28 March to 27 June 1974 and by multiplying it by its corresponding percentage weight. For example, the average value of the DM against the SDR for that three-month period is [3.0330DM/SDR] × 27.3% = .828, the number of Deutsche marks in the EUA basket. Similarly, the average value of the French franc against the SDR over that three-month period is [5.8974FF/SDR] × 19.5% = 1.15, the number of French francs in the EUA basket. A similar operation is performed for the other seven currencies to define the number of units of each currency in the basket.

Once the composition of the EUA basket is established, the EUA *value* of any component currency on any given day can be easily calculated. The Commission, on the basis of the Council Decision of 21 April 1975, used a two-step procedure. First, the EUA value of the Belgian franc is calculated (BFR/EUA). This is done by summing the nine ratios obtained by dividing each component currency composing the EUA basket by its corresponding bilateral market exchange rate vis-à-vis the Belgian franc observed in Brussels at 2:30 p.m. each business day. Secondly, the EUA value of the *i*th currency (where *i* is any component currency other than the Belgian franc), is calculated by taking the product of the BFR/EUA rate obtained in the first step and the *i*th currency's bilateral market exchange rate vis-à-vis the Belgian franc. It should be noted that the Commission published a Communication on 28 December 1978 (reproduced in Monetary Committee of the European Community 1989: 129–130), just prior to the entry into force of the ECU, somewhat modifying the methodology of calculating the EUA value in terms of its component currencies. This new methodology will also be applied to calculate the value of the ECU in terms of any currency.

Paragraph 2.1 of the Brussels Resolution stipulates that, at the outset, the *value* of the ECU is to be identical to the *value* of the EUA. On the day of transition when the ECU comes into force, there is a continuity between the EUA and the ECU: 1 EUA = 1 ECU. However, immediately thereafter, on 13 March 1979, the concept of the EUA disappears. The values of the EUA/ECU against each currency, calculated on 12 March 1979 and using the methodology described below, are shown in column 3 of Table 2.1.[4]

The ECU (theoretical) rate calculated by the Commission

Each business day, the Commission calculates the ECU (theoretical) rate in terms of each Member State's currency and of other currencies as of 2:15[5] p.m., Brussels time. The general principle used is the same as the one applied in the calculation of the EUA value of the *i*th currency from 1975 to 1978. There is, however, one major difference. Instead of calculating the ECU exchange rate of the *i*th currency by first calculating the ECU rate of the Belgian franc, the Commission first calculates the ECU rate of the US dollar.

The Commission calculates the ECU rate of the US dollar by summing the ratios obtained by dividing the quantity of each component currency of the ECU basket by its corresponding exchange rate against the US dollar, as observed and recorded at 2:15 p.m. (Brussels time) each business day by the central banks of the Member States. Using as an example the original composition of the EUA/ECU basket shown in column 2 of Table 2.1, the ECU value (theoretical) of the US dollar is calculated as follows:

$$(US\$/ECU) = [3.66 \div (BFR/US\$)]$$
$$+ [0.217 \div (DKR/US\$)]$$
$$+ [0.828 \div (DM/US\$)]$$
$$+ [1.15 \div (FF/US\$)]$$
$$+ [0.286 \div (HFL/US\$)]$$
$$+ [0.00759 \times (US\$/IRL)]$$
$$+ [0.140 \div (LFR/US\$)]$$
$$+ [109.0 \div (LIT/US\$)]$$
$$+ [0.0885 \times (US\$/UKL)]$$

where   3.66 is the number of Belgian francs in the ECU basket; BFR/US\$ is the market exchange rate (mid-point) of the Belgian franc–US dollar observed on the Brussels foreign exchange market at 2:15 p.m. and recorded by the Banque nationale de Belgique;

0.217 is the number of Danish kroner in the ECU basket; DKR/US\$ is the market exchange rate (mid-point) of the Danish krone–US dollar observed on the Copenhagen foreign exchange market at 2:15 p.m. and recorded by the Danmarks Nationalbank;

... etc.; and finally,

0.0885 is the number of British pounds in the ECU basket; US\$/UKL is the market exchange rate (mid-point) of the British pound–US dollar observed on the London foreign exchange market at 2:15 p.m. (Brussels time) and recorded by the Bank of England. (N.B.: since traditionally the British and Irish pounds are quoted as US\$/UKL and US\$/IRL, respectively, on the foreign exchange markets, the Commission *multiplies* the number of pounds by the exchange rate for these two currencies in the above expression.)

To calculate the ECU (theoretical) rate of any other currency, such as, for example, the French franc, the Commission performs a second operation, namely:

$$FF/ECU = US\$/ECU \times FF/US\$$$

where each exchange rate on the right-hand side of the equation is already given above. The Commission calculates the ECU rate in terms of its component currencies and of a dozen other currencies. These rates are published daily, correct to six significant figures, in the 'C' edition of the *Official Journal of the European Communities [European Union]*. These ECU rates are sometimes qualified as 'theoretical' or 'synthetic' to distinguish them from the ECU market rates directly quoted by market makers on all the major foreign exchange markets twenty-four hours around the clock. Under normal circumstances, any significant spread between a given ECU market rate (mid-point between the bid and offer rate) and its 'synthetic' ECU rate would be almost instantaneously eliminated by arbitrage. During periods of uncertainty regarding the future status of the ECU, it is not unusual to observe a significant discount on the ECU market rate relative to its 'synthetic' rate (see Chapter 5 for more details).

Changes in the composition of the ECU basket

Paragraph 2.3 of the Brussels Resolution provides that the composition of the ECU basket is to be re-examined and, if necessary, revised six months later and thereafter every five years or, on request, if the weight of any currency has changed by 25 percent or more since the last revision of the ECU basket. Any change in the composition of the ECU basket is to be decided by the Ecofin Council, acting unanimously on a proposal from the Commission and after consultation with the Monetary Committee and of the Board of Governors of the EMCF. Changes in the composition of the ECU basket are to be made in line with underlying economic criteria and are to take into account the relative changes which occur as new countries accede to the Community and are included in the ECU basket. The basket revision must be done in such a way that the 'external' value of the ECU, i.e. its 'synthetic' value in terms of any individual currency, such as the US dollar or any component currency, remains unchanged at the moment of the shift so as to preserve *value continuity*, on the day of the change, between the 'old' and 'new' ECU basket. In concrete terms, this means that the US$/ECU synthetic value, on the day prior to the revision, must be the same whether calculated with the 'old' currency composition or with the 'new' currency composition. On the basis of the formula given above to calculate the synthetic ECU value against any participating currency, the 'value continuity' rule also implies that the synthetic ECU rate against any participating currency must also be the same, on the day prior to the revision of the composition of the basket, whether calculated with the 'old' currency composition or with the 'new' currency composition.

Since the introduction of the ECU basket, two revisions were made to its composition: one in September 1984, at which time the Greek drachma was introduced in the ECU basket, and the other in September 1989, at which time the Spanish peseta and Portuguese escudo were introduced. Each of these two revisions also gave an opportunity to the Council, to change the currency composition of the ECU basket so as to bring back the weight of each currency in line with the underlying economic criteria (see Table 2.2).[6] No revision of the composition of the ECU basket has been made since September 1989 and none is permitted since the coming into force of the Maastricht Treaty (Chapter 4). The ECU basket has become a closed basket composed of twelve currencies, in quantities determined last September 1989.

Table 2.2 Revisions of the composition of the ECU basket, 1984 and 1989

Currency	1984 composition of ECU basket	1984 weight[a] on revision day (%)	1984 weight[a] on the previous day (%)	1989 composition of ECU basket	1989 weight[a] on revision day[b] (%)	1989 weight[a] on the previous day (%)
BFR	3.71	8.2	8.1	3.301	7.6	7.6
DKR	0.219	2.7	2.7	0.1976	2.45	2.7
DM	0.719	32.0	36.9	0.6242	30.1	34.7
DRA	1.15	1.3	—	1.440	0.8	0.6
ESC	—	—	—	1.393	0.8	—
FF	1.31	19.0	16.7	1.332	19.0	18.7
HFL	0.256	10.1	11.3	0.2198	9.4	10.9
IRL	0.00871	1.2	1.0	0.00855	1.1	1.1
LFR	0.14	0.3	0.3	0.130	0.3	0.3
LIT	140.0	10.1	7.9	151.8	10.15	9.4
PTA	—	—	—	6.885	5.3	—
UKL	0.0878	15.0	15.1	0.08784	13.0	13.0

Notes:
(a) The weight of the ith currency $w(i) = x(i)/z(i)$ where $x(i)$ is the quantity of the ith currency in the ECU basket and $z(i)$ is the value of the ECU in terms of the ith currency.
(b) Although the composition of the new ECU basket was announced on 21 September 1989, the Council, in a departure from the procedure used in September 1984, announced, on 19 June 1989, both the *weights* [$w(i)$'s] of the new future basket and the immediate participation of the Spanish peseta in the ERM. 'Pursuant to the present decision, the Commission will determine the amounts of the currencies to be included in the ECU on the basis of these weighting coefficients and of the rates of exchange of the ECU against each of these currencies observed on the markets on 20 September 1989' (Council Regulation No. 1971/89 (EEC) of 19 June 1989, reproduced in Monetary Committee of the European Community 1989: 127–128). This unusual procedure was followed so as to eliminate the uncertainty of the impact an ECU basket revision has on the ECU interest rate and thus to continue to encourage the development of the private ECU as a financial instrument. Briefly, reducing the weight of currencies with low interest rates (e.g. the Deutsche mark) while at the same time increasing the weight of currencies with high interest rates (e.g. the peseta and the escudo) increases the ECU interest rate. Anyone holding an ECU bond while the components of the ECU basket are modified in such a fashion will suffer a capital loss. Knowing in June the new weights of the component currencies in the ECU basket which will prevail as of September, allowed new ECU bond issues to be priced without factoring in a risk premium for the uncertainty of the future weights of the component currencies in the ECU basket due simply to a change in the ECU composition of the basket. (See Chapter 5 for more details on this point.)

ECU as a reserve asset

Under the provisions of the EMS, the ECU is not only a unit of account, but also an official reserve asset used as a means of settlement between monetary authorities of the Member States of the European Community. The EMCF 'receives'[7] monetary reserves in the form of gold and US dollars from the Member States and, in turn, issues ECUs to the monetary authorities of the Member States which may use them as a means of settlement. These official ECUs are created as three-month revolving swaps between the national central banks and the EMCF. As a result, the creation of ECUs as a reserve asset is not definitive; the 'transfers' are renewed each trimester and, unlike the IMF's *ex nihilo* creation of SDRs, ECUs do not increase liquidity since they are substituted for gold and US dollars. It is clear from this arrangement that funds do not really belong to the EMCF but to each national central bank. The EMCF is not designed to be like a true 'European Monetary Fund', as was envisaged in the Werner Report and in the original provisions of the EMS after a two-year transition period.

An initial supply of ECUs is provided by the EMCF against the 'transfer' of 20 percent of gold and 20 percent of US dollar reserves held by each national central bank. The periodical review, each trimester, of the gold and US dollar reserves ensures that each central bank maintains a deposit (bookkeeping entry) of at least 20 percent of these reserves with the EMCF. A Member State not participating in the ERM may participate in this operation, as the United Kingdom, and later (1986) Greece, chose to do. The ECU deposits with the EMCF are to be used in connection with the settlement operations related to the intervention obligations of each Member State's central bank under the rules of the Exchange Rate Mechanism of the EMS. Initially, some ECU23,000 million were created through these swap accounts. The volume of ECUs created can change at the time the swaps are renewed, as a result of changes either in members' gold and dollar reserves or in the ECU value of gold and the dollar. The total outstanding amounts from 1991 to 1996 of these swap accounts are shown in Table 2.3.

THE EXCHANGE RATE MECHANISM (ERM)

The Exchange Rate Mechanism of the EMS is a compromise between France which wanted the exchange rate band to be defined around the ECU and Germany which wanted the exchange rate band to be defined bilaterally. Consequently, the currency of a Member State participating in the ERM has a band defined around each of its bilateral central rates and another band defined around its ECU central rate.

Bilateral central rate

At the centre of the Exchange Rate Mechanism lies the defined ECU central rate of each Member State's currency. A bilateral central rate between two participating currencies is defined as the ratio of the two ECU central rates. Accordingly, whenever a Council regulation is adopted to realign the currencies participating in the ERM,[8] the ECU central rates must be modified in such a way as to change the bilateral central rates. At the outset, the calculated synthetic ECU value of each Member State's currency on 12 March 1979 is defined as the ECU central rate (shown in column 3 of Table 2.1). Currencies of Member States participating in the ERM have margins of fluctuation around their bilateral central rates.

Table 2.3 Swap operations (Gold, USD/ECU) of the EC central banks with the EMCF

Date	Gold transfers (Million ounces)	US dollar (thousand million)	Gold price (ECU/ ounce)	Exchange rate USD/ECU	Counterpart (ECU thousand mill.)		
					Gold	USD	Total
01–91	93.5	27.4	285.2	1.40	26.7	20.0	46.6
04–91	93.5	27.7	277.6	1.22	26.0	22.6	48.6
07–91	93.5	27.9	290.3	1.12	27.2	24.9	52.1
10–91	93.5	28.2	286.9	1.23	26.8	22.9	49.8
01–92	93.5	28.9	263.3	1.34	24.6	21.6	46.3
04–92	93.5	29.6	276.5	1.26	25.9	23.6	49.4
07–92	92.2	30.9	253.9	1.35	23.4	22.9	46.3
10–92	92.2	32.7	250.2	1.37	23.1	23.8	46.9
01–93	92.2	32.6	258.6	1.20	23.9	27.2	51.1
04–93	89.6	29.7	271.7	1.21	24.3	24.5	48.8
07–93	89.6	28.9	287.8	1.15	25.8	25.1	50.9
10–93	89.6	31.3	298.6	1.17	26.7	26.7	53.5
01–94*	89.6	31.8	327.3	1.11	29.4	28.6	58.0
04–94	89.9	32.7	334.7	1.13	30.1	28.9	59.0
07–94	89.9	34.0	317.1	1.21	28.5	28.0	56.5
10–94	89.9	34.8	318.5	1.25	28.6	28.0	56.6
01–95	93.9	34.8	312.3	1.22	29.3	28.5	57.8
04–95	94.9	35.4	290.4	1.35	27.6	26.3	53.9
07–95	93.8	35.8	289.9	1.35	27.2	26.6	53.8
10–95	93.7	35.7	290.5	1.32	27.2	27.0	54.2
01–96	93.5	35.0	292.8	1.31	27.4	26.8	54.2
04–96	92.1	36.7	301.7	1.27	27.8	28.8	56.6
07–96	92.1	39.0	304.6	1.26	28.0	31.0	59.1

Notes:
For purposes of the swap operations, the value of the reserve components contributed to the EMCF are established as follows:
(i) for the gold portion, the average of the prices, converted into ECU, recorded daily at the two London fixings during the previous six calendar months, but not exceeding the average price of the two fixings on the penultimate working day of the period;
(ii) for the US dollar portion, the market rate two working days prior to the value date.
*As provided by the Maastricht Treaty, on 01.01.1994 the European Monetary Institute (EMI) took over all the activities of the EMCF.
Source: Table I.4, *Ecustat*, Luxembourg: Statistical Office of the European Communities (Eurostat), various issues.

Paragraph 3.1 of the Brussels Resolution of 5 December 1978 (reproduced in Monetary Committee of the European Community 1989: 46) provides that around each bilateral central rate, margins of ±2.25 percent are established. Member States whose currencies were not in the 'snake' may temporarily establish fluctuation margins of ±6 percent, but should reduce these margins as soon as economic conditions permit. Italy decided to make use of this option until January 1990, at which time it began to participate in the narrow margins. Around any given bilateral central rate, *both* central banks – the one with the weak currency *and* the one with the strong currency – have a legal obligation to intervene in unlimited amounts to defend these margins.

On the recommendation of the Commission and after consultation of the Monetary Committee, a decision to modify any or all bilateral central rates – and therefore the structure of the ECU central rates – must be agreed unanimously by the Ecofin Council, composed of the Finance Ministers of the participating Member States, and by the Governors of the participating Central Banks. The bilateral central rates were realigned eleven times between 1979 and 1987, once in 1990, and five times between September 1992 and May 1993. The last realignment took place in March 1995, bringing to eighteen the total number of realignments made since the inception of the EMS. In September 1992, two Member States, the United Kingdom, which had only joined the Exchange Rate Mechanism on 8 October 1990, and Italy, suspended their participation in the ERM. Table 2.4 summarizes the pre-Maastricht realignments of the currencies participating in the ERM. The post-1990 realignments are shown and discussed in Chapter 4.

EMS realignments between 1979 and 1983

During this period, realignments (cf. Table 2.4) were frequent as a result of largely divergent economic policies. The currencies of Belgium (1979, 1981, 1982 [twice], 1983), Denmark (1979 [twice], 1981, 1982 [twice], 1983), France (1979, 1981, 1982, 1983), Italy (1979, 1981 [twice], 1982, 1983), Ireland (1979,

Table 2.4 EMS realignments: percentage changes in bilateral central rates:[a] 1979–90

	24 Sept. 1979	30 Nov. 1979	23 Mar. 1981	5 Oct. 1981	22 Feb. 1982	14 June 1982	21 Mar. 1983	22 July 1985	7 Apr. 1986	4 Aug. 1986	12 Jan. 1987	8 Jan. 1990
BFR					−8.5		+1.5	+2.0	+1.0		+2.0	
DKR	−2.9	−4.8			−3.0		+2.5	+2.0	+1.0			
DM	+2.0			+5.5			+4.25	+5.5	+2.0	+3.0	+3.0	
FF				−3.0			−5.75	−2.5	+2.0	−3.0		
LIT			−6.0	−3.0			−2.75	−2.5	−6.0			−3.7
IRL							−3.5	+2.0		−8.0		
HFL				+5.5			+4.25	+3.5	+2.0	+3.0	+3.0	

Notes:
(a) Calculated as the percentage change against the group of currencies whose bilateral parities remained unchanged in the realignment, except for the realignments of 21 March 1983 and 22 July 1985. For these, the percentages are shown as in the official communiqué of the Commission, and are calculated from the ECU central rates. Using the first column as an example, the figures in this table are to be interpreted in the following manner: the bilateral central rate of the Deutsche mark against the Danish krone was revalued by 4.9%, while the bilateral central rate of the DM against the FF was revalued by 2%, etc.
+ is a revaluation; − is a devaluation.
Source: Ungerer *et al.* 1990: 55

1981, 1982, 1983) and the Netherlands (1979, 1983) were devalued against the Deutsche mark. After the March 1983 devaluation, France abandoned its unilateral expansionary policies, which were launched in 1981 under a new socialist government, and chose to re-establish its international competitiveness by way of restrictive monetary and budgetary policies.

EMS realignments between 1983 and 1987

This is a period of significant nominal convergence of unit labour cost, inflation rates and monetary policies, with the DM emerging as the nominal anchor of the EMS and as an alternative international reserve currency. This meant that the exchange relationships between the US dollar and the ERM currencies were primarily determined by the dollar–DM policies. With the appreciation of the dollar from 1983 to 1985, no significant exchange rate tensions existed between ERM currencies. Between March 1983 and July 1985, no realignments occurred in the EMS. The July 1985 and August 1986 realignments were devaluations of the Italian lira and Irish punt, respectively, against all other ERM currencies. With the April 1986 devaluation of the French franc against all other ERM currencies, the French government once again took restrictive fiscal and monetary measures. The 1987 realignment, prompted by ERM tensions linked to dollar weakness, which in turn led to large marginal intervention by the Bundesbank in support of the French franc, became unavoidable when the Bundesbank considered that the total intervention compromised its domestic monetary policy (see Collignon *et al.* 1994: 30). No specific policy measures were taken by any government in support of this realignment. Instead, Ministers of Finance and the central bank Governors examined measures to strengthen the operating mechanism of the EMS. These measures are known as the Basle/Nyborg Agreement, described below.

Marginal intervention rules around bilateral central rates

The rules of the EMS call for unlimited intervention whenever any two ERM currencies reach their bilateral margins of fluctuation, originally defined as ±2.25 percent for those currencies participating in the narrow band and ±6 percent for those currencies participating in the wide band. A currency reaching the weak edge of its bilateral band implies that the other currency is on its bilateral strong edge. When this happens, the two central banks are legally required to intervene so as to prevent the currencies from crossing their bilateral margins.

In order to allow interventions to be made in Community currencies, the participating central banks open for each other – in their respective currencies – lines of credit in unlimited[9] amounts. These lines of credit, known as the Very Short-Term Financing (VSTF) facility or mechanism, are administered by the EMCF. When utilized, these accounts are debited or credited, using a common numéraire, the ECU. The bookkeeping is done by the Bank for International Settlements (BIS), an agent of the EMCF.[10] The conversion of currencies into ECU is done at the daily rates established for the ECU by the Commission on the value day of the intervention or the repayment operation.

Taking as an example the narrow ±2.25 percent French franc–Deutsche mark bilateral band, with the French franc on its weak edge (343.05 FF/100 DM in Table 2.6) and thus with the DM/FF on its strong edge (29.15 DM/100 FF in Table 2.6), the Banque de France is required to buy its own currency against the DM on the Paris foreign exchange market. Since, in accordance with Article 15 of the 1979 Agreement between central banks relative to the operating procedures of the EMS (Central banks 1979), the Banque de France is not allowed to hold the currencies of the other Community central banks in any significant amounts beyond working balances, the Deutsche Bundesbank has an obligation to lend DMs to the Banque de France so that the latter can purchase franc commercial bank deposits with the DMs. As a result the monetary base decreases in France while the monetary base in Germany increases as the intervention has supplied the German banking system with additional amounts of DM central bank deposits. Since the Banque de France has to repay its intervention credit (see below for terms and conditions) in DMs or other foreign exchange reserves (e.g., ECUs), its reserves are immediately reduced (liability towards the EMCF is recorded) while the Bundesbank's reserves are immediately increased (a claim against the EMCF is recorded).

In support of the intervention of the Banque de France on the Paris foreign exchange market, the Bundesbank is required to sell its currency against the French franc on the Frankfurt foreign exchange market. When the Bundesbank intervenes, the results on the monetary base in each country are similar to the ones described above. The monetary base in Germany increases while the monetary base in France decreases. Moreover, in view of the rules established between the central banks, the French francs that the Bundesbank purchases on the foreign exchange market must be immediately transferred to the Banque de France since the former may not hold French francs or other ERM member currencies acquired by intervention. As a result of these transactions, the Bundesbank has a claim against the EMCF (an increase in reserves) and the Banque de France has a liability with the EMCF (a decrease in reserves). In short, whether the obligatory intervention is done by the Banque de France or by the Bundesbank, the effects on the monetary base and foreign exchange reserves are the same, namely a decrease in monetary base and foreign exchange reserves in France and an increase in the monetary base (if not sterilized) and foreign exchange reserves in Germany.

The Bundesbank will probably sterilize the impact on its monetary base via open market operations (see Mastropasqua *et al.* 1988); the Banque de France will not be able to do so since sterilization of the impact of intervention on its monetary base would lead to a further reduction in its foreign exchange reserves. To that extent, the impact of intervention is *asymmetric* on the Member State with the strong currency compared to the Member State with the weak currency. The interest rate does not have to change in Germany whereas the interest rate in France rises. Thus, the monetary policy of the central bank with the strong currency becomes the 'anchor' of the system. Whether German monetary policy has been in fact the 'anchor' of the ERM is the subject of an empirical controversy (see Fratianni and von Hagen 1990a and Mélitz 1988). It should be noted that a small country with a strong currency could not become the 'anchor' of the EMS since that country would be technically unable to sterilize the impact of intervention on its monetary base (Collignon *et al.* 1994: 22–23).

Terms and conditions of VSTF facility

The Agreement between central banks, signed on 13 March 1979, reinforced the terms and conditions of the VSTF facility. The VSTF facility was originally established under the terms of the 1972 Basle Agreement to implement the European exchange rate system known as the 'snake'. The terms and conditions of the 1979 EMS Agreement between central banks, with minor amendments introduced in 1985 and more important ones introduced in 1987 which are known as the Basle/Nyborg Agreement, are as follows:

• The debtor central bank, which borrows the currency of the creditor central bank, is given seventy-five days from the *end* of the month in which the debt is incurred to reimburse, with interest, the creditor central bank. This is known as the 'initial settlement date'. However, at the request of the debtor central bank, the initial settlement date for a financing operation may be extended for a period of three months. This request is granted automatically, provided that the *total* amount of indebtedness of the central bank in the VSTF facility does not exceed a ceiling equal to twice (200 percent) the debtor quota of the central bank concerned under the Short-Term Monetary Support facility. Moreover, any debt already renewed automatically for three months may be renewed for a further three months, subject to the agreement of the creditor central bank(s).

Prior to the 1987 Basle/Nyborg amendments, the initial settlement date was forty-five days from the *end* of the month in which the debt was incurred and the three-month extension was automatically granted, provided that the total amount of indebtedness of the central bank in the VSTF facility did not exceed a ceiling equal to (100 percent) its debtor quota under the STMS facility.

- Any debt exceeding the 200 percent ceiling mentioned above may be renewed once for three months, subject to the agreement of the creditor central bank, or central banks if the debtor central bank has loans outstanding with more than one creditor central bank.
- When a reimbursement of a financing operation falls due, settlement by the debtor central bank is to be effected as far as possible in the creditor's currency. However, since a central bank's holdings of the currencies of other central banks are limited to specific amounts of working balances, repayment in this way will only be possible to the extent that a reversal of exchange-market conditions enables the debtor central bank to buy the creditor's currency in the market. Any debt not settled in the creditor's currency may be wholly or partly settled by transfers of ECU assets, and/or by transferring other reserve components in accordance with the composition of the debtor central bank's reserves. In general, the creditor central bank is not obliged to accept settlement in ECUs of an amount exceeding 50 percent of the claim being settled but, pursuant to the 1987 amendment, this percentage may go to 100 percent provided that this does not bring about an ECU disequilibrium in the creditor's composition of reserve assets.
- Since the unit of account of the VSTF facility managed by the EMCF is the ECU, debtor and creditor balances are denominated in ECUs. However, since the loans and reimbursements are usually effected in assets denominated in national currencies, the conversion from the national units of account to the ECU is done on settlement day on the basis of the daily rate for the ECU established by the Commission. Under those rules of accounting, a central bank that lends its currency may find itself reimbursed, months later after its currency has appreciated against the ECU, in fewer units of its own currency.
- Interest payments apply to loans granted under the very short-term financing operations. Following the 1985 amendment, the interest rate is calculated as a weighted average of the most representative rates on the domestic money market of the countries whose currencies make up the ECU basket. The weights are based on the weighting of the currencies in the ECU basket derived from the ECU central rates in force. The interest liability of the debtor central bank is payable in ECUs.

Intramarginal interventions

An intervention effected before a currency reaches its bilateral floor or ceiling is known as an intramarginal intervention. Although not legally required under the terms of the ERM, intramarginal interventions became, within a relatively short time of the launching of the EMS in 1979, the rule rather than the exception (see Table 2.5). Micosi (1985) states that up to June 1985, intramarginal interventions represented

Table 2.5 Deutsche mark interventions in the EMS (in thousand million Deutsche marks)

		Obligatory	Intramarginal	Total
1979	Purchases	—	2.7	2.7
	Sales	3.6	8.1	11.7
	Balance	+3.6	+5.4	+9.0
1980	Purchases	5.9	5.9	11.8
	Sales	—	1.0	1.0
	Balance	−5.9	−4.9	−10.8
1981	Purchases	2.3	8.1	10.4
	Sales	17.3	12.8	30.1
	Balance	+15.0	+4.7	+19.7
1982	Purchases	—	9.4	9.4
	Sales	3.0	12.8	15.8
	Balance	+3.0	+3.4	+6.4
1983	Purchases	16.7	19.1	35.8
	Sales	8.3	12.9	21.2
	Balance	−8.4	−6.2	−14.5
1984	Purchases	—	28.9	28.9
	Sales	4.7	7.6	12.3
	Balance	+4.7	−21.4	−16.6
1985	Purchases	—	29.1	29.1
	Sales	0.4	30.8	31.1
	Balance	+0.4	+1.6	+2.0
1986	Purchases	19.0	33.6	52.6
	Sales	4.1	74.0	78.1
	Balance	−14.8	+40.4	+25.5
1987	Purchases	—	47.8	47.8
	Sales	15.0	61.7	76.8
	Balance	+15.0	+13.9	+28.9
1988	Purchases	—	26.8	26.8
	Sales	—	16.3	16.3
	Balance	—	−10.5	−10.5
1989	Purchases	—	20.4	20.4
	Sales	5.0	8.6	13.6
	Balance	+5.0	−11.8	−6.8
1990	Purchases	1.5	32.5	34.1
	Sales	—	12.3	12.3
	Balance	−1.5	−20.2	−21.8
1991	Purchases	—	6.4	6.4
	Sales	—	21.9	21.9
	Balance	—	+15.5	+15.5
1992	Purchases	—	75.1	75.1
	Sales	63.7	199.7	263.4
	Balance	+63.7	+124.6	+188.3
1993	Purchases	—	92.0	92.0
	Sales	25.1	168.8	193.9
	Balance	+25.1	+76.8	+101.9

Table 2.5 Continued

		Obligatory	Intramarginal	Total
1994	Purchases	—	52.6	52.6
	Sales	—	5.5	5.5
	Balance	—	–47.1	–47.1
Selected periods, net 3 June 1992 to 25 September 1992		+63.7	+120.4	+184.2
8 July 1993 to 1 August 1993		+24.7	+82.4	+107.0

Note: Deutsche mark intervention by other central banks participating in the EMS Exchange Rate Mechanism and EMS intervention by the Bundesbank. Plus (+) equals Deutsche mark sales on the foreign exchange markets. Minus (-) equals Deutsche mark purchases on the foreign exchange markets.
Source: Deutsche Bundesbank, Annual Reports–1989; 1994: 99

two-thirds to three-quarters of total ERM interventions. Most central banks participating in the ERM preferred to keep the exchange rate well within the margins to forestall, in case of temporary weakness, any speculative attacks. Since central banks are not allowed to accumulate beyond working balances Community currencies in their foreign exchange reserves, except with the consent of the partner central bank concerned, dollars had to be used for intramarginal interventions. The Basle/Nyborg Agreement (1987) between central banks eliminated this anomaly of the EMS by allowing, within the framework of the VSTF facility, a central bank to borrow Community currencies for intramarginal interventions, with the presumed permission of the creditor central bank(s), in a cumulative amount not exceeding 200 percent of the country's debtor quota in the STMS facility.

In tandem with this new provision, it was also agreed, at the behest of the Bundesbank, to have more frequent recourse to changes in interest rate differentials to defend bilateral central rates and to reinforce the multilateral surveillance exercised by the Monetary Committee and the Committee of Central Bank Governors on the basis of indicators and projections in order to highlight any policy inconsistencies between EMS countries (Vissol 1989).

A major test of intramarginal intervention with Community currencies and the use of interest rate differential occurred in October 1987 with the fall of the US dollar against the DM and the resulting downward pressures on the French franc against the DM. The monetary authorities of France and Germany reacted swiftly by undertaking massive intramarginal intervention, financed to the maximum amounts allowed under the Basle/Nyborg Agreement and by an additional bilateral credit from the Bundesbank to the Banque de France. At the same time, the French franc was allowed to depreciate within the band against the DM. This action was combined with coordinated interest rate moves by the central banks of France and Germany.

Bilateral parity grid of the ERM

Since 2 August 1993, and in order to prevent one-way risk to speculators whenever two currencies reached their ERM bilateral edge (see Chapter 4 for further details), the margins of fluctuation around each bilateral central rate have been 'temporarily' established at ±15 percent for all the currencies participating in the ERM (which, as of the end of 1996, includes the currencies of the fifteen Member States, except the Greek drachma, the British pound and the Swedish krona), with the exception of the bilateral central rate of the Deutsche mark–Dutch guilder, which has kept the pre-August 1993 narrow margins of ±2.25 percent. Thus, on the basis of ECU central rates set at each realignment of EMS exchange rates, a bilateral grid is defined with a ceiling and floor around each bilateral central rate, as shown in Table 2.6. With eleven currencies currently participating in the ERM (counting the Belgian and Luxembourg francs as one currency), the bilateral grid has 121 cells, minus the diagonal, or 110 cells. In fact, fifty-five of these cells are the inverse of the other fifty-five. For example, the FF/DM rate is the inverse of the DM/FF rate. Table 2.6 shows the ceiling and floor around the bilateral central rates (BCR) in effect since 6 March 1995, with the ±15 percent margins of fluctuation. Since ERM participants are still targeting the former ±2.25 percent margins of fluctuation in force prior to 2 August 1993, these unofficial margins of fluctuation are also shown for the currencies that have not been bilaterally realigned or introduced into the ERM since that date (BFR–LFR, DKR, DM, FF, HFL, IRL).

ECU central rate

In addition to the band defined around each bilateral central rate, each participating currency in the Exchange Rate Mechanism of the EMS has a band defined around its ECU central rate. This latter band is designed to act as an automatic early warning signal to each Member State that its weighted average exchange rate, equivalent to its ECU rate calculated by the Commission, is deviating from the established benchmark, its ECU central rate. An ECU rate which reaches the floor or ceiling around its ECU central rate, defined as the 'threshold of maximum divergence', is designed to be an early warning signal to the Member State that its economic policies and/or its fundamentals are not consistent with the established and agreed-upon ECU central rate. In other words, the average exchange rate of the Member State is deviating from its established average benchmark,

Table 2.6 Bilateral central rates and the obligatory ±15.0% intervention limits in force since the last realignment of 6 March 1995 and, for comparative purposes, the unofficial ±2.25% margins for the BFR-LFR, DKR, DM, FF, HFL, IRL in force prior to 2 August 1993

Currency and ECU central rate[a]	Ceiling and floor around BCR[a]	BFR/LFR 100 =	DKR 100 =	DM 100 =	ESC 100 =	FF 100 =	FMK 100 =	HFL 100 =	IRL 1 =	LIT 100 =	ÖS 100 =	PTA 100 =
BFR/LFR 39.7191 (8.3%/ 0.33%)	+15.0%		627.880	2,395.20	23.3645	714.030	787.830	2,125.60	57.7445	24.1920	340.420	28.1525
	+2.25		553.000	2,109.50		628.970		1,872.15	50.8605			
	BCR	*100*	*540.723*	*2,062.55*	*20.1214*	*614.977*	*678.468*	*1,830.54*	*49.7289*	*20.8337*	*293.163*	*26.0696*
	−2.25%		528.700	2,016.55		601.295		1,789.85	48.6230			
	−15.0%		465.665	1,776.20	17.3285	529.660	584.290	1,576.45	42.8260	17.9417	252.470	20.8795
DKR 7.34555 (2.7%)	+15.0%	21.4747		442.968	4.32100	132.066	145.699	393.105	10.6792	4.47400	62.9561	5.20640
	+2.25%	18.9143		390.160		116.320		346.240	9.40600			
	BCR	*18.4938*	*100*	*381.443*	*3.72119*	*113.732*	*125.474*	*338.537*	*9.19676*	*3.85294*	*54.2270*	*4.48376*
	−2.25%	18.0831		373.000		111.200		331.020	8.99220			
	−15.0%	15.9266		328.461	3.20460	97.943	108.057	291.544	7.92014	3.31810	46.6910	3.86140
DM 1.92573 (32.4%)	+15.0%	5.63000	30.4450		1.13280	34.6250	38.1970	b	2.80000	1.1729	16.5050	1.36500
	+2.25%	4.95900	26.8100			30.4950		90.7700	2.46600			
	BCR	*4.84837*	*26.2162*	*100*	*0.975561*	*29.8164*	*32.8948*	*88.7526*	*2.41105*	*1.0101*	*14.2136*	*1.17548*
	−2.25%	4.74000	25.6300			29.1500		86.7800	2.35700			
	−15.0%	4.17500	22.5750		0.84014	25.6750	28.3280	b	2.07600	0.8699	12.2410	1.01230
ESC 197.398 (0.71%)	+15.0%	577.090	3,120.50	11,903.3		3,549.00	3,915.40	10,564.0	286.983	120.24	1,691.80	139.920
	BCR	*496.984*	*2,687.31*	*10,250.5*	*100*	*3,056.35*	*3,371.88*	*9,097.55*	*247.145*	*103.541*	*1,456.97*	*120.493*
	−15.0%	428.000	2,314.30	8,827.7		2,632.10	2,903.80	7,834.70	212.838	89.170	1,254.70	103.770
FF 6.45863 (20.6%)	+15.0%	18.8800	102.100	389.48	3.79920		128.107	345.65	9.3895	3.93379	55.3545	4.55780
	+2.25%	16.6310	89.9250	343.050				304.440	8.2703			
	BCR	*16.2608*	*87.9257*	*335.386*	*3.27188*	*100*	*110.324*	*297.661*	*8.08631*	*3.38773*	*47.6706*	*3.94237*
	−2.25%	15.8990	85.9700	327.920				291.040	7.9064			
	−15.0%	14.0050	75.7200	288.81	2.81770		95.0096	256.35	6.964	2.91750	41.0533	3.39510

Table 2.6 Continued

Currency and ECU central rate[e]	Ceiling and floor around BCR[a]	BFR/LFR 100 =	DKR 100 =	DM 100 =	ESC 100 =	FF 100 =	FMK 100 =	HFL 100 =	IRL 1 =	LIT 100 =	ÖS 100 =	PTA 100 =
FMK[c] 5.85424 (0.0%)[f]	+15.0%	17.1148	92.5438	353.008	3.44376	105.253		313.295	8.51107	3.5670	50.1744	4.14938
	BCR	14.7391	79.6976	304.000	2.96570	90.6422	100	269.806	7.32960	3.07071	43.2094	3.57345
	−15.0%	12.6931	68.6347	261.801	2.55402	78.0597		232.353	6.31217	2.64438	37.2114	3.07740
HFL 2.16979 (10.1%)	+15.0%	6.3434	34.3002	b	1.27637	39.0091	43.0378		3.1545	1.32156	18.5963	1.93793
	+2.25%	5.58700	30.2100	115.235		34.3600			2.77840			
	BCR	5.46286	29.5389	112.673	1.09920	33.5953	37.0636	100	2.71662	1.13811	16.0149	1.32445
	−2.25%	5.34150	28.8825	110.167		32.8475			2.65620			
	−15.0%	4.70454	25.4385	b	0.946611	28.9381	31.9187		2.33952	0.980132	13.7918	1.14060
IRL 0.798709 (1.1%)	+15.0%	2.33503	12.6261	48.16964	0.469841	14.3599	15.8424	42.7439		0.486472	6.84544	0.566120
	+2.25%	2.05664	11.1208	42.4268		12.6480		37.6478				
	BCR	2.0109	10.8734	41.4757	0.404620	12.3666	13.6433	36.8105	1	0.418944	5.89521	0.487537
	−2.25%	1.96616	10.6315	40.5515		12.0915		35.9919				
	−15.0%	1.73176	9.36403	35.7143	0.348453	10.6500	11.7494	31.7007		0.360789	5.07688	0.419859
LIT[e] 1906.48 (8.0%)	+15.0%	5,573.60	30,138.0	114,956.0	1,121.500	34,276.0	37,816.0	102,027.0	2,771.70		16,339.0	1,351.30
	BCR	4,799.91	25,954.2	99,000.4	965.805	29,518.3	32,565.8	87,864.7	2,386.95	100	14,071.5	1,163.72
	−15.0%	4,133.60	22,351.0	85,259.0	831.700	25,421.0	28,045.0	75,668.0	2,055.61		12,118.0	1,002.20
ÖS[c] 13.5485 (0.0%)[f]	+15.0%	39.6809	214.174	816.927	7.97000	243.586	268.735	725.065	19.6971	8.25219		9.60338
	BCR	34.1107	184.444	703.55	6.86356	209.773	231.431	624.417	16.9929	7.10655	100	8.27008
	−15.0%	29.3757	158.841	605.877	5.91086	180.654	199.305	537.740	14.6082	6.12032		7.12200

Table 2.6 Continued

Currency and ECU central rate* around BCR[a]	Ceiling and floor* around BCR[a]	BFR/LFR 100 =	DKR 100 =	DM 100 =	ESC 100 =	FF 100 =	FMK 100 =	HFL 100 =	IRL 1 =	LIT 100 =	ÖS 100 =	PTA 100 =
PTA 163.826 (4.2%)	+15.0%	438.944	2,589.80	9,878.50	96.3670	2,945.40	3,249.50	8,767.30	238.175	99.7800	1,404.10	
	BCR	412.461	2,230.27	8,507.18	82.9927	2,536.54	2,798.41	7,550.30	205.113	85.9311	1,209.10	100
	−15.0%	355.206	1,920.70	7,326.00	71.4690	2,184.40	2,410.00	6,502.20	176.641	74.0000	1,041.30	
DRA 295.269 (0.49%) notional[d]												
UKL 0.793103 (11.1%) notional[d]												

Notes:

(a) BCR: Bilateral Central Rate is equal to the ratio (row/column) of the two corresponding ECU central rates indicated in the first column. For example, BCR of the DM/FF is 1.92573/6.45863; BCR of the FF/DM is 6.45863/1.92573: etc. Since the ceiling around one BCR (for example, of the FF/DM in Paris) must be exactly equal to the inverse of that BCR (the DM/FF in Frankfurt) so that both central banks receive a simultaneous signal for intervention requirements, the inverse of the result obtained by applying the positive (negative) percentage rate to any bilateral central rate must be precisely equal to the result obtained by applying the negative (positive) percentage rate to the inverse of that bilateral central rate. The usual methodology of calculating percentages does not provide such results. The 'proper' methodology is shown in a footnote in Lelart (1994: 43). For example, the general formula for the ±2.25% margins is: BCR·X − BCR÷X = 0.045·BCR where X is the number, whose solution is 1.0227 in this case, by which the BCR is multiplied and divided to obtain the ceiling and floor, respectively.

(b) DM–HFL retained margins of ±2.25%.

(c) The Austrian schilling and the Finnish markka joined the ERM on 9 January 1995 and 14 October 1996, respectively. The Italian lira re-joined the ERM on 25 November 1996.

(d) The grids for UKL and DRA are not shown since these currencies do not currently participate in the ERM. The British pound participated in the ERM with the ±6 percent margins from 8 October 1990 to 16 September 1992; the DRA has never participated in the ERM. Notional ECU central rates are given for those two currencies. The Swedish krona (SKR) is not shown at all in this table since this currency neither participates in the ERM nor is included in the ECU basket.

(e) The ECU central rates established on 25 November 1996, date of the re-entry of the LIT in the ERM. The weight, shown in parentheses, is equal to the number of units of currency in the ECU basket (as defined in September 1989) divided by its ECU central rate.

(f) Although an ECU central rate is established, the Austrian schilling and the Finnish markka are not part of the composition of the ECU basket by virtue of Article 109G of the Maastricht Treaty; therefore, each currency has a zero weight in the ECU basket.

Source: Any EU central bank or the European Monetary Institute.

its ECU central rate. This signal is designed to be set off before the currency reaches any of its bilateral margins, which would avert the need for marginal intervention.

In the provisions of the EMS (para. 3.6 of the Resolution of the European Council of 5 December 1978), there is a presumption that, whenever the 'threshold of maximum divergence' is reached, the Member State concerned must take adequate measures to correct the situation, namely:

(i)   *Diversified intramarginal intervention:* intervention on the foreign exchange market in various currencies rather than in the single currency which would deviate the most from the currency of the country concerned.
(ii) *Measures of domestic monetary policy:* changes in interest rates designed to have a direct influence on capital flows and thus reduce exchange rate tensions.
(iii) *Change of the central rates:* modification of bilateral central rates if the divergence is due to persistent fundamental real disparities between the Member State concerned and the other Member States.
(iv) *Other economic policy measures:* including fiscal policy changes if necessary.

The 'threshold of maximum divergence' or floor and ceiling around the ECU central rate is defined in the following manner. If the 'synthetic' ECU rate of the ith currency, as calculated by the Commission each day,[11] deviates from its ECU central rate by a percentage equal to, or more than

1   $75\% \times [\pm2.25\%(1 - w(i))]$ where the ith currency is in the narrow band of the ERM,[12] or
2   $75\% \times [\pm6.00\%(1 - w(i))]$ where the ith currency is in the wide band of the ERM,[13] or
3   $75\% \times [\pm15.00\%(1 - w(i)]$ where the ith currency participates in the post-July 1993 ERM band,[14]

then the ith currency has reached its 'threshold of maximum divergence'. The weight of the ith currency, w(i), is defined as the ratio of the ith currency composition of the ECU basket and the ECU *central* rate of the ith currency, i.e. its *theoretical* weight and not its *effective* weight. Since the ith currency is part of the ECU basket, in general the ith currency could deviate bilaterally against every other currency in the basket by more than ±2.25 percent and still have deviated by less than ±2.25 percent against its ECU central rate. This argument becomes all the more important for the currency with a large weight in the ECU basket. In order to avoid this situation, the theoretical weight of the ith currency has to be subtracted from the basket, which has a weight equal to 1, when defining the threshold around the ECU central rate of the ith currency.

Since the threshold of maximum divergence is defined at 75 percent of the ±2.25 (or ±6 or ±15) percent divergence of its ECU rate around its

ECU central rate, adjusted for its theoretical weight in the basket, it is generally true that a currency will reach its ECU threshold *before* it attains any given bilateral margin. Thus, the Member State concerned would presumably have taken corrective measures *before* reaching a bilateral margin, avoiding the need for obligatory marginal intervention. There are two problems with this argument. One is technical; the other is legal. It is possible for a currency to reach a bilateral margin against another currency before reaching its ECU 'threshold of maximum divergence'. The very design of the indicator based on a composite of all the currencies causes it to respond only in situations where one currency is clearly divergent from the average of the other currencies. Whenever just two currencies strongly move in opposite directions, it is possible that neither currency crosses its threshold of maximum divergence. This indicator does not always efficiently act as an 'early warning system' (Commission of the European Communities 1979: Annex; Salop 1981; Rey 1982; Spaventa 1982). Moreover, even if it did act efficiently, in practice the bells and whistles that the threshold of maximum divergence is supposed to signal are mostly ignored by the Member States concerned since they have no legal obligation to take corrective measures. No legal obligations were imposed because of the Bundesbank's view that an ECU-based exchange rate mechanism would be less stability prone (read: price stability for Germany) than a parity grid of bilateral intervention rates. For example, if most Member States participating in the ERM were to pursue inflationary policies while Germany did not, the ECU divergence indicator would place the burden on Germany to adjust its monetary policy in line with the Community average. Such a policy would be clearly inconsistent with the price stability mandate of the Bundesbank. Therefore, the EMS *legal* obligations only included unlimited marginal interventions with respect to the bilateral parity bands. And, as explained in Chapter 4, the Bundesbank effectively reserved the right to suspend this legal obligation if such unlimited lending of Deutsche marks to central banks with weak currencies were to undermine its control of the German money supply.

THE CREDIT MECHANISMS

The Brussels Resolution of the European Council of 5 December 1978 maintained and reinforced the credit mechanisms created in the early 1970s. The Short-Term Monetary Support (STMS) facility, established in February 1970, had its effective available credit increased from approximately 3,320 million ECU (or EUA) in December 1977 to ECU14,000 million. The Medium-Term Financial Assistance (MTFA) facility, established in January 1972, had its effective available credit increased from approximately 4,300 million ECU (or EUA) available in January 1978 to ECU11,000 million.

Short-Term Monetary Support facility

The Short-Term Monetary Support facility, like the VSTF facility, is governed by an Agreement between the central banks of Member States and is administered by the EMCF, with the Bank of International Settlements (BIS) as its agent. The granting of short-term monetary support is linked to the need for short-term financing caused by a temporary balance-of-payments deficit (current or capital account). Credits are granted without economic policy conditions, but they trigger subsequent consultations. They are extended for a period of three months, orginally with the possibility of renewal for another period of three months. With the amendments introduced in the context of the European Monetary System, a new agreement allows credits under the STMS facility to be renewed for an additional three months, raising the maximum duration from six to nine months.

As mentioned in Chapter 1, each Member State has a 'debtor quota' (borrowing ceiling) and a 'creditor quota' (commitment ceiling), the latter being twice as high as the former to safeguard the viability of the system under varying distributions of payment imbalances among Member States (see Table 2.7). In addition, extensions beyond the debtor and the creditor quotas – the so-called *rallonges* – can be applied to any Member State. The central bank of a Member State may *borrow* from its partners under the STMS facility a total amount equal to its 'debtor quota' plus one-half of the total available (creditor) *rallonge*. The central bank of a Member State is committed to *lend* to its partners under this facility a maximum amount equal to its 'creditor quota' plus the total (creditor) *rallonge*. Accordingly, a central bank may have to lend twice the amount that it may borrow. Overall, if the central banks of the Member States representing 66.6 percent of the 'debtor quota' draw on this facility which is financed by the other central banks of the Member States representing 33.3 percent of the 'creditor quota', the *maximum net* total amount of credit is mobilized, plus, of course, the total creditor *rallonge*. Normally, the STMS is denominated in the currency of the creditor central bank, but it must be denominated in ECUs when it is granted in the form of a prolongation of a debt contracted under the VSTF facility. As indicated in Chapter 1, the STMS facility was used by Italy in 1974, but has not been used since the EMS came into operation.

Medium-Term Financial Assistance (or Support) facility

The Medium-Term Financial Assistance facility, governed by an Ecofin Council decision, extends loans to any Member State in 'difficulties or seriously threatened with difficulties as regards its balance-of-payments (current or capital account)'. Credits are extended for a period of two to five years and subject to economic policy conditions to be laid down by

Table 2.7 Short-Term Monetary Support facility, March 1979 and January 1995

	Debtor quotas (million ECU)	Creditor quotas (million ECU)	Percentage
March 1979			
Banque Nationale de Belgique	580	1,160	7.34
Danmarks Nationalbank	260	520	3.29
Deutsche Bundesbank	1,740	3,480	22.03
Banque de France	1,740	3,480	22.03
Central Bank of Ireland	100	200	1.27
Banca d'Italia	1,160	2,320	14.67
De Nederlandsche Bank	580	1,160	7.34
Bank of England	1,740	3,480	22.03
Total	7,900	15,800	100
Rallonge	4,400	8,800	

Note: If the central banks holding 66.6% of the debtor quotas borrowed up to their limit from the other central banks holding 33.3% of the creditor quotas, the total amount of credit outstanding would be ECU5,261 million. Adding to this number the *rallonge* of ECU8,800 million also available to the borrowers, the total amount of credit outstanding would be ECU14,000 million. This is the figure indicated in the text as the maximum total amount available under the terms of this facility.

January 1995
With the enlargement of the European Community since 1979, the 1995 debtor and creditor quotas for this facility are as follows:

Banque Nationale de Belgique	580	1,160	5.81
Danmarks Nationalbank	260	520	2.60
Deutsche Bundesbank	1,740	3,480	17.43
Bank of Greece	150	300	1.50
Banco de España	725	1,450	7.26
Banque de France	1,740	3,480	17.43
Central Bank of Ireland	100	200	1.00
Banca d'Italia	1,160	2,320	11.62
De Nederlandsche Bank	580	1,160	5.81
Oesterreichische Nationalbank	350	700	3.50
Banco de Portugal	145	290	1.45
Suomen Pankki	220	440	2.20
Sveriges Riksbank	495	990	4.96
Bank of England	1,740	3,480	17.43
Total	9,985	19,970	100

Note: The total creditor and debtor rallonges remained the same as in 1979. Therefore, using the same calculation as above, the total amount of credit available from this facility is ECU15,450 million.

Source: These data are available from any of the central banks of the European Union or from the European Monetary Institute. The author obtained them from the Banque de France.

the Council of Ministers. In formulating conditions and in monitoring the performance of a debtor country, important advisory roles are assigned to the Commission and the Monetary Committee. The MTFA has creditor (commitment) ceilings but no debtor ceilings for individual countries, except that normally no Member State may draw more than 50 percent of the total of credit ceilings. There is no *rallonge*.

A Council Regulation (1969/88/EEC), adopted at the same time as the Council Directive of 24 June 1988 regarding the liberalization of all capital movements within the Community, merged the MTFA facility with the Community Loan Mechanism (Chapter 1) to form a new facility called the Medium-Term Financial Support (MTFS). This was done with a view to provide a flexible financial 'safety net' in order to encourage all Member States to proceed with the full liberalization of capital transactions. The terms and conditions of the Community Loan Mechanism (CLM) established in 1975 had been amended in 1981. As of that date, Member States with balance-of-payments difficulties unrelated to the oil price shock could use the facility and the Community could borrow up to ECU6,000 million to lend to Member States. France was granted a loan of ECU4,000 million in May 1983. By 1985, the CLM borrowing limit of the Community had been established at ECU8,000 million, of which any Member State could borrow up to 50 percent. Greece was granted a loan of ECU1,750 million in December 1985, of which ECU500 million is still outstanding at the end of February 1996.

As with its two predecessors – the MTFA and the CLM – borrowings under the MTFS facility are subject to conditions aimed at re-establishing a sustainable balance-of-payments position. The outstanding amount of borrowing under the new MTFS facility is limited to ECU16,000 million. This total may include up to ECU14,000 million of market borrowing by the Community, which becomes the main form of financing envisaged for medium-term balance-of-payments assistance. As of 1988, the original MTFA facility has been effectively replaced by the CLM. Under the MTFS facility, Italy was granted a loan of ECU8,000 million (or its equivalent in other currencies) in four tranches on 18 January 1993, of which ECU4,045 is still outstanding at the end of February 1996.

ASSESSMENT OF THE EMS FROM 1979 TO 1990

The EMS period between 1979 and 1989 is examined in this chapter. The period 1990–95, which includes the ERM currency turmoil of 1992–93, is examined in the following chapter, since the latter period is marked by a clear 'regime change', with the implementation of Stage I of the Economic and Monetary Union section of the Maastricht Treaty, which included the complete liberalization of capital flows and the expectation that the Community was on a well-defined path towards a monetary union by the end of the century.

The EMS and convergence

In general terms, convergence between countries is the narrowing of international differences in national economic characteristics and performances. Nominal convergence between two countries refers to the narrowing of their nominal variables such as inflation rates, costs (measured by unit labour costs) and interest rates. Real convergence between two countries refers to the narrowing of differences in real variables such as productivity, real growth rate of GDP and unemployment rates.

Starting in the late 1960s, the term 'convergence' began to appear discreetly in Community texts, but only to describe the coordination of national budgetary and monetary policies, not – as we shall see in Chapter 4 – to describe economic performance. The Barre Plan of 1969 spoke of the 'convergence' of the national medium-term economic policies between the Member States. Yet, the Council Decisions of 1969 and 1971 (see Chapter 1) only used the expression 'co-ordination of short-term economic policies of the Member States'. It was only with the 1974 Council Convergence Decision, which replaced the previous two Decisions, that the term 'convergence' was clearly associated with the economic policies of the Member States: to 'attain a high degree of convergence of the economic policies of the Member States' (cf. Chapter 1). The convergence of economic policies was to be achieved by using the various committees that had been established in the 1960s to implement some of the provisions of the Treaty of Rome establishing the EEC.

With the failure of policy convergence in the 1970s by means of committees, the emergence of the EMS in the 1980s provided an opportunity to redefine the instruments used to achieve policy convergence. The Exchange Rate Mechanism, with the ECU at its centre, was to provide an automatic indicator to the national authorities with regard to the convergence of their macroeconomic policies. Converging in terms of policy was to be simplified in this system, without the need to centralize the decision-making. Whenever the ECU exchange rate of a currency deviated from its ECU central rate, market forces were presumably indicating to the national authority that its economic policies were not converging towards the Community average. By virtue of the definition of the ECU as a weighted average of Community currencies, the Community average was defined in terms of the average policy stance of all the participating Member States of the ERM. Of course, in practice the measure of the Community average was not used as the benchmark. Convergence in the 1980s effectively came to mean economic policies converging on the German benchmark since what mattered was the exchange rate of the participating ERM currency deviating from the bilateral central rate against the Deutsche mark, not the ECU exchange rate deviating from its ECU central rate. Giavazzi and Pagano (1988) and Giavazzi and Giovannini (1989) argue that Germany was acting as the centre of the system. The other ERM members adapted their monetary policies to maintain fixed parities with Germany. The evidence of this asymmetry is based on the fact the Bundesbank only engaged in marginal bilateral intervention whereas the other ERM members engaged in intra-marginal intervention. Additional evidence of this hypothesis is provided by the asymmetrical behaviour of interest rates in Germany and the other ERM members. In the period just prior to realignments, German interest rates did not change whereas the interest rates of the other ERM members clearly changed.

An indirect assessment of macroeconomic policy convergence between the Member States during the EMS period of 1979–89 is provided by examining the stability of the bilateral nominal exchange rates between the currencies participating in the ERM and by examining the convergence of inflation rates, unit labour costs, and interest rates between the Member States participating in the ERM.

Variability of exchange rates: 1979–89

A measure of short-term nominal exchange rate variability must be calculated either around a trend or a constant value, depending on whether the expected exchange rate follows a trend value or has constant value. Ungerer *et al.* (1990) use both measures to assess the short-term variability of ERM currencies before and after the inception of the EMS, i.e. for the periods of 1974–78 and 1979–89, respectively. They compare the variability of currencies of the ERM with that of non-ERM currencies. The study indicates that, on average, the variability of bilateral nominal exchange rates of ERM countries against their partners declined substantially between the periods 1974–78 and 1979–89, irrespective of the method of measurement. By contrast, bilateral nominal exchange rate variability for non-ERM countries against non-ERM countries did not change significantly between these same two periods. The study also indicates that, on average, the variability of bilateral nominal exchange rates of ERM currencies against non-ERM currencies increased considerably between the two time periods, while the variability of bilateral exchange rates of non-ERM currencies against non-ERM currencies increased much less. These results are shown in Table 2.8. Further evidence along these lines is provided by Fratianni and von Hagen (1990b). However, they argue that the reduced intra-ERM volatility was at the expense of increased volatility of exchange rates outside the ERM.

Convergence of inflation rates

In general, the evidence on the performance of the ERM of the EMS shows that inflation rates between participating Member States converged in the latter half of the 1980s (Ungerer *et al.* 1990: table 17 and Collignon *et al.*

Table 2.8 Variability of bilateral nominal exchange rates, 1974–89

	Coefficient of variation		Variation of log changes	
	1974–78	1979–89	1974–78	1979–89
	Against		ERM	Currencies
Belgium	20.3	10.6	10.6	6.0
Denmark	25.0	12.3	12.8	6.7
France	31.6	13.8	16.8	6.8
Germany	29.2	13.2	14.7	6.0
Ireland	36.0	12.9	18.4	7.9
Italy	36.0	15.5	19.3	7.5
Netherlands	21.1	10.6	11.1	5.2
Average ERM	28.4	12.7	14.8	6.6
Austria	20.3	9.6	9.9	4.3
Canada	44.1	49.1	22.5	24.9
Japan	44.5	44.4	21.1	20.4
Norway	25.3	26.6	13.3	12.8
Sweden	30.2	27.2	14.6	14.3
Switzerland	44.0	22.5	20.5	12.0
UK	32.7	38.9	16.8	19.7
US	34.7	51.3	18.8	26.4
Average non-ERM	34.5	33.7	17.2	16.8
	Against		Non-ERM	Currencies
Belgium	36.7	43.8	17.9	21.9
Denmark	32.3	41.5	17.0	21.6
France	37.8	46.5	18.7	22.5
Germany	35.7	40.1	18.0	20.7
Ireland	37.0	43.3	14.4	22.9
Italy	38.0	44.3	20.1	20.0
Netherlands	36.8	43.8	18.4	22.5
Average ERM	36.3	43.3	17.8	21.7
Austria	39.5	44.6	18.6	23.1
Canada	23.4	19.0	12.4	12.1
Japan	46.7	52.0	20.1	27.2
Norway	35.6	36.9	18.7	18.9
Sweden	39.9	38.0	18.6	18.2
Switzerland	48.0	46.2	23.6	24.5
UK	49.6	46.4	18.9	23.5
US	34.2	37.1	16.0	20.3
Average non-ERM	39.6	40.0	18.4	21.0

Notes: The exchange rate variability is defined either as the coefficient of variation (standard deviation divided by the mean) of monthly exchange rates or as the standard deviation of the monthly changes in the natural logarithm of exchange rates in a year. The first concept of measurement appears more appropriate if the expected exchange rates remain unchanged while the second concept appears to apply when the expected exchange rates follow a trend. The bilateral exchange rates are a weighted average (MERM weights) against ERM or non-ERM currencies.
Source: Ungerer *et al.* (1990: Table 10).

1994: table 7). By 1990, all the ERM countries, with the exception of Italy and Spain who both participated in the wide ERM bands, had converging inflation rates with a mean of 2.7 percent and a standard deviation of 1.0 percent. The United Kingdom, a non-ERM country, had an inflation rate of 5.3 percent. The question is whether the converging disinflation for the countries participating in the narrow ERM band during the latter half of the 1980s was due to the effects of the EMS. Collins (1988) shows that ERM membership may not have been responsible for the reduced and converging inflation rates.

Realignments: the case of the French franc–Deutsche mark

The French franc–Deutsche mark exchange rate has been front and centre in the European Monetary System and still is in the period leading up to the establishment of the monetary union. That bilateral exchange rate deserves special attention. From 1979 to 1987, there were six bilateral devaluations of the French franc against the Deutsche mark (1979, 1981, 1982, 1983, 1986, 1987) with a cumulative devaluation of 45.2 percent. This percentage is measured on the basis of the FF/DM bilateral central rate of 2.3095 established on 13 March 1979, compared to the FF/DM bilateral central rate of 3.35386 established on 12 January 1987. It has not been changed since January 1987. The bilateral central rates of the FF/DM between 1979 and 1987 are shown in Table 2.9.

The French franc against the Deutsche mark clearly shows a trend, explained in large part by the spread between the French and German inflation rates, as measured by the GDP implicit price indexes. The data are consistent with a realignment rule that approximates the simple version of the relative purchasing power parity theory in international

Table 2.9 French franc/Deutsche mark bilateral central rates and price indexes

Date	FF/DM bilateral central rate	French GDP price index, 1980 = 100	German GDP price index, 1985 = 100
13 Mar. 1979	2.30950	88.37	80.46
24 Sept. 1979	2.35568	93.38	82.64
5 Oct. 1981	2.56212	117.54	90.43
14 June 1982	2.83396	124.19	92.19
21 Mar. 1983	3.06648	131.79	94.63
7 Apr. 1986	3.25617	162.89	102.90
12 Jan. 1987	3.35386	166.44	104.76
Cumulative % change: 1979–87	45.2% devaluation of FF vs DM	88.3% increase	30.2% increase

Source: Price indexes are taken from the OECD quarterly data diskette

economics. From 1979 to 1987, the GDP implicit price index increased by 88.3 percent and 30.2 percent in France and Germany, respectively, resulting in an inflation differential of 58.1 percentage points. Over that same time period, the cumulative nominal bilateral devaluation of the French franc against the Deutsche mark was, as indicated above, 45.2 percent.

CONCLUSION

The rules established under the EMS were the result of a compromise between the views of Member States with strong currencies (led by Germany) and of Member States with weak currencies. Unlike the case of the snake arrangement, the exchange rate band of the EMS was defined both bilaterally and against the ECU. Under the snake regime, the burden of bilateral marginal interventions rested primarily on the Member States with the weak currencies. Under the EMS, although the burden of bilateral marginal interventions still effectively rested on the Member States with the weak currencies, albeit with more flexible terms for the repayment of intervention credits, the ECU 'divergence indicator' was designed to share the burden of economic adjustments between Member States with weak and strong currencies. The terms 'weak' and 'strong' were defined vis-à-vis a weighted average of the Community currencies, not bilaterally with respect to any given Community currency. Thus, if the Deutsche mark was characterized as 'too strong' according to the ECU 'divergence indicator', the German government and/or the Bundesbank would therefore have the burden of adjustment in this case. However, the 'divergence indicator' only carried a presumption of action by the Member State concerned, as the Deutsche Bundesbank did not want to be legally forced to loosen its monetary policy – and as a consequence lose control of its price stability objective – in the event its currency was sending signals of diverging in the direction of 'too strong'. The Basle/Nyborg amendments to the 1979 Agreement between central banks also had the effect of placing more responsibility on the central banks with weak currencies since they were expected to intervene before reaching their weak bilateral margin(s) and to make more use of interest rate variations to prevent the weak currency from reaching its bilateral margin. The central banks with the strong currencies had few significant, if any, additional bilateral obligations in this case.

The EMS, in contrast to the previous European 'snake' system, provided a certain flexibility, such as the ±6 percent margins of fluctuation around the bilateral central rate and the more concerted effort on the part of the Council to modify those bilateral central rates whenever the 'fundamentals' indicated the need to do so. In the final analysis, the original EMS was not designed to be an end in itself, but only as a step towards the economic and monetary union (cf. Commission of the European

Communities 1979: 74). The original EMS arrangement made reference to a future 'final system' that would entail the establishment of a European Monetary Fund, with the creation *ex nihilo* of ECU assets to be used as a means of settlement between central banks. This was to occur no later than two years after the start of the EMS. However, this part of the agreement was never implemented because of the Bundesbank's concern about the risks of the creation of additional international liquidity leading to inflation.

APPENDIX

Table A2.10 Member States' participation in various aspects of the EMS since 1979

Member State (currency)	In VSTF/STMS	In ERM	In ECU basket
Belgium (BFR)	Yes	±2.25% margins*	Yes
Denmark (DKR)	Yes	±2.25% margins*	Yes
Germany (DM)	Yes	±2.25% margins**	Yes
Greece (DRA)	Yes since 1/1986	No	Yes since 9/1984
Spain (PTA)	Yes since 5/1987	±6.0% margins since 6/1989*	Yes since 9/1989
France (FF)	Yes	±2.25% margins*	Yes
Ireland (IRL)	Yes	±2.25% margins*	Yes
Italy (LIT)	Yes	±6.0% margins until 1/1990; ±2.25% margins until 9/1992; No from 9/1992 to 11/1996; ±15.0% margins since 11/1996	Yes
Luxembourg (LFR)	Yes	±2.25% margins*	Yes
Netherlands (HFL)	Yes	±2.25% margins**	Yes
Austria (ÖS)	Yes since 1/1995	±15.0% margins since 1/1995	No***
Portugal (ESC)	Yes since 11/1987	±6.0% margins since 4/1992*	Yes since 9/1989
Finland (FMK)	Yes since 2/1995	±15.0% margins since 10/1996	No***
Sweden (SKR)	Yes since 4/1995	No	No
United Kingdom (UKL)	Yes	No, except ±6.0% margins between 10/1990 and 9/1992	Yes

*   Since 2 August 1993, the bilateral margins are widened to ±15%.
**   Since 2 August 1993, the bilateral margins are widened to ±15%, with the exception of the DM–HFL which retains the narrow margins.
*** Therefore this currency has a weight of zero for the calculation of the threshold of maximum divergence.

because the tariffs between the Member States are reduced to zero. Trade is distorted because price discrimination is increased – a zero tariff if the good comes from another Member State but an external tariff if that same good comes from outside the group. Jacob Viner (1953) called these two characteristics trade creation and trade diversion, whose net effect can either improve or worsen the economic welfare of the members of a preferential trading arrangement (see also Moore 1994).

In a free-trade area, each member country can retain its previous tariff on imports from outside the area. In a customs union, all member countries agree on a common external tariff. In order to comply with GATT regulations requiring that the level of protection be no greater than before the establishment of a customs union, the EEC decided to set its common external tariff at the arithmetic average of the previous tariffs of member countries. This therefore raised the level of protection against third countries in those member countries with liberal trade regimes and lowered it in more protectionist ones. A customs union candidate which has both relatively more trade with third countries and a more liberal trading regime than its partners is more likely to suffer a net loss from the sum of the trade diversion and trade creation effects of joining the customs union. In the 1950s, Britain had relatively more trade with third countries (i.e. countries other than the Member States composing the original EEC, known as EUR6) and a more liberal trading regime than most Continental European states. An indication of the relative importance of the effects of trade diversion on Britain may be obtained by considering the following data. In 1957, the year prior to entry into force of the Treaty of Rome, the UK's exports to EUR6 was 13.8 percent of its total exports. By contrast, France's exports to the other six countries (including the UK) was 27 percent of its total exports; Germany's exports to the other six countries was 31.2 percent of its total exports; Italy's exports to the other six countries was 30.4 percent of its total exports. In each case, similar figures are observed for the structure of imports. Thus, the issue of the potential effects of trade diversion had to be more important for the UK than for the countries composing EUR6. This fact may partly explain Britain's reluctance to join a customs union with EUR6 at that time and its preference to enter into a large European free-trade area.

Preferential trading arrangements lead to increasing economic integration. A measure of the increasing economic integration of the European Community may be obtained by examining over time the share of intra-Community trade. Using the countries composing EUR12 (EUR6 plus the UK, Ireland, Denmark, Greece, Spain and Portugal) as a benchmark, the share of intra-Community exports of goods and services has been growing since 1958. In 1958, the share of 'intra-Community' exports out of the total exports of EUR12 was 37.2 percent. By 1970, this share increased to 53.4 percent. In 1991, intra-Community exports represented 61.6 percent of the total exports of goods and services of these twelve

Member States. Another indication of increasing economic integration among the original six Member States of the EEC is the increasing share of EUR6 intra-Community trade for each of the three largest Member States. In 1958, the share of French exports of goods and services going to the other five Member States was 22.1 percent. By 1991, that figure rose to 45 percent. Comparable figures for Germany are 27.3 percent and 38 percent. For Italy, the figures are 23.6 percent and 42.8 percent.

THE SINGLE MARKET IN GOODS, SERVICES, CAPITAL AND LABOUR

Although the elimination of internal tariffs and quotas between the Member States of EUR6 was for the most part completed by 1968, the goal of a barrier-free, single market in the movement of goods, services, labour and capital still had not been achieved by the mid-1980s. Many legal, non-tariff barriers remained in place.

The Single European Act (SEA), which came into force in July 1987, reinforced the original provisions of the Treaty of Rome to create a single market within the Community by removing all hitherto legal obstacles to the free movement of goods, services, capital and labour. In keeping with these objectives, some 280 Directives were adopted by Council, acting by a qualified majority and by using the newly adopted SEA cooperation procedure with the European Parliament. In general, these Directives were to be transposed into national laws by the end of 1992. The goal, which still has not been entirely achieved in all areas, is to remove non-tariff barriers between Member States of the following nature:

- *physical* frontiers, which include stoppages at intra-Community customs posts at geographical frontiers;
- *technical* frontiers, which include restrictions on intra-Community trade related to different national technical regulations and norms for goods and services, or to discrimination against non-national bids for public purchases of goods and services;
- *fiscal* and *subsidy* frontiers, which include non-harmonized national value-added and excise taxes on goods and services, as well as non-harmonized national state aid to industry.

For purposes of economic analysis, these non-tariff barriers or frontiers have been classified by the Commission (1988: 33) in terms of the following catagories:

- Cost increasing barriers, which include the cost of delays at customs posts for the purposes of value-added or excise tax assessment, of the collection of statistics, or of the verification of technical regulations, and the cost of meeting different technical regulations in production, packaging or marketing in effect in other Member States.

- Market-entry restrictions, which include government procurement restrictions, the right of establishment of various service industries and professions, restrictions in some service sectors that prevent or limit direct cross-border trade (e.g. insurance, investment services, energy) and the right to enter some monopolized or highly regulated markets (e.g. airline and telecommunications industries, cross-border branch banking).
- Market-distorting taxes, subsidies and practices, which include non-harmonized value-added taxes and subsidies and market-distorting competition rules due to the lack of common, European-wide rules on merger policy.

Estimated economic benefits of completing the single market

The anticipated economic benefits of a completed, competitive single market were estimated by a research team headed by Mr Paolo Cecchini. This research project was financed by the Commission. Many independent economic experts, consultants and research institutes contributed to this project, with support from the Commission's departments. The methodology, the economic analysis, and the results were published by the Commission (1988). The microeconomic (the partial equilibrium consumers' and producers' surplus) gains derived from the economies of scale of restructuring, from the removal of barriers and from the competition effects were estimated between 4.3 and 6.4 percent of Community (EUR12) GDP, with a mid-point estimate of 5.8 percent. By contrast, the static gains from the complete removal of duties between the Member States of EUR6 in 1968 was estimated at that time to be about 1 percent of GDP. In addition to the 'welfare gains' of partial equilibrium analysis, the Cecchini report also estimated the dynamic, macroeconomic gains, using the Interlink and Hermes multinational macroeconomic models. This dynamic gain, due to the combination of a decline in consumer prices, an increase in employment, a reduction in public sector deficit and an improvement in the current account, was estimated to be a 4.5 percent increase of GDP over a six-year period.

The methodology and data used in the Cecchini sectoral studies were criticized and believed to be the source of the over-estimated gains derived from completing the single market (cf. Peck 1989, Flam 1992 and Dornbusch 1989). More recently, the Commission (1996g) estimated the overall economic effects (static and dynamic effects) of the single market measures to be in the order of an extra increase in EU GDP (EUR12) of 1.1–1.5 percent over the period 1987–93, or 60,000 to 80,000 million ECUs.

As the single market measures have been implemented, cross-border mergers and acquisitions between Community firms and between firms from the same Member State increased. Between 1986 and 1995, the number of mergers and acquisitions has increased from 720 to 2,296 in industry and from 783 to 2,602 in services. However, 70 percent are purely mergers and acquisitions between firms from the same Member State (Commission 1996g), which the Commission interprets as a defensive strategy at the national level. In the manufacturing sector, the concentration at the EU level has increased between 1987 and 1993. The share of the four largest firms increased from 20.5 percent of the total, on average, of European turnover, to 22.8 percent over that time period. Yet, there also has been a decline in concentration at the national level. These facts may be interpreted as evidence of a pan-Europeanization of the manufacturing sector with a simultaneous increase in competition at the national level. Europe-wide, large firms' volume of activity has grown with relative declines on home markets due to the variation in the geographic distribution of the firms in this sector. The creation of a single market, with an increased competition at the national level, has resulted in the convergence of prices across Member States. Between 1985 and 1993, the coefficient of variation for prices (including taxes) between Member States for identical consumer goods decreased from 22.5 percent to 19.6 percent, and for services from 33.7 percent to 28.6 percent (Commission 1996g).

Harmonization of indirect tax rates

The harmonization of indirect taxes, such as the value-added tax (VAT), reduces price discrepancies and distortions in the pattern of competition between Member States. As a preliminary step, the Community agreed, effective 1 January 1993, to set minimum VAT rates. The 'standard' VAT rate in any Member State may not be *less* than 15 percent (Germany and Luxembourg have the minimum rate; Denmark and Sweden have the highest rate of 25 percent) and the 'reduced' VAT rates on essential goods and services of a social or cultural nature such as food, medicine, water distribution, books, newspapers and cinema admissions may not be *less* than 5 percent. Not more than two 'reduced' VAT rates may be established. Member States which applied zero or extra low rates (less than 5 percent) may retain them on a transitional basis. Since 1993, private individuals crossing internal frontiers are no longer subject to any customs check or merchandise declaration. Thus, under the new VAT system, private individuals pay the VAT applicable in the Member State where they make the purchase (except for new automobiles, boats and planes for which the destination VAT rate is applicable). For intra-Community transactions between traders who use VAT registration numbers (wholesale trade), the VAT rate of the Member State where the goods are imported is applicable. Similarly, the Community agreed, effective 1 January 1993, on minimum excise duty rates for alcoholic beverages (some equal to zero), mineral oils (such as petrol) and manufactured tobacco.

The goal of the European Union is ultimately to introduce harmonized VAT rates and to remove any distinction between domestic and cross-border intra-Community transactions when applying the VAT rate. Harmonization and reduction of indirect taxes imposed on labour is another fiscal area where the Commission believes progress must be made. These indirect taxes must be reduced to lower the relative cost of labour so as to reduce the unemployment rates. Moreover, these indirect taxes on labour must be harmonized to eliminate market distortions with respect to the location decisions of production taken by firms in the single market.

Removal of physical and technical barriers

The removal of physical barriers, such as the numerous internal border checks for merchandise crossing internal frontiers, reduces the cost of goods. Since 1993, the burdensome consignment declarations at each internal frontier have been replaced by exchanges of information between the tax administrations of the Member States based on minimal sales details supplied at regular intervals by traders who sell goods to other traders in other Member States. The savings of implementing these measures for cross-border shipments have been estimated to be 0.7 percent of the value of intra-EU trade, or 5,000 million ECUs per annum.

The differences between the national product standards in the Community create technical barriers to the free movement of goods within the single market and make it more difficult, and sometimes impossible, to import products manufactured in accordance with the standards in certain Member States into other Member States. The new, single market Community approach is to require that all Member States grant access to their national markets to products which conform to the European standards referred to in a harmonization Directive. The European standards are drafted by the various private national standards organizations meeting together under a European umbrella. By following these European standards, manufacturers and retailers can be sure that their products are entitled to free movement within the single market. For products that do not require a harmonization directive, which represents about 25 percent of manufactured products, Community legislation is no longer required. The free movement of goods is automatically guaranteed by the principle of mutual recognition – a good legally manufactured and marketed in one Member State should be able to be sold in another. By 1996, this is still proving difficult to enforce.

Removal of market-entry restrictions

One type of market-entry restriction on the supply of professional services is the lack of recognition by one Member State of the diplomas or professional qualifications obtained in another Member State. Single market directives have addressed this problem. If a specific diploma must be held in order to practice the professional activity in question (i.e. it is a regulated profession), the host Member State must apply the mutual recognition machinery provided for in the Community Directives. The recognition is automatic where training for the profession has been harmonized at the Community level, such as in the medical profession; it is semi-automatic and involves checks where training for the profession has not been harmonized. If the practice of the profession concerned is not dependent on obtaining a specific diploma, the employer is free to assess the relevance of the qualification. Since January 1991, there are twenty-two Community systems, from road hauliers and pharmacists to architects and lawyers, establishing automatic recognition for professional qualifications. Since June 1994, semi-automatic recognition is based on the presumed equivalence of education and training, which can always be contested by the host Member State.

In some service sectors, market-entry restrictions prevent or limit direct trading across borders. Many of these service sectors are either state monopolies (telecommunications, airlines, electricity, rail transport services or postal services) or highly regulated industries (banking and financial services). Directives, based on either the single market provisions of the Treaty of Rome (EEC) and the SEA or the competition rules of the Treaty of Rome, have set the following deadlines for the creation of a competitive, single market in the following sectors:

- Banking services, January 1993.
- Insurance services, July 1994.
- Investment services, January 1996.
- Airlines, January 1993, right of consecutive cabotage and abolition of market share limitations, freedom to set fares, and common airline licensing [consecutive cabotage is the right of an airline to disembark and embark passengers in all other Member States on the onward legs of a flight originating from, or terminating to, the airline's home country]; April 1997, right of full cabotage, which is the right of an airline to fly on any route in the EU.
- Road hauliers, unrestricted cabotage, July 1998.
- Telecommunications, January 1998, for voice telephony with a five-year derogation for Ireland, Greece, Portugal and Spain and a two-year derogation for Luxembourg.
- Electricity, partial opening, as of January 1999, to cross-border competition for customers consuming more than 40 GWh per year (22 percent of the market), and falling to 20 GWh and 9 GWh (28.5 percent and 32 percent of the market, respectively) by January 2000 and January 2003, respectively, with a two-year derogation for Greece and a one-year derogation for Belgium and Ireland; Member States can choose between two methods of market opening – 'third party access',

whereby large electricity users can conclude supply contracts directly with foreign generators, and the more restrictive 'single buyer' system, favoured by France, where a designated national electricity buyer would conclude contracts on behalf of customers.

- Rail transport, a 1991 Directive, introduces the principle of the separation of the provision of capital-intensive rail infrastructure from the commercial operation of railway services; the latter must eventually be liberalized and open to competition on a commercial basis; the infrastructure (i.e. tracks and equipment) must be harmonized between the Member States so as to allow competition on the provision of cross-border railway services; the 1991 Directive only opened-up access to cross-border rail transport of freight which combined 'train and truck'; the Commission proposed in 1996 to introduce limited competition on freight and international passenger services.
- Postal services, 1 January 1998, the liberalization of the postal market for letters weighing more than 350 g; further liberalization with respect to 'direct' mail and in-bound cross-border mail will have to be taken by 2000 to enter into force 1 January 2003.

In the air transport sector, the deregulation and liberalization measures taken since 1993 to increase competition in European air-space have resulted in an increase in the number of routes flown from 520 at the end of 1996 against 490 in 1993, with 30 percent of the routes in 1996 served by two carriers. Six percent of the routes are served by three or more carriers (against 2 percent in 1993). Taking into account charter flights, which represent 50 percent of the market, 90 to 95 percent of the passengers benefit from lower fares than those of 1993. However, on some routes, the fares per kilometre remain high: Strasbourg–Vienna is six times more expensive than London–Palma de Majorca.

The single market in telecommunications

The directives to establish an open, competitive, single market in telecommunication services are based on Article 90 of the Treaty of Rome (EEC), which deals with rules governing competition in respect of public enterprises, and on a Commission (1987) *Green Paper* on telecommunications policies.

In the telecommunications service sector, a two-step approach has been adopted by the Commission to create a single market. First, national governments are encouraged either to privatize the state-owned monopoly or to change the legal status of the state-owned public enterprise so that it will be able to compete once the market has been liberalized. Then, the Commission initiates legislation to promote intra-Union competition when the physical networks (trunk routing, exchanges, 'local loop') are opened up and equal access is guaranteed by 1 January 1998. The legislation includes rules on mutual recognition of certificates and standardization to ensure inter-operability between equipment in telecommunications.

Prior to the deadline, Member States must also notify the Commission of their licensing procedures to allow competition in the provision of telecommunication services. The notification must be completed by January 1997, after which the Member State must publish by July 1997 the licensing conditions, as well as the terms and conditions for inter-connection. Each Member State must also establish a regulatory structure that nurtures commercial rivalry and effectively works against anti-competitive behaviour. Regulation is essential when telecoms markets are opened to competition for the following reasons:

● to ensure that a basic telephone service is available to all at a reasonable price – the so-called universal service obligation, which Member States are allowed to enforce by virtue of certain provisions in the Treaty of Rome;
● to ensure that new competitors are able to interconnect their networks with that of the former monopoly operator at reasonable cost;
● to prevent established operators from stifling competition at the outset through their stranglehold on the final connection to the home or office;
● to ensure fair competition in new services expected through the 'information highway'.

European legislation also requires that the so-called 'alternative telecom networks' be able to compete with state telecoms. These alternative networks, such as those controlled by television cable networks, energy supply networks and railway power cables, should be free to provide any telecoms services, such as data transmission and GSM (mobile communication) except basic voice telephony, as of July 1996.

Currently, the largest telecommunications market in Europe is served by the monopoly operator Deutsche Telekom, which has been partially privatized (20 percent of the shares) in November 1996. In anticipation of an open, competititive telecoms market, most of the European telecoms operators are forming strategic alliances with each other and with American telecoms operators. These alliances are a means by which the operators can win business from large multinational customers and can position themselves for the future global competition. Deutsche Telekom is pursuing a global strategy through an alliance with France Télécom, dubbed Atlas. In addition, Deutsche Telekom and France Télécom will purchase 20 percent of Sprint (US) to form an alliance dubbed Global One.

With the new freedom allowed to the 'alternative' telecoms networks to compete with Deutsche Telekom (excluding basic voice telephony prior to 1998), German utilities and other companies are seeking partnerships with each other and with foreign telecoms operators. Veba and RWE, two of Germany's largest conglomerates, have formed an alliance to compete with Deutsche Telekom. RWE and Veba together operate private networks with 70,000 km of modern optical-fibre cabling. Mannesmann, a large German company, bought a 50 percent stake in DBKom, the telecoms network of Germany's railway system, the second biggest telecommunications network of fixed lines behind Deutsche Telekom. Mannesmann and Veba, like Deutsche Telekom, are also securing international partners to improve their chances of operating outside Germany. Mannesmann joined with the US group AT&T, and Veba created a joint venture with Cable & Wireless, the UK-based telecoms group. Viag, the German electricity utility which has an extensive fibre-optic network, created a joint venture with British Telecommunications to provide telecoms services to corporate and residential clients in direct competition with Deutsche Telekom.

France Télécom controls a monopoly market for the traditional voice telephony in France. In anticipation of the 1998 deadline, the French government is to sell 49 percent of the shares of France Télécom to its employees, private investors and to other telecoms. In late 1997, the first tranche, equivalent to 20 percent of the shares, will be sold on the private market. The French government will also introduce an independent telecommunications regulator to ensure fair competition, which would require the competitors of France Télécom to share in the cost of providing the 'public service' mandate of telecommunications, such as basic telephone service to rural areas and public telephone booths. France argues in favour of the state retaining a dominant position in certain 'public service' sectors such as telecommunications, power transmission (Electricité de France), postal services (La Poste), and passenger railway (la SNCF) in order to guarantee 'affordable' tariffs to consumers across the country.

British Telecom, whose privatization was initially launched in 1984, is an entirely private company since 1993. BT now operates in Europe's most liberal market, facing competition from more than forty licensed operators. BT, which has joint ventures in Germany, Italy, Spain, Sweden, the Netherlands, France, Switzerland and Austria, announced in late 1996 merger plans with MCI (US) to create a global telecoms operator called Concert. Concert will compete with Global One for the business of large international companies. BT has also formed a strategic alliance with Cegetel, the telecoms subsidiary of the French utility Compagnie Générale des Eaux, which in turn has formed an alliance with the SNCF's (Société Nationale des Chemins de Fer Français) telecoms subsidiary. The SNCF plans to compete with France Télécom in fixed and mobile telephone services.

Telecom Italia is 59.3 percent owned by STET, a holding company owned by the Italian Treasury. In early 1997, the Italian government announced that Telecom Italia will be entirely absorbed by STET, which in turn will be privatized.

Telecoms operators who currently enjoy a monopoly must 'rebalance' their local and long-distance tariffs or fall victim to savage competition when the EU markets for basic voice telephony are opened to competition in 1998. This is already happening in Germany and France. For example, in 1996 Deutsche Telekom has increased by 156 percent the price of a local call while at the same time granting rebates of up to 39 percent to large corporate clients on their phone bills, primarily composed of long-distance charges. France Télécom has already reduced long distance domestic and international rates while increasing the monthly basic charges and the price of local calls. France Télécom will reduce domestic long-distance charges by an additional 17.5 percent and 21 percent, effective March 1997 and October 1997, respectively. International calls will be reduced a further 20 percent and 17 percent on these two dates. Monthly basic charges will again be increased.

The single financial market

The creation of a single financial market involves the principle of the *free movement of capital* between Member States, the principle of the *right of establishment* of financial institutions from one Member State into another Member State, and the principle of the *right to supply* cross-border financial services from the home country.

Free movement of capital

The general principle of unrestricted movement of capital, set out in Article 3C of the Treaty of Rome is circumscribed by Article 67.1, which provides for the *gradual* abolition of restrictions on the movement of capital belonging to persons resident in Member States, with a timetable to be defined by Council directives and only 'to the extent necessary to ensure the proper functioning of the common market'. Moreover, the Treaty's provision allows scope for the application of protective measures – safeguard clauses – if circumstances require. Such circumstances include disruptions in the functioning of the capital market in any Member State (Article 73) and balance-of-payments difficulties (Articles 108 and 109). In the Treaty, a distinction is made between movement of capital associated with the capital account of the balance of payments, and movement of capital, such as interest and dividend payments, associated with the current account of the balance of payments. The restrictions on the movement of capital in the latter category had to be abolished four years after the Treaty came into force.

The basic Directives on the liberalization of capital movements were adopted in 1960 and 1962. These Directives defined the various movements of capital into four different categories, each of which was subject to a different degree of liberalization. Priority was given to the deregulation of capital transactions associated with short-term and medium-term credits in respect of commercial transactions, with investments in plant and equipment, with personal capital movements and with trade in quoted securities (Lists A and B). List C included transactions, such as the issue and placing of securities on a capital market, and long-term credits related to commercial transactions, to be deregulated conditionally. List D included short-term transactions chiefly associated with currency speculation. These transactions were not deregulated.

These Directives did not add much to the liberalization measures on capital movements which the Member States had already adopted on their own initiative. Nonetheless, these Directives set out specific obligations on Member States such as the prohibition of repealing unilaterally the liberalization measures that a Member State had already adopted.

In the 1970s, liberalization of capital movements came to a standstill. In fact, with the international crises related to the breakdown of the Bretton Woods international monetary system and the oil price shocks, some Member States used the safeguard clauses in Articles 108 and 109 to re-impose controls on capital movements included in Lists A and B when faced with exchange rate disturbances. In 1968, France, in the face of a domestic crisis, was obliged to reintroduce substantial controls on movements of capital. These controls were maintained when France faced the international crises of the 1970s. Italy too, in the wake of the first oil crisis of 1974, reintroduced certain capital controls. When Denmark, Ireland and the United Kingdom joined the Community in 1973, these three countries maintained strict controls on capital movements, which they were initially allowed to keep by virtue of the transitional provisions of the accession treaties.

In the 1980s, a number of events converged to provide a new impetus to the liberalization of capital movements. The increasing globalization of financial markets, combined with the lifting by Britain and Germany of all restrictions on capital movements in 1979 and 1981, respectively, created a challenge to the compartmentalization of the Community's individual financial markets, notably in France, Italy, Denmark and Ireland. Moreover, by the mid-1980s, the Community was launching measures to complete the single market; restrictions on the movements of capital were seen as incompatible with that goal. Accordingly, in 1986 the Council adopted a Directive (86/566/EEC), which provided for the unconditional (see List C above) liberalization of capital movements associated with long-term credits related to commercial transactions and with the integration of the national securities markets. The latter included the admission to the capital market of one Member State of securities issued by a company in another Member State and the cross-border acquisition of unlisted foreign securities (bonds, shares or units issued by undertakings for collective investment in transferable securities, UCITS, i.e. by investment funds).

Soon after, in June 1988, another Directive (88/361/EEC) lifted all the remaining restrictions on capital movements between Member States. The aim of the Directive was to extend the principle of liberalization to all capital movements, not only to those transactions indicated in certain lists contained in the 1960, 1962 and 1986 Directives. This 1988 Directive effectively meant the end of restrictions imposed on transactions of a monetary or quasi-monetary nature, such as the opening of accounts abroad and cross-border transactions in money-market instruments. The Directive also stipulated that Member States should endeavour to attain the same degree of liberalization of capital movements to and from third countries. Except for those Member States granted a transitional period, the Directive provided for capital movements to be fully liberalized by 1 July 1990. Ireland and Spain were given until the end of 1992 to implement this directive; Portugal and Greece were given until the end of 1995. By 1 January 1993, only Greece had not fully liberalized capital movements. It did so by 16 May 1994. Belgium and Luxembourg eliminated their dual foreign exchange market by 2 March 1990, ahead of the December 1992 deadline.

The Directive contained a special safeguard clause to allow the Member States to take protective measures against short-term capital movements, for a period not exceeding six months, in cases where their monetary and exchange rate policies should be disrupted as a result of the liberalization programme. This safeguard clause was in addition to, and did not replace, the more general safeguard clauses (Articles 73, 108 and 109) of the Treaty of Rome.

Freedom of establishment and to provide services

After adopting the directives necessary to establish the complete liberalization of capital movements, the Commission, in the context of completing the single market in the financial area of banking, investment (brokerage) services and insurance, proposed measures to implement the principles of 'freedom of establishment' and 'freedom to provide services'. The approach was as follows (Servais 1991: 49):

- harmonization of the essential elements of prudential rules and standards;
- mutual recognition by Member States of each other's legislation and supervision of financial institutions;
- on these bases, the principle of supervision by the country of origin: all the activities of financial institutions carried out in the Community – whether through a branch (by virtue of the right of establishment) or through trans-border suppliers (by virtue of the freedom to provide services) – must be supervised by the Member State in which the head office is established.

The Second Banking Directive (89/646/EEC), which came into force on 1 January 1993, is a good example of this approach to financial integration. A credit institution, duly authorized to operate in its Member State of origin, may establish itself (branch) or provide trans-border services in any other Member State without having to seek additional licences (the principle of a single licence or 'passport'). The Member State which issues the licence is responsible for the supervision of all activities of the credit institution throughout the Community. However, the supervisory authorities of the host country retain responsibility for monitoring the liquidity – not the solvency – of the branches of the credit institution. The credit institution is allowed to carry out any banking activity in the host country, provided that it may carry the activity out in its country of origin. Harmonization of minimum capital requirements for the authorization to issue a licence to a credit institution is set at ECU5 million. In related directives, harmonization of solvency ratios and minimum deposit insurance levels have been legislated.

In May 1994, the Council adopted a directive relative to the deposit insurance system, which came into force in January 1995. Each Member State must guarantee deposits of credit institutions in an amount of at least ECU20,000 per depositor. The deposit insurance must not only cover the banks located in the Member State which issued the licence but also the branches of these banks located in the host Member States. However, until the end of 1999, the insurance coverage of the branches located in the host Member State may not be greater than the insurance ceilings available in the host Member State. Four Member States – Portugal, Greece, Spain and Luxembourg – were granted until the end of 1999 to implement this directive.

The principle of the single licence or 'passport' issued by the national regulatory authority from the country of origin to provide financial services throughout the Community has also been applied to the insurance and the investment service sectors, effective July 1994 and January 1996, respectively. For the latter sector, the EU Investment Services Directive extends the right to non-bank firms (banks already have this right under the Second Banking Directive) to provide investment services, and allows all investment firms, banks and non-bank companies to have access to stock exchange membership in all the Member States and to set up branches or subsidiaries there. When operating outside their home countries, the investment firms will be subject to rules on the conduct of business devised by the local regulators. Foreign banks will not gain direct access to stock exchanges in Spain, Portugal and Greece until 1999. The Council adopted accompanying rules to the Investment Services Directive: the Capital Adequacy Directive for banks and securities firms to set aside capital to cover risks in securities trading and a directive providing minimum protection for small investors in case the investment firm goes bankrupt. Effective December 1996, investment firms will be required to provide a minimum insurance coverage of ECU15,000 until 1999.

After that, the firms will be required to provide a minimum 90 percent of ECU20,000.

A setback to the completion of the European financial common market is the lack of an agreement to set minimum withholding tax rates on interest payments, with no distinctions made between residents and non-residents, to prevent tax-induced distortions in the allocation of savings. The Commission proposal, in 1989, provided for the introduction of a common system of withholding tax (minimum rate of 15 percent) on interest paid to residents and non-residents and for strengthening of cooperation between national tax authorities. Member States could also retain the option of not applying the withholding tax to interest paid to residents of third countries. A few Member States are unwilling to accept such a system, arguing that it would provoke a major flight of capital to third countries. Currently, some Member States – Germany, Austria, Luxembourg, Sweden, Denmark – have no withholding tax on interest payments.

Another setback to the completion of the single market in the financial sector is the right of Member States to restrict capital transfers where permitted by their fiscal law. The most significant restrictions in this area affect investment undertaken by pension funds. Six Member States restrict a range of pension fund investments to their national market.

CONCLUSION

The coming into force of the Single European Act in the mid-1980s provided the Community with the necessary instrument to complete the goal of removing the obstacles to the free movement of goods, services, capital and labour. As of April 1996, the overall rate of transposition of single market directives into national laws of the Member States was 89.7 percent (Commission 1996b). Denmark had the highest rate of transposition (96.6 percent) followed by the Netherlands, the United Kingdom, Luxembourg and Spain. The sectors which presented the most problems in terms of the implementation of the White Paper directives to complete the single market were public procurement, insurance, and intellectual and industrial property.

For federalists and for those with a functionalist approach towards integration, the next logical step, after the SEA, was to take Europe on the road towards a monetary union. By 1988, the generally positive attitude of the public towards Europe, characterized as 'Europhoria', paved the way for federalists like Delors and Mitterrand to grab the opportunity to push for further European integration. Delors, with the support of France, proposed to re-launch the goal of progressively achieving a monetary union, which had been temporarily suspended in 1974, but which had not been entirely forgotten.[1] In June 1988, the Heads of State or Government created a committee, chaired by Delors, to draft proposals for an economic and monetary union.

4 The Maastricht road to a monetary union: 1989–99

OPTIMUM CURRENCY AREA

The economic literature dealing with the issue of establishing irrevocably fixed nominal exchange rates, or what amounts to a single currency, is treated by the theory of the optimum currency area (OCA). This theory goes back to Mundell's (1961) famous article in which he poses the question of what determines an optimal currency area. Starting with the assumption of sticky prices and wages, Mundell argues that the economic space which has labour and capital mobility is a candidate for a single currency. Labour mobility within the defined zone maintains full employment over the entire zone as demand shifts from one good produced in one part of the zone to another good produced in another part of the zone. There is no need for a variation of an exchange rate between the parts of this economic space to maintain full employment. Accordingly, a single currency provides benefits in terms of microeconomic efficiencies (eliminates transactions costs) without imposing any macro-stabilization cost as a result of the loss of the exchange rate instrument. Further refinements were later added to the OCA theory.

Kenen (1969) added another relevant criterion to the determination of an OCA, namely the production structure of the various economic zones that are candidates for the single currency. Industrial countries with a high degree of within-country product diversification are good candidates for defining an OCA, even with the existence of little labour mobility between these countries. Under these circumstances, Kenen argues that 'economic diversification [in each industrial country], reflected in export diversification, serves, ex ante, to forestall the need for frequent changes in terms of trade and, therefore, for frequent changes in national exchange rates' (Kenen 1969: 49). Assume that one good, produced only in a given country, suffers a negative demand shock, and further assume that the demand shifts from this good to all other goods that are produced domestically and abroad. Then, the diversified production structure means that aggregate production need not change in the country which suffers the product-specific negative demand shock. There is no need for an exchange rate change.

On the basis of the Mundell labour-mobility criterion to define an OCA, the European Union would be ill-suited as a geographic unit to have a single currency. The Commission, in a recent report (Emerson *et al.* 1990) acknowledges that European workers move around less within the Union than American workers within the US because of language and cultural barriers. By contrast, on the basis of the Kenen criterion, the European Union is a possible candidate for an OCA. Calculations by Bini-Smaghi and Vori (1993) show that, on average, the Member States of EU12 have relatively more product diversification in the manufacturing sector than the twelve US Federal Reserve Districts. However, this empirical evidence based on comparative analysis with the US is a weak argument in favour of OCA since the US may not be an optimal currency area. Moreover, as Krugman (1991) argues, the creation of a monetary union may increase the regional specialization of a union over time. In other words, the European monetary union may lead to a less diversified production structure in each Member State.

Extending the Kenen criterion to the European case, Emerson *et al.* (1990) argue that the loss of the nominal exchange rate variation between the Member States participating in a monetary union may not represent the loss of a macro-stabilization instrument. Within the European Union, and especially among those Member States which are candidates for the initial monetary union in 1999, product market integration tends to be of the intra-industry type, not of the inter-industry type. With the exception of Portugal and Greece, the share of intra-industry trade in intra-Community trade between Member States of EU12 varied between 57 and 83 percent in 1987 (Commission 1990b). This means that the Community is characterized by intra-Community trade based on different products within the same industry. In other words, product differentiation across Member States tends to dominate product specialization. The consequence of this phenomenon is that Member States are more likely to receive symmetric shocks rather than asymmetric shocks. This renders the nominal exchange rate variable an ineffective adjustment instrument to stabilize the economies. For example, if all Member States have an automobile production sector with intra-European trade of various automobile products, all the Member States cannot have a devaluation of their currencies vis-à-vis each other to cushion a shock emanating from the automobile sector. Thus, the Emerson argument attempts to buttress the idea that Europe is an OCA. The first important assumption underlying this conclusion is that Member States of the Community will not be subjected to real asymmetric shocks. Examples of real asymmetric shocks are the reunification of Germany and major social disturbances, which have important economic consequences on real wages, in one Member State and not in the others. The second assumption is that a Member State in the monetary union does not have a 'differential policy response' to a change in the single monetary policy of the monetary union. An example of a differential policy response would be the case of the single European central bank deciding to tighten monetary policy, causing a differential impact on various Member States participating in the monetary union. If British mortgages have short-term variable interest rates while French ones have long-term fixed rates, the impact of the single monetary policy will be different in the UK and in France. The monetary (nominal) shock is symmetric, but the response is asymmetric. Differences in the monetary transmission process in the Member States are described in the Annual Report of the European Monetary Institute (1995a: 36–37).

If the EU – or even the hard core of the EU – is not an OCA (e.g., Eichengreen 1992 and Taylor 1995), the loss of the exchange rate instrument as a macro-stabilizer will create significant costs to the Member States which form the monetary union. Comparisons with the US or Canada to argue the case in favour of a monetary union have limited applicability to the EU. These two North American countries are federal states, each with a large federal budget designed to play the role of an automatic stabilizer with the net transfer of funds to various regions. By contrast, the EU budget, which will represent only 1.27 percent of the Union's gross national product by 1999, is not intended to play – and cannot given its size – the role of an automatic stabilizer for Member States which receive asymmetric shocks. The Union's structural and cohesion funds, which represent 31 percent of the total budget expenditures (see Box 4.3) are designed as development aids for particular regions within the Union, not as automatic stabilizers.

It is difficult to estimate the cost of eliminating the nominal exchange rate instrument. The estimated cost depends on the importance and the duration of the asymmetric shock that a Member State may receive and on that Member State's ability to use its budgetary policy as a macroeconomic stabilizer. It also depends on the assumptions made with respect to degree of real wage flexibility between the Member States of the monetary union. If wage setting is responsive to local labour market conditions, a change in the real relative wages between the Member States can provide the equivalency of an exchange rate variation in a single currency area.

The Commission (Emerson *et al.* 1990) tried to compare the impact of repeated random shocks under a single currency and under the ERM whereby Germany sets its monetary policy independently and the other ERM countries (France, Italy and the United Kingdom) pursue their own monetary policies provided that their exchange rate remains in a narrow band with respect to the DM. Moreover, in the ERM regime, there is a stylized realignment rule whereby the DM parity is devalued by 4 percent whenever the accumulated price differential with Germany reaches 8 percent. The simulation exercise, carried out using the IMF's Multimod model and based on the criterion of minimizing deviations in output and prices from baseline levels, shows that the single currency regime outperforms the ERM regime. The results 'provide an indication that for the Community as a whole the [single currency] regime contains features which could to an important extent offset the costs in terms of macroeconomic stability incurred from the loss of the exchange rate instrument' (Emerson *et al.* 1990: 155). However, Masson and Symansky (1992), using the same IMF model with a different methodology, concluded that the single currency is not clearly superior to the ERM regime.

Direct benefits of a single currency

Directs benefits of introducing a single currency are related to the microeconomic efficiencies created as a result of reduced transaction costs and to the macroeconomic advantages of having the domestic currency developing as an international medium of exchange and as a reserve asset. The indirect benefits of price stability and low interest rates, attributed to the monetary union, are not so much benefits derived from the creation of a monetary union as the benefits derived from the rules imposed by the Maastricht Treaty to achieve a monetary union. In fact, the presumed dynamic benefits derived from price stability and low interest rates could be obtained without a monetary union.

Microeconomic efficiency

The Mundellian efficiency benefits of lower transactions costs in a single currency area are easily estimated. These benefits are calculated by estimating the foreign exchange transactions costs (bid-ask spread) and the costs related to hedging foreign exchange risk. These benefits are estimated by the Commission (Emerson *et al.* 1990) to be between 0.3 and 0.4 percent of GDP. This is the equivalent of 20,000 million and 25,000 million ECUs per year for EU15. Against these efficiency benefits, the one-off costs of the changeover from the national currencies to the single currency have to be offset. The banking sector estimates these costs to be in the order of 10,000 million to 15,000 million ECUs for the entire EU banking industry (Banking Federation of the European Union 1995). The European Union retailers estimate the conversion costs to be of the order of 27,000 million ECUs (*Financial Times*, 25 October 1996: 16). These costs include the problems of temporarily handling two currencies in the shops (the national currency and the Euro), the temporary dual display of prices, computer changes, staff training and public information campaigns. Adding to these figures the conversion costs that the other sectors (private and public) of the economy will face, the total costs could easily approach an amount significantly greater than the entire microeconomic efficiency benefits obtained in the first year of the monetary union.

Development of a European currency capable of rivalling the US dollar

Since the end of the Second World War, the US dollar has played a predominant role as the official international reserve asset of central banks and as an international vehicle currency for international trade and invest-ment. An international vehicle currency is a currency used in international transactions for invoicing or for settlement, or for both.

In light of the economic size and expected monetary stability of the European Union, the single currency of that monetary union will develop *over time* into a major international currency that may rival the US dollar as an international reserve asset and vehicle currency. To give an indica-tion of the potential use of the Euro as an international reserve asset and international vehicle currency, the following facts are considered:

- With the breakdown of the Bretton Woods international monetary system in the 1970s, the US dollar's share (80 percent) of global foreign exchange official reserves began to decline until 1990. Thereafter, this pattern was subsequently reversed, and the US dollar share at the end of 1995 was approximately 62 percent of foreign exchange reserves (IMF 1996: table I.2). The Deutsche mark's share is 17 percent.
- By the mid-1990s, 50 percent of world trade is still invoiced in dollars, far above the United States' 12 percent share of world merchandise exports in 1995 (World Trade Organization 1996).
- Excluding intra-EU trade, the EU15 represents in 1995 20 percent of world merchandise exports whereas the US represents 16 percent of world merchandise exports.
- In Europe, the share of local currency trading against the US dollar is still predominant. In the major ERM financial centres (excluding London, Frankfurt and Milan), the share of local currency trading against the US dollar represented 61 percent of all transactions in 1995. In those same centres, the share of local currency trading against the Deutsche mark represented 31 percent of all transactions. In major non-ERM financial centres in the EU (London and Milan) the share of local currency trading against the US dollar and the Deutsche mark represented 72 percent and 20 percent, respectively, of all transactions.

As the Euro, over the long run, shares the traditional role of the US dollar in the international monetary system, the EU will reap three poten-tial benefits: seignorage, transactional efficiency gains and economic power in international economic negotiations.

Just as the US dollar is willingly held as an international reserve asset by central banks, the Euro would also be willingly held by non-EU central banks as a form of reserve. The central bank, whose currency is held as a reserve asset by another central bank, receives an economic gain or surplus called 'seignorage'. Seignorage is created by virtue of the fact that the country whose central bank issued the reserve currency receives goods and services with a costless *quid pro quo*, namely the reserve currency.

The expansion of the European single currency as an international vehicle currency will yield some small microeconomic efficiency gains for the European Union, by reducing transaction costs on the exchange market for trade with non-EU countries and by reducing exchange rate risks due to the development of single currency for invoicing with non-EU countries.

As the European single currency becomes a major international currency alongside the US dollar, the European Union would have more influence in various international forums in encouraging developments favourable to its interests. For instance, the EU could more easily negotiate with the US and Japan on a world policy mix and an international exchange rate regime (target zones for the Euro) favourable to its interest.

Indirect benefits of the European Monetary Union

The dynamic benefits described below are not necessarily generalized to all monetary unions. These benefits are obtained in the European case as a result of the rules imposed by virtue of particular provisions in the Maastricht Treaty.

Benefits relating to price stability

Price stability provides an efficient allocation of resources. A low inflation rate is associated with a low variability of inflation. This fact has two macroeconomic consequences, both of which have a positive impact on long-run output.

- First, low variability of inflation reduces the problem entrepreneurs face, in order to make the correct production and investment decisions, in distinguishing between absolute price changes and relative price changes in an inflationary environment. In an economy with a high variability of the inflation rate, entrepreneurs have a 'signal extraction problem' to solve in order to determine what proportion of the observed price variation can be attributed to an absolute price change and to a relative price change. The Commission (Emerson *et al.* 1990) has estimated that a 1 percent decrease in relative price variance could increase real output by 0.3 percent of GDP.
- Secondly, with a low variability of inflation, the market-determined real interest rate does not incorporate a risk premium to cover for that variability. Thus, a lower real interest rate allows entrepreneurs to undertake investment projects which would be rejected in an environment with a high variability of inflation. Empirical estimates show that a reduction in the risk premium of only 0.5 percentage points could raise income in the Community by 5 to 10 percent in the long run.

There are, of course, transitional costs of reducing the inflation rate. These costs are a temporary loss of output combined with a temporary higher level of unemployment[1] due to wage and price stickiness and the difficulty of securing credibility for the price stabilization objective. Moreover, a monetary union is not necessary to ensure price stability in the long run; it is only necessary to have national central banks committed to such a goal. Since the Maastricht Treaty requires the European central bank to be a politically independent institution, committed to price stability, many European countries, which could not have made such a credible commitment on their own, will benefit by joining the monetary union (cf. Giavazzi and Pagano 1988; Kydland and Prescott 1977).

Benefit relating to public finance rules

The Maastricht Treaty imposes a ceiling on the public deficit/GDP ratio and on the public debt/GDP ratio of Member States participating in the monetary union. Accordingly, an unsustainable budgetary position in a Member State, such as a public deficit/GDP ratio resulting in a forever increasing public debt/GDP ratio, is forestalled. The binding rules on public finance ratios imposed on the participating Member States of the monetary union allow the financial markets to eliminate the fiscal risk premium incorporated into the long-term interest rate of countries who would otherwise run unsustainable public deficits. The risk premium is the result of what Ball and Mankiw (1995) call the 'hard landing' or 'portfolio saturation'[2] effects of continuously rising public debt ratios. These effects are usually anticipated, and telegraphed to the market, by private credit agencies who downgrade a government's debt (the sovereign debt of Canada and Sweden are recent examples). Thus, the Member States of the monetary union with strict budget rules reap the dynamic growth benefits of a lower real interest rate. Although fiscal consolidation may in the short run reduce aggregate demand from the Keynesian effects of decreased public expenditures and/or higher taxes, the long-run effect of lower real interest rates and a higher capital stock on growth may be more than offset by the short-run effect (Giavazzi and Pagano 1995). Again, any economic advantage derived from budgetary discipline could be obtained simply by each country legislating such binding rules. However, it can be argued that the multilateral surveillance by Community institutions, coupled with penalties for violations of the public finance ratios, provides a credibility to the financial markets that a particular country could not obtain by legislating its own budgetary policy rules.

THE EMU SECTION OF MAASTRICHT

The Economic and Monetary Union (EMU) section of the Maastricht Treaty[3] appears primarily in Title II, Articles 102A to 109M, and in some eleven Protocols and six Declarations. Table 4.1 indicates the applicability of each article to the three stages of the EMU. This proposed union is one of the major objectives of the Maastricht Treaty, involving not only the introduction of a single currency, but also the transfer of monetary powers away from national authorities to a newly created European central bank. It also transfers some national budgetary powers to the

Table 4.1 The provisions of Title II of the Treaty on European Union and their applicability to the three stages of EMU

Article	Description	I	II	III
102a	Objectives and principles of economic policy	X	X	X
103	Formulation of economic policy, ensuring its implementation	X	X	X
103a(1)	Rules governing severe supply difficulties	X	X	X
103a(2)	Rules governing severe economic difficulties			X
104	Rules governing credit facilities		X	X
104a(1)	Rules governing privileged access to financial institutions		X	X
104a(2)	Defining application of Article 104a(1)	X		
104b	Financial liability of the Community		X	X
104c (1, 9, 11)	Rules governing government deficits			X
104c(2–8, 10, 12–13)	Rules governing government deficits		X	X
104c(14)	Rules governing government deficits	X	X	X
105	Tasks and objectives of ESCB			X
105a	Issuance of notes and coins			X
106	Composition of ESCB		X	X
107	Independence of ESCB			X
108	Independence of central banks		X	X
108a	ECB regulatory instruments			X
109	Relations with non-Community currencies			X
109a	Composition of ECB			X
109b	ECB relations with other EC institutions			X
109c(1)	Tasks and composition of the Monetary Committee	X	X	
109c(2–4)	Tasks and composition of the Economic and Financial Committee			X
109d	Role of Commission, Council and Member States	X	X	X
109e	General details concerning Stages I, II and III	X	X	X
109f	Tasks, composition and regulatory instruments of EMI		X	
109g	Currency composition of ECU	X	X	X
109h	Rules governing balance-of-payments difficulties	X	X	
109i	Rules governing balance-of-payments crises	X	X	
109j	Transition to Stage III		X	
109k	Derogations from Stage III		X	X
109l(1–3)	Details concerning composition and tasks of ECB		X	X
109l(4–5)	ECU value			X
109m(1)	Exchange rate policy	X	X	
109m(2)	Exchange rate policy			X

Source: Church and Phinnemore (1994:152).

Council. It thus represents a clear shift from intergovernmental cooperation to supranational integration on some economic and monetary matters.

In principle, all the Member States are eventually to join the EMU, but since 'state-contingencies' have to be satisfied before joining the single currency area, the process is designed to have 'multiple transitions'. All the Member States participate in the step-by-step approach towards a monetary union. As the final target date approaches to launch the initial monetary union, only the Member States that have satisfied the entry requirements are designated to join the single currency area. The laggards are expected to join the initial monetary union as soon as they meet the same 'state-contingencies'. This approach can be viewed in the context of the 'multi-speed' design to the construction of Europe (see Introduction).

The rest of this chapter examines in some detail the three stages of the EMU time-and-state-dependent scenario, as spelled out in the Maastricht Treaty. At the end of the chapter, an overall assessment of this approach is presented. The EMU section of the Treaty is the product of numerous compromises between the various positions of the Member States, most notably between the Commission and France on the one hand, and Germany and the Netherlands on the other hand.[4] The Treaty is a legal document, drafted in 1991, signed in February 1992, and ratified by the end of 1993 by all Member States. As there is an informal agreement not to revise any of the EMU provisions of the Treaty at the intergovernmental conference of 1996–97, there is a strong presumption that its provisions must be implemented.

STAGE I: JULY 1990 TO DECEMBER 1993

Background

In June 1988, the European Council agreed in Hanover to establish a Committee on Economic and Monetary Union, chaired by the Commission President, Jacques Delors, to draw up a plan for establishing full economic and monetary union. The Delors Report entitled *Report on the Economic and Monetary Union of the European Community* (Commission of the European Communities 1989b, 1989c), released on 17 April 1989, suggested a three-stage plan towards EMU, with the implementation of Stage I, involving closer monetary and economic cooperation, starting at the latest, on 1 July 1990, to coincide with the beginning of the complete liberalization of capital flows within the Community.[5, 6] The then Prime Minister of the United Kingdom, Margaret Thatcher, would not accept the linkage of an agreement to start Stage I with a commitment to implement the provisions of the other stages in the Delors Report, which would lead to a full currency union. Thus, at its meeting of June 1989 in Madrid, the European Council only agreed to start Stage I on the proposed date and reaffirmed the commitment, already stated in the Single European

Act (1986),[7] to reach an economic and monetary union in undefined subsequent steps, which were to be laid down at an intergovernmental conference.

The revolutionary events which occurred in Europe in 1989–90 with the fall of the Berlin Wall (10 November 1989) and the inevitability of German reunification (3 October 1990) accelerated the commitment to achieve the EMU.[8] The European Council agreed, at its meeting of December 1989 in Strasbourg, to launch the EMU intergovernmental conference (IGC) as of December 1990. This intergovernmental conference, which worked until December 1991, drafted the provisions of each stage of the EMU, which was finally adopted as part of the Maastricht Treaty.

Position of the United Kingdom

Although the British government was in favour of the single market policy with its liberalization and deregulation of economic activity, and of the capital movement policy of eliminating all cross-border restrictions during Stage I, it had no intention of accepting the subsequent stages towards a monetary union, as proposed in the Delors Report, which ultimately imposed a single currency with a single European central bank and binding fiscal policy rules. In short, it would lead to a form of federalism and would further undermine the principle of British self-government (United Kingdom 1989a). The British government's immediate response to the Delors Report was published in a paper entitled *An Evolutionary Approach to Economic and Monetary Union* (United Kingdom 1989b), which set out the basic framework of how to proceed with monetary cooperation in the Community. It preferred a market-determined, evolutionary process towards an arrangement that would effectively be like a monetary union. According to this proposal, the fixed exchange rates between European currencies would not be imposed by decree but would be established by market forces. As in the Delors proposal, during Stage I all the restrictions on capital movement between Member States would be removed. All the currencies would participate in the Exchange Rate Mechanism. During Stage II, with the removal of restrictions on the use of all Community currencies, Community currencies would evolve into 'parallel currencies' with the national currency. With rising currency substitution, the monetary authority of each Member State would have strong incentives to pursue non-inflationary policies. Exchange rate stability would emerge and the EMS would evolve into a system of more or less fixed exchange rates, a sort of monetary union.

As soon as the decision was taken in December 1989 to launch an intergovernmental conference in late 1990 to draft the EMU section of the Maastricht Treaty, the British government, with John Major as Chancellor of the Exchequer, presented a new proposal (United Kingdom 1990, 1991), which supplemented the one presented in 1989. During Stage II, a Hard

ECU (HECU), issued on demand against Community currencies by a European Monetary Fund, would be introduced. The HECU would become the *common* currency of the Community circulating in parallel to all the other Community currencies. The central parity of the HECU would never be devalued against any Member currency. Over time, the superiority of the HECU would gradually diminish the role of the other currencies; the HECU would become the dominant currency of the European Union and, in the very long run, the single currency.

This British proposal did not gather much support, in particular since the Bundesbank (see Pöhl 1990) did not want to see the creation of a European currency without an independent European central bank to manage it. The European Monetary Fund did not meet that requirement. When, in October 1990, the Heads of State or Government of all Member States, except the United Kingdom, agreed on the broad outline and timetable for Stage II and Stage III, the United Kingdom would eventually request for an option not to participate in Stage III:

> The United Kingdom is unable to accept the approach set out. . . . But it agrees that the overriding objective of monetary policy should be price stability, that the Community's development should be based on an open market system, that excessive budget deficits should be avoided, and that there should be no monetary financing of deficits nor the assumption of responsibility on the part of the Community or its Member States for one Member State's debts. The United Kingdom, while ready to move beyond stage one through the creation of a new monetary institution and a common Community currency, believes that decisions on the substance of that move should precede decisions on its timing. But it would be ready to see the approach it advocates [as described above] come into effect as soon as possible after ratification of the necessary Treaty provision. . . .
>
> (Excerpts from Conclusions of the Presidency,
> European Council, Rome, 27 and 28 October 1990)

Provisions of Stage I

Although Stage I began in July 1990 before the Maastricht Treaty was even signed and ratified by the twelve Member States in February 1992 and October 1993, respectively, some provisions of Stage I did not require a new legal framework as it was essentially a commitment to start the process within the existing legal institutional framework of the EMS and the post-SEA Treaty of Rome.

Convergence in terms of economic performance

The Council 'Convergence Decision' of 12 March 1990 (90/141/EEC), which replaced the 18 February 1974 Council Decision on the convergence of economic policies (see Chapter 1), provided the legal basis during Stage I for economic and monetary policy coordination between the Member States. However, the policy convergence objectives went beyond the 1974 notion of simply attaining 'a high degree of convergence of the economic policies of the Member States'; the 1990 decision also included convergence in terms of economic performance which included the achievement of price stability, sound public finances, sound overall balances of payments and open, competitive, markets.

The economic policies were to be undertaken in the context of the Community policy guidelines written in the Commission's *Annual Economic Report*. This document, which was adopted by the Council, embodied the existing common view on policy matters which would form the backdrop to each Member State's multi-annual programmes describing its convergence objectives in terms of performance and the means it intended to use to achieve them (Colasanti 1994). These programmes were to receive wide domestic dissemination and were then to be 'endorsed' at the Community level, which would presumably strengthen the hand of each government to implement the proposed measures. The Ecofin Council was to engage in multilateral surveillance of each Member State's multi-annual programmes. This Council 'Convergence Decision' of 1990, recommended in the Delors Report (1989b: Chapter III, Section 3) and adopted just a few months before the start of Stage I of the EMU, reappears in the Treaty on European Union (1992), with some modifications, in the form of Article 103. This article, applicable during all three stages, is discussed below under 'Stage II' since the Treaty came into force on 1 November 1993 just as Stage II was to begin on 1 January 1994.

Other provisions applicable during Stage I

The other provisions of Stage I are clearly indicated in Articles 109E.2.a, first indent, and 109G of the Treaty. They include:

- The adoption, if not already done, of measures to comply with the complete liberalization of capital movements and payments between Member States and between Member States and third countries provided in Article 109E.2.a, first indent. This measure does not apply to Member States that have been granted extensions under the Council Directive of 24 June 1988.
- The adoption, *but not the immediate implementation*, of national laws to comply, as of the start of Stage II, with the provisions prohibiting national central banks (with the exception of the Bank of England) to grant credit facilities to governments or public authorities, *and* prohibiting government and Community institutions to have privileged access to financial institutions [Article 109E.2.a, first indent]. To this effect, legislative action was taken in Belgium, Germany, Greece, Spain, France, Italy, the Netherlands, Portugal and Sweden.

- The freezing, as soon as the Maastricht Treaty comes into force on 1 November 1993, of the currency composition of the ECU basket (Article 109G). This provision is a clear departure from the provisions of the EMS. Thus, until it disappears on the first day of Stage III, the ECU *basket* is composed of twelve currencies in the quantities agreed in 1989 when the ECU basket was last revised. This measure reduces uncertainty in the future valuation of the ECU basket. The stronger currencies will progressively have greater weights in the basket while the weaker ones will have lesser weights. The measure also eliminates part of the uncertainty on ECU interest rates, attributable to the potential future changes in the composition of the ECU basket. This should encourage the use of the private ECU as a financial instrument (see Chapter 5).

The ERM crises of September 1992 to August 1993

Although Stage I did not end as anticipated by the framers of EMU because of the currency tensions that marked the period September 1992 to August 1993, the transition to Stage II was made in accordance with the timetable imposed by the Maastricht Treaty. In fact, the Council concluded at the end of 1993, pursuant to Article 109E.2.b regarding the progress made with respect to economic and monetary convergence, that all the conditions of Stage I had been satisfied and therefore the European Union could move into Stage II.

During the period 1992–93, there were five realignments of bilateral central rates, two currencies – the British pound and the Italian lira – withdrew from the Exchange Rate Mechanism, and the exchange rate bands were widened from ±2.25 percent to ±15 percent (except for the HFL/DM). Table 4.2 summarizes these events. Only the Deutsche mark, French franc, Benelux currencies and Danish krone were not realigned against each other. Among those currencies, the French franc, Danish krone and the Belgian-Luxembourg francs probably could not have maintained their bilateral central rates against the two 'hard currencies' (the Deutsche mark and Dutch guilder) if the margins of fluctuation had not been widened to ±15 percent in August 1993 (see Chart 4.1).

The September 1992 ERM crisis[9]

The ERM crisis began in September 1992 and continued in 1993. It is recalled that from 1987 to September 1992, the ERM functioned without any realignment – except for the Italian lira in 1990 when it joined the narrow ERM margins of fluctuation. As explained above, in mid-1989, Member States agreed that Stage I of the Economic and Monetary Union process would begin in mid-1990. The Council 'Convergence Decision' of March 1990 would ensure voluntary convergence programmes regarding

Table 4.2 EMS realignments: percentage changes in bilateral central rates:[a] 1992–95

Currencies	14 Sept. 1992	17 Sept. 1992	22 Nov. 1992	1 Feb. 1993	13 May 1993	6 Mar. 1995[c]
BFR/LFR	+3.5					
DKR	+3.5					
DM	+3.5					
ESC	+3.5		–6.0		–6.5	–3.5
FF	+3.5					
HFL	+3.5					
IRL	+3.5			–10.0		
LIT	-3.5	b				
ÖS	d					
PTA	+3.5	–5.0	–6.0		–8.0	–7.0
UKL	+3.5	b				

Notes:
(a) Calculated as the percentage change against the group of currencies whose bilateral parities remained unchanged in the realignment.
(b) On 16 September 1992 and 17 September 1992, the UKL and LIT withdrew, respectively, from the ERM.
(c) Since 2 August 1993, the bilateral margins of fluctuation are widened to ±15 percent, except for the HFL/DM.
(d) ÖS joins EMS and ERM in January 1995 when Austria accedes to the EU.
+ is a revaluation; – is a devaluation.
Source: Official Communiqués from the Commission.

inflation and fiscal and monetary polices of Member States throughout Stage I. By October 1990, all Member States, with the exception of Greece and Portugal, were participating in the ERM. The Economic and Monetary Union section of the Maastricht Treaty was being drafted at an intergovernmental conference. It was completed by the end of 1991 and signed in February 1992. Some two decades after the vague declarations of the European Summit of December 1969 in The Hague regarding the goal of achieving an economic and monetary union, the Community had finally enshrined *in a treaty* a clearly defined process to reach a monetary union with a legally binding timetable. The final step was the ratification process of the Treaty by each Member State. The process towards the economic union was progressing with the expectation that most single market directives would be implemented by January 1993. 'Europhoria' prevailed. With the 'convergence play' and the institutional prerequisites in place, the market had formulated expectations that the majority of Member States would glide into a monetary union by the late 1990s, *without any major realignment of ERM currencies.* As an IMF study (Goldstein *et al.* 1993: 49–50) indicates:

In the five years preceding the crisis [currency crisis of September 1992], cross-border [between Member States] investment flows increased

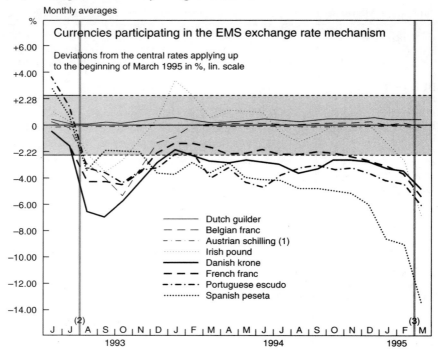

Chart 4.1 Movements of selected EC currencies against the Deutsche mark

(Source: Deutsche Bundesbank Annual Report 1994)
Notes:
(1) Joined the exchange rate mechanism at the start of 1995.
(2) Previous fluctuation margins of ±2¼% and ± 6%, respectively, widened to a uniform ± 15%. Depiction of the narrow fluctuation margin (± 2¼%) for the period after July 1993 serves merely to facilitate assessment of exchange rate movements.
(3) Peseta and escudo devalued by 7% and 3½%, respectively, with the two currencies' central rates being largely adjusted to the market trend.

substantially as investors took advantage of new opportunities to diversify their portfolios internationally. Also in the 'convergence play' strategy, institutional investors had sought to exploit the existing interest rate differentials in Europe, given the perception that the macroeconomic performance of ERM member countries would gradually converge. They pursued this strategy, for example, by borrowing funds in the countries with relatively low interest rates such as Germany, and by investing in high-yield countries such as Italy and Spain.

An investor who believed that interest rates would gradually converge toward the levels observed in the low-interest-rate countries without exchange rate realignments on the way, would invest in long-term,

high-yielding securities in anticipation of earning significant capital gains
as interest rates fell. . . . In the United Kingdom, long-term (and short-
term) interest rates were approximately 6 percentage points higher, on
average, than German rates between 1987 and 1990. The differential
came down sharply in the fourth quarter of 1990 following sterling's
entry into the ERM, so that by early summer 1992 the differential was
below 100 basis points. In Spain the differentials against German rates
hovered around 7 percentage points for 1987–1990, before dropping
sharply in the first quarter of 1991 to approximately 300 basis points.
French interest rate differentials, reflecting France's strong performance
in controlling inflation, were low and declined steadily through 1987–91
[to less than 50 basis points].

Then, rather suddenly, a set of events converged to change the market's
prior assumptions:

- In June 1992, the people of Denmark, in a referendum, rejected the
  Maastricht Treaty, casting uncertainty as to whether the monetary
  union scenario could ever be realized since Community treaties must
  be ratified by all Member States to come into force.
- Polls were indicating that the outcome of the French referendum on
  the ratification of the Maastricht Treaty, scheduled for 20 September
  1992, was too close to call. This was an even more serious threat to
  the EMU than the Danish rejection. Whereas a Community 'deus ex
  machina' could be envisaged in the face of a Danish 'nej', a French
  'non' would immediately create a stillborn Maastricht Treaty.
- It was becoming clear that the effects of German reunification with its
  inflationary tendencies were going to pressure the Bundesbank to
  maintain German interest rates high. The deepening recession and
  record unemployment in certain Member States would pressure these
  countries to decouple their monetary policies from the German benchmark. This, together with the uncertainty regarding the ratification of
  the Maastricht Treaty, would result in a realignment of their currencies vis-à-vis the Deutsche mark.
- Once this stage was set and in place, the pressures within the ERM
  were so great that the credibility could not be re-established without
  taking one of the following actions: (1) realigning currencies, as in the
  case of the Italian lira initially, of the Spanish peseta, of the Portuguese
  escudo and of the Irish punt; (2) withdrawing the currency from the
  ERM, as in the case of the British pound and of the Italian lira later;
  (3) reassuring the financial markets by deeds that the monetary policy
  would not deviate from the German one, as in the case of the Banque
  de France when it issued with the Bundesbank a joint communiqué in
  support of maintaining the 1987 FF/DM bilateral central rate, which
  provided a concrete signal to the market that the Banque de France
  was committed to follow the Bundesbank monetary policy.

Selected examples of measures taken by central banks

During the ERM crisis of September 1992, the central banks had recourse to the two instruments usually used under a regime of fixed exchange rates: official central bank intervention on the foreign exchange market and short-term interest rate variations. When those measures were unsuccessful to maintain the exchange rates within the ERM bilateral bands, the Member States either suspended their participation in the ERM, adjusted the bilateral parities, or attempted to convince the markets that the central banks would do whatever is necessary in terms of mutual support for intervention to maintain the fundamentally correct bilateral parity. This section focuses on the measures taken by the central banks of Germany, France, the United Kingdom and Italy.

Official Intervention

Central banks of Member States participating in the ERM have access to three sources of international reserves. They can:

(i)   use their own stock of reserves,
(ii)   borrow from international capital markets,
(iii) borrow from official sources under the terms of the VSTF facility (multilateral credits) and/or special arrangements between two central banks (bilateral credits).

Several countries whose currencies came under attack resorted to the international syndicated loan markets (an example of point (ii) above). To signal its support for the ERM parity of the pound sterling set in October 1990, the United Kingdom announced on 3 September 1992 a foreign currency borrowing programme valued at ECU10,000 million. According to the Deutsche Bundesbank (1992: 46), the Bundesbank, through the VSTF facility of the EMCF (an example of multilateral credits of point (iii) above) and its own interventions, provided to the foreign exchange market DM92,000 million during the September 1992 crisis, of which DM33,000 million and DM11,000 million were lent to the Bank of England and the Banca d'Italia, respectively, when the pound sterling and the lira touched their weak edge against the DM on 16/17 September 1992 (see also the *Economist*, 10 October 1992: 71, and the *Financial Times*, 1 October 1992: 1).

According to the Banque de France, in the seven days ending 22 September 1992, the period just prior to, and just after, the French referendum on the Maastricht Treaty, a total of FF160,000 million was spent on the currency's defence – all from its own stock of reserves (an example of point (i) above). In an unusual move, the Banque de France and the Bundesbank issued a joint statement on 23 September 1992 on the unequivocal support for the existing bilateral central rate of the French franc–Deutsche mark. This suggested to the market that the Bundesbank was entering into a bilateral credit arrangement with the Banque de France (an example of (iii) above), not subject to a rigid repayment schedule under the multilateral credit arrangement of the EMCF. The statement was backed by heavy intramarginal intervention on the foreign exchange market by the Banque de France and the Bundesbank and was successful, with the accompanying interest rate changes described below, to maintain the French franc in the narrow margins of fluctuation against the Deutsche mark.

Even if the amount of funds available under the VSTF facility is said to be unlimited, this is not literally true. Because of the fear that domestic price stability might have to be sacrificed for external exchange rate stability (i.e. that the central bank with the strong currency might no longer be able to control its own money supply), the Bundesbank privately insisted right from the start of the ERM in 1979 on an opt-out clause. According to an article in Pringle (1992: 12–21), this clause was confirmed in a letter to the German government by the then president of the Bundesbank, Otmar Emminger. The Bundesbank indicated that it was not prepared to finance interventions of unlimited amounts in favour of countries whose fundamental exchange rate misalignment required adjustment, which may explain the distinction made by the Bundesbank in September of 1992 between, on the one hand, the pound sterling and the lira and, on the other hand, the French franc. This agreement between the Bundesbank and the German government was acknowledged by the then Minister of Economy Graf Lamsdorff, who stated, with respect to the EMS provisions, on 6 December 1978 in the Bundestag: 'the Bundesbank has the responsibility to intervene and the option not to intervene if it is of the opinion that it is unable to do so'. This opt-out clause on the part of the Bundesbank was not invoked before the 1992 ERM crisis of the British pound and Italian lira. In 1993, the Governors of the Central Banks of the European Community (Committee of Governors of the Central Banks of the Member States of the European Economic Community 1993: 5) in a post-mortem to the 1992 ERM crisis, wrote that intervention must not interfere with the 'control over domestic monetary conditions in the country issuing the intervention currency [and must be] consistent with the primary objective of achieving price stability in the Community' (see also Kenen 1995a: 182–184).

Defensive increases in interest rates

Examples of central bank changes of official short-term interest rates during the month of September 1992 are as follows.

United Kingdom   On 16 September, the Bank of England raises its base lending rate from 10.0 percent to 12.0 percent and within a few hours announces another increase to 15.0 percent, effective 17 September. Then, the Bank of England retracts the second base rate increase as the pound sterling withdraws from the ERM.

Italy   On 4 September, the Bank of Italy raises its discount rate and its rate on fixed-term advances by 175 basis points (b.p.) each to 15.0 percent and 16.5 percent, respectively.

France   On 18 September, the Banque de France temporarily closes five-to-ten-day repurchase market, but reopened it when call money rates rose to 20.0 percent. The five-to-ten-day repurchase rate is the interest rate set by the Banque de France on its repurchase agreements available as emergency funding at the *discretion of financial institutions*. This rate is typically above short-term market rates and serves as an upper bound. On 23 September, the Banque de France increases the five-to-ten-day repurchase rate by 250 b.p. to 13.0 percent but keeps the 'taux des pensions sur appels d'offres' (auction rate) constant at 9.6 percent while commercial banks agree not to increase rates. The 'taux des pensions sur appel d'offres' is the interest rate established for official repurchase agreements, offered at the *discretion of the Banque de France*. This rate typically serves as the lower bound for short-term market rates.

Germany   On 15 September, the Bundesbank lowers its official discount rate by 50 b.p. to 8.25 percent, its Lombard rate by 25 b.p. to 9.5 percent, and offers the next securities repurchase agreement at a fixed rate of 9.2 percent. The discount rate is the interest rate charged by the Bundesbank for rediscounting eligible assets of financial institutions. This rate is typically the lower bound for short-term rates. The Lombard rate is the interest rate charged by the Bundesbank for collateralized short-term loans to financial institutions designed to bridge temporary reserve shortages. This rate is typically higher than short-term market interest rates and generally serves as an upper bound. The repurchase rate (repo) is the interest rate at which the Bundesbank agrees to buy securities from the banking system, which increases liquidity, for a fixed period of two, three or four weeks at the end of which time the banks have to buy them back. This rate is typically between the Lombard rate and the discount rate. The repo rate may be either a 'fixed-rate tender' or a 'market-determined' rate.

The July 1993 ERM crisis

When, following the French parliamentary elections of March 1993, the new majority centre-right government of Balladur was sending ambiguous signals regarding its commitment to the Maastricht 'convergence play' and the 'franc fort' policy of the previous Socialist government, and also was indicating its desire to see French interest rates below German ones, with the French franc possibly replacing the DM as the anchor of the ERM, the 1987 FF/DM bilateral central rate could only be maintained either by a re-affirmation of the Bundesbank's unlimited intervention to support the French franc, or by restricting capital movements, or by increasing the riskiness of speculation against the French franc.[10] This time, the Bundesbank was unwilling to provide unlimited credit to the Banque de France in the face of a new French government that had not yet demonstrated its commitment to monetary and fiscal stability. Re-imposing restrictions on short-term capital movements related to foreign exchange markets would have been legally possible (Article 4 of Council Directive 88/361/EEC). However, it would have been contrary to the spirit of the measures taken at the start of Stage I. Moreover, Article 73B of the Maastricht Treaty would have prohibited such restrictions as of 1 January 1994. That left the Community with the third option, namely to widen the bilateral margins of fluctuation to ±15 percent. As long as the French franc did not depreciate by 15 percent from its 1987 central rate against the Deutsche mark, this measure would obviate the need for intervention. It would also avoid creating the incentives for one-way bets of a devaluation on the part of speculators when a currency is on the weak edge of a narrow exchange rate band (see Kenen 1995b: 173; and Williamson and Henning 1994). Finally, this measure would maintain the existence of the ERM, to which explicit reference is made in certain provisions of the Maastricht Treaty (e.g. Article 109J).

As soon as the bilateral bands were widened and intervention ceased, the French franc quickly fell some 4.5 percent from its bilateral central rate against the DM. For the July 1993 ERM crisis, which, in addition to the French franc also involved the Danish krone, and to a lesser extent the Belgian franc, the Irish punt, the Spanish peseta and Portuguese escudo, support operations, just prior to the widening of the exchange rate bands, by the Bundesbank and by other ERM central banks, had resulted in Deutsche mark intervention of DM107,000 million (see Table 2.5), of which DM60,000 million was intervention by the Bundesbank in the Frankfurt foreign exchange market. These amounts, while less than during the September 1992 crisis, had of course been much more concentrated on the French franc. As the French franc returned by the end of 1993 to within its narrow margins against the Deutsche mark, the Bank de France later announced that the whole of the FF107,000 million (equivalent to about DM30,000 million) borrowed through the EMCF had been repaid on 14 January 1994 (Bank for International Settlements 1994b).

After returning within its narrow margins against the Deutsche mark during most of 1994, the French franc in 1995 again made use of its wider margins of fluctuation. In the period May–June 1995, the financial markets reacted to the uncertainties raised by another new government of France, under – this time – a new centre-right president. When the government announced its priority to reduce the high unemployment rate of 12.1 percent in France without indicating how it would finance the proposed labour programmes and thus giving the impression that its avowed determination to reduce the public deficit ratio might be compromised, the French franc fell significantly (some 4.7 percent from its bilateral parity) against the Deutsche mark within the wider margins of fluctuation.

These episodes convinced the central bank governors and ministers of economics and finance that the Stage II Maastricht road to a monetary union with the complete liberalization of capital flows, combined with the reluctance of the Bundesbank to provide unlimited ERM credits for marginal intervention, must be based on enough flexibility of the ERM to accommodate temporary national 'shocks', such as an expected departure from the nominal 'convergence' criteria (see below).

STAGE II: JANUARY 1994 TO DECEMBER 1998

Background

The Treaty on European Union, drafted between December 1990 and December 1991, allowed for a short Stage II, starting in January 1994 and ending in December 1996, with just enough time to complete the 'convergence play' of a majority of the Member States and to establish the technical, operational framework for a European central bank with its single monetary policy. The Treaty stipulates that the first decision regarding the launching of a monetary union must be made, *at the latest*, by 31 December 1996 (Article 109J.3). Accordingly, it even left the door open to an earlier date. With the longer than expected duration of the ratification process of the Treaty and with the 1992–93 ERM crises, the first possible date for the beginning of Stage III was indeed 1 January 1997. But even that date was effectively abandoned in mid-1995 (Ecofin Council informal decision of 19 June 1995) when it became clear that a majority of the Member States would not meet the Maastricht convergence criteria discussed below. It appears that Stage II will be a lengthy process and that it may even have to be extended beyond December 1998. As explained below, this can be done within the framework of the *original* provisions of the Treaty, without the need to introduce amendments. Although Article N(2) of the Treaty on European Union provides for the convocation of an intergovernmental conference in 1996–97 (see Introduction) to negotiate revisions to the Treaty, Mr de Silguy, the Commissioner responsible for monetary affairs, indicated that the EMU part of the Maastricht Treaty should not be revised at all, explaining that any attempt to re-open those provisions of the Treaty would necessarily kill EMU (*Le Monde*, 25 May 1995: 3).

Provisions of Stage II

Broad economic guidelines and multilateral surveillance

As explained above, Article 103 of the Treaty on European Union became applicable as soon as the Treaty entered into force on 1 November 1993 and continues to apply without any time limit, i.e. throughout Stages II and III. Article 103 supersedes the Council Decision of 12 March 1990, which was in force throughout the duration of Stage I.

Article 103.2 provides the legal framework for setting the 'broad guidelines' of economic policies for the Community and the Member States. These broad economic guidelines are formulated in the following manner. On the basis of its *Annual Economic Report*, the Commission draws up the recommendations that are to serve as the basis for the conclusions on the broad economic policy guidelines submitted first to the Ecofin Council, which in turn submits its 'draft' guidelines to the European Council for discussion. The latter submits its conclusions back to the Ecofin Council which, acting by a qualified majority, adopts a 'recommendation setting out these guidelines'. The Ecofin Council informs the European Parliament of its recommendations. These guidelines, which in 1994 and in 1995 included price and exchange rate stability, sound public finances and the creation of more employment (see *Bulletin of the European Union*, 7/8 – 1994, 1995 and 1996; Commission 1995a), form the core of all future 'multilateral surveillance' of Member States by the Commission and the Council (see Box 4.1). For the purpose of the multilateral surveillance procedure, Member States have to forward information to the Commission about important measures taken by them in the field of their economic policy. This is done by means of their multi-annual programmes which Member States have been required to submit since the beginning of Stage I in 1990. It should be emphasized that the broad economic policy guidelines are only a recommendation, and therefore are not legally binding. However, in view of the fact that these guidelines are 'adopted' at the highest political level, the European Council, there is considerable 'peer pressure' to respect them, not to mention Article 103.4 which allows the Ecofin Council to address a public recommendation to a Member State whose policies are not considered to be consistent with the guidelines.

Budgetary discipline of Member States

Throughout the duration of Stage II, the Commission shall examine periodically compliance of each Member State with budgetary discipline on the basis of two criteria: whether the ratio of planned or actual government deficit to gross domestic product exceeds 3 percent and whether the ratio of government debt to gross domestic product exceeds 60 percent. If one or both of these public finance threshold ratios are exceeded or if

Box 4.1 'Broad guidelines of economic policies' and 'multilateral surveillance' in accordance with Article 103

In conformity with the Maastricht Treaty, Broad Economic Policy Guidelines were adopted by the Ecofin Council in December 1993, July 1994, July 1995 and July 1996. The Guidelines are first drafted by the Commission, then examined by the Ecofin Council, which in turn submits them to the June meeting of the European Council to be endorsed by the Heads of State or Government. The Guidelines are then re-submitted to the Ecofin Council for final adoption. On 14 February 1994, the Ecofin Council agreed to adopt the yearly 'broad economic guidelines' at the middle of the year and to have one formal 'multilateral surveillance' session at the end of the year.

For 1996, the 'broad guidelines' essentially corroborate and augment the policy recommendations formulated in mid-1995 (Commission of the European Communities 1995a, 1996b). Without compromising the convergence criteria of low inflation, exchange rate stability, and the sustained efforts to consolidate the public finances consistent with the timetable and the objectives of the Maastricht Treaty, the Commission recommends in its 'broad guideline' submission to the Council that, in keeping with the resolution of the Essen European Council meeting of December 1994, Member States implement structural reforms of their labour markets so as to stimulate productivity and improve the functioning of the labour market, both of which are necessary to reduce the unemployment rate in the European Union. In 1995, the average unemployment rate for EU15 was 10.9 percent, ranging from 22.9 percent for Spain to 2.9 percent for Luxembourg. By contrast in the US, the unemployment rate was 5.8 percent. Against the projected background of sluggish growth and an increase in the size of the labour force in the Community during 1996–97, the unemployment rates in most Member States are not expected to be significantly different in 1996 (EU15 average = 10.8 percent in December 1996) and 1997.

The recent recession (1990–93) had a severe impact on employment in most Member States. The numbers employed in the European Union as a whole declined by 4 percent in the three years 1991–94, twice as much as any previous fall over comparable periods since the war. As a result, 6 million jobs – some 60 percent of the 10 million or so net increase in jobs generated during the record period of employment expansion between 1985 and 1990 – were effectively lost over this period. Of these, 1 million jobs lost were in the former East Germany. In order to reduce the high level of structural unemployment, the proposed labour market measures are as follows:

- more investment in labour training by small and medium-size firms;
- the introduction on a firm-by-firm basis of work-sharing schemes without any decrease in productivity;
- the reduction of non-wage labour costs, especially for unskilled labour, without increasing the national budget deficits;
- the improvement of government assistance targeted to the long-term unemployed, i.e. re-training and special incentives given to firms to hire the long-term unemployed.

Although the Commission does not share the view that the unemployment rate should be added to the list of convergence criteria ('real convergence') that must be met for entry into the monetary union, it proposed that multilateral surveillance under Article 103.3 include the measures taken by each Member State to reduce in a sustainable way the unemployment rate. This was done for the first time at the Madrid European Council meeting of December 1995, in a joint report from the Ecofin and Social Affairs Councils and from the Commission. At the Community level, the President of the Commission proposed in 1996 a Confidence Pact for Employment which would include the national labour market reforms mentioned above, as well as measures to improve the competitiveness of the Community economies by reinforcing Community efforts in the particular areas of research and development, in the implementation of Trans-European Network projects in the transport, telecommunications and energy sectors, and in completing the internal market by transposing directives in the sectors of public procurement, insurance and intellectual property. Finally, the Scandinavians are proposing a 'jobs chapter' in the revised Maastricht Treaty. This chapter would include the creation of an employment committee, drawn from the Member States and the Commission, which would monitor each Member State's employment policies to attain the Treaty's employment goals. These labour market policies may include investing in training and lowering non-wage costs. In September 1996, the Council approved the creation of an Employment Committee, composed of two representatives from each Member State and two representatives from the Commission. This new committee is to be the 'counterparty' to the long-standing Economic Policy Committee (see Chapter 1), which is composed of officials from the Ministries of Finance and the national central banks. The Employment Committee is to have advisory status to promote coordination between Member States on employment and labour market policies.

the Commission considers that there is a risk of an excessive deficit in a Member State, it notifies the Ecofin Council who, acting by qualified majority, decides on the basis of the Commission report and of the opinion of the Monetary Committee whether an excessive deficit exists. If an excessive deficit exists, the Council then makes recommendations to the Member State concerned.[11] If no effective action is taken by the Member State, the Council may make the recommendations public. Beyond that, the Council has no power to enforce these guidelines during Stage II.[12]

The 3 percent reference value for the public *deficit* ratio may be overridden if either the ratio has declined substantially and continuously and reached a level that comes close to the reference value, or the excess over the reference value is only exceptional and temporary and the ratio remains close to the reference value. This provision seems to capture the important (i) macroeconomic distinction between a 'structural' deficit and an 'observed' deficit, which may be different from the former concept due to the purely temporary, cyclical factors, and (ii) distinction between the temporal tendency, or change over time, of a structural deficit and its value in any given calendar year. 'Government' for purposes of these criteria means general government, including social security funds. Revenues from the privatization of government enterprises are not to be included in government receipts, but reduce the gross government debt. Similarly, the 60 percent reference value of the public *debt* ratio may be overridden if the ratio is sufficiently diminishing and approaching the reference value at a satisfactory pace.

Prohibition of central bank financing of governments or Community institutions

As of the start of Stage II, national central banks, with the exception of the Bank of England, are prohibited from granting credit facilities to, or outright financing of their governments or Community institutions. Governments include central, regional, local governments or public bodies, such as publicly-owned credit institutions, except in the context of supply of reserves by central banks or of 'lender of last resort'. Moreover, governments may not have privileged access to financial institutions such as the imposition on financial institutions to hold liabilities of the public sector. All of these activities are considered incompatible with the process of convergence towards monetary stability.

Prohibition of mutual guarantees between Member States of their public debt

From the start of Stage II, a Member State shall not be liable for, or assume the commitments of, central governments, regional, local or other public authorities of another Member State. The same applies to the Community vis-à-vis any Member State. These rules are imposed so as to provide incentives for fiscal discipline to Member States who might otherwise compromise the monetary stability objective of the convergence criteria towards a monetary union. During Stage II, the 'no bail-out' clause – as it is sometimes called – does not preclude the possibility that whenever a Member State is in difficulties as regards its balance of payments and where such difficulties are liable to jeopardize the functioning of the common market, the Council, acting by a qualified majority on the recommendation of the Commission, may adopt decisions to grant financial assistance to the Member State.

Legislation leading to national central bank independence

During Stage II, each Member State shall begin the legislative process leading to the independence of its central bank from the government, with a clear mandate that the central bank's primary objective shall be price stability (see Table 4.3 for the status and features of each central bank as of 1994). During 1993–95, Belgium, France, Italy, Spain and Portugal significantly modified the status of their central bank to comply with these Treaty requirements. Although the monetary association between Belgium and Luxembourg will remain unchanged during Stage II, a draft law on the Institut Monétaire Luxembourgeois (IML) was submitted to the national Parliament in December 1993 to establish an independent IML (i.e. central bank) in conformity with the provisions of the Maastricht Treaty. By October 1995, amendments to the statutes of national central banks were pending in Belgium and Luxembourg while in Ireland, the Netherlands, Finland and Sweden preliminary or preparatory work on such amendments was being undertaken. The Swedish Riksbank is still not independent from the Riksdag (Parliament); it even has members of the Riksdag on its board. Should Sweden decide to join Stage III, the Swedish constitution will have to be changed in this regard to be in compliance with the Maastricht Treaty.

With the exception of the Bank of England – provided that the United Kingdom does not notify the Council of its intention to participate in Stage III – the independence of each national central bank from its government is to be effective by the date of the *establishment* of the European central bank, which for practical reasons will occur before the start of Stage III and immediately following the designation by the Heads of States or Government of the Member States that are to form the initial single currency area. At the crucial time during the closing months of Stage II when the final preparations are undertaken to render the future European central bank operational, the Governors of the central banks of the Member States designated to join the single currency area and the Executive Board of the European central bank must not be influenced by their national government and EU institutions when they make those decisions.

Table 4.3 Institutional characteristics of European Union Central Banks, 1994

	Nationale Bank van België	Danmarks Nationalbank	Deutsche Bundesbank	Bank of Greece	Banco de España	Banque de France
Principal Statutory Objective	None, although safeguarding the currency implicit	To maintain safe and secure currency system	To safeguard the currency	To control currency in circulation and credit	To ensure price stability	Ensuring price stability
Legal authority for:						
1. Exchange rate regime	Government	Government	Government	Government	Government	Government
2. Setting targets for: ● monetary growth	Central Bank*	Central Bank*	Central Bank	Central Bank**	Central Bank**	Central Bank**
● inflation	Central Bank*	Central Bank*	Central Bank	Government*	Central Bank	Central Bank
3. Changing key interest rates	Central Bank	Central Bank	Central Bank	Central Bank	Central Bank	Central Bank
4. Payment system services	Central Bank	Central Bank	Central Bank	Central Bank	Central Bank	Central Bank
5. Supervision of financial institutions	No	No	No		Central Bank	Central Bank & Comm. Bancaire
6. Safeguard financial stability	Central Bank	Central Bank	Central Bank	Central Bank	Central Bank	Central Bank
Appointment of Governor	Crown, on proposal of government, 5 years (renewable)	Crown, on proposal of government, no fixed term	Federal President on proposal of government after consultation of Central Bank Council, normally 8 years with 2 years minimum (renewable)	Pres. of Republic on Government proposal after nomination by the general Council, 4 years (renewable)	Crown, on proposal of President of government, 6 years (non-renewable)	Council of Ministers, 6 years (renewable)

Table 4.3 Continued

	Nationale Bank van België	Danmarks Nationalbank	Deutsche Bundesbank	Bank of Greece	Banco de España	Banque de France
Recent and planned changes	Legislation prohibiting 'monetary financing' and ensuring independence adopted on 22 March 1993 and entered into force in April 1993	None	None	Proposal to draft legislation to make central bank more independent and to change statutes in conformity with Treaty on European Union	Law 13/1994 of 1 June 1994 on the Autonomy of the Banco de España introduced the provisions of the Treaty on European Union	Laws of 4 August 1993 and 31 Dec. 1993 on the Statute of the Banque de France introduced provisions of the Treaty on European Union

	Central Bank of Ireland	Banca d'Italia	Institut Monétaire Luxembourgeois	Nederlandsche Bank	Oesterreichische Nationalbank	Banco de Portugal
Principal Statutory Objective	To safeguard the integrity of the currency	None, although safeguarding the currency implicit	Includes the promotion of the stability of the currency	To safeguard the value of the currency	To maintain the internal and external value of the Austrian currency	To maintain internal monetary stability and the external solvency of the currency
Legal authority for:						
1. Exchange rate regime	Government	Government	Government	Government	Central Bank in cooperation w/Government	Central Bank in Government after consulting CB
2. Setting targets for:						
• monetary growth	Central Bank*	Joint. w/Gov.	Central Bank*	Central Bank*	Central Bank*	Central Bank*
• inflation	Central Bank*	Government	Joint. w/Gov.*	Central Bank*	Central Bank*	Central Bank*

Table 4.3 Continued

	Central Bank of Ireland	Banca d'Italia	Institut Monétaire Luxembourgeois	Nederlandsche Bank	Oesterreichische Nationalbank	Banco de Portugal
3. Changing key interest rates	Central Bank	Central Bank	Central Bank	Central Bank	Central Bank	Central Bank
4. Payment system services	Central Bank	Central Bank	Central Bank	Central Bank	Central Bank	Central Bank
5. Supervision of financial institutions	Central Bank	Central Bank	Central Bank	Central Bank	No	Central Bank
6. Safeguard financial stability	Central Bank	Central Bank	Central Bank	Central Bank	Central Bank	Central Bank
Appointment of Governor	President on proposal of government, 7 years (renewable)	Board of directors, with approval of government, life tenure	Grand Duke, on proposal of Council of Ministers, 6 years (renewable)	Nominated by joint meeting of Governing Board and Supervisory Board and appointed by Crown on proposal of Council of Ministers, 7 years (renewable)	President of the Federal Republic on nomination by the Federal Government, 5 years (renewable)	Council of Ministers on proposal of Minister of Finance, 5 years (renewable)
Recent and planned changes	Bill to modify minor points	None	A bill to effect the changes required by the Treaty on European Union is pending in Parliament	The law of 9 Dec. 1993 introduced provisions of the TEU. Final adjustments are under consideration	None	Amendments to reinforce the independence of the central bank in line with Articles 109E(5) and 108 of the TEU are under consideration

Table 4.3 Continued

	Suomen Pankki	Sveriges Riksbank	Bank of England
Principal Statutory Objective	To maintain a stable and secure monetary system and to assist and facilitate the circulation of money in Finland	None, although safeguarding of the currency implicit	None, although safeguarding the currency implicit
Legal authority for:			
1. Exchange rate regime	Government on proposal of the central bank	Central Bank	Government
2. Setting targets for:			
● monetary growth	Central Bank	Central Bank*	Government**
● inflation	Central Bank	Central Bank	Government
3. Changing key interest rates	Central Bank	Central Bank	Central Bank***
4. Payment system services	Central Bank	Central Bank	Central Bank
5. Supervision of financial institutions	No	No	Central Bank
6. Safeguard financial stability	Central Bank	Central Bank	Central Bank
Appointment of Governor	President of the Republic on a proposal of the Parliamentary Supervisory Council, indefinite tenure	Governing Board, 5 years (renewable)	Crown, on proposal of Prime Minister, 5 years (renewable)
Recent and planned changes	Legislation in order to comply with the requirements of the TEU is under consideration	Legislation in order to comply with the requirements of the TEU will be proposed during the current legislative period	Changes will be needed if the United Kingdom participates in Stage III

*No targets set at present.
**No targets set at present; only monitoring ranges used.
***Since May 1997, CB has operational, not statutory, responsibility for setting interest rates.
Source: European Monetary Institute, Annual Report, 1994.

The establishment of the precursor to the European central bank

At the start of Stage II, the European Monetary Institute (EMI) is established as the precursor to the European central bank. The EMI, which is composed of all the national central bank governors, one of whom is elected Vice-president, and a President[13] appointed by the Heads of State or Government, contributes to the realization of the conditions necessary for the transition to Stage III by strengthening the coordination of monetary policies of the Member States with a view to ensure price stability, by making the preparations required for the establishment of the single central bank with its single monetary policy, and by overseeing the development of the private ECU, including the smooth functioning of the ECU clearing system (see Chapter 5). In fact, under Article 109F.3, the EMI must be able to specify by 31 December 1996 the proposed regulatory, organizational and logistical framework necessary for the European central bank to perform its tasks in Stage III. The framework will then be submitted to the European Central Bank (ECB) for a final decision, at the date of establishment of the ECB, which is scheduled to take place in mid-1998. The EMI has eight sub-committees studying the following topics:

- instruments (required reserves, open market operations, standing credit facilities) and procedures (centralization vs decentralization) for conducting a single monetary policy and the transmission mechanisms of monetary policy in Member States (see below);
- the functioning of the ERM and the development of the private ECU;
- banking supervision regarding prudential issues;
- harmonization of monetary and banking statistics;
- clearing and settlement systems (see Chapter 5);
- the design, manufacture and distribution of the Euro banknote, the future single currency (see Chapter 5, endnote 6);
- the implementation of a technical strategy for information and communications systems for the European System of Central Banks (ESCB), the future European central bank;
- harmonization of accounting rules and standards in the ESCB.

The EMI has already published the proposed operational framework for the single monetary policy in Stage III (European Monetary Institute 1997a).

In addition to the *primary tasks* cited above, the EMI also has:

- *Advisory functions*: such as formulating opinions and recommendations on the overall orientation of monetary policy and exchange rate policy, or making recommendations to the monetary authorities of the Member States concerning the conduct of their monetary policy, or formulating a reference scenario on the changeover to the single currency (European Monetary Institute 1995d).

- *Operational and technical functions*: such as the administration of the operations of the VSTF and STMS mechanisms of the former EMCF, which the EMI absorbed in January 1994, and the administration of borrowing and lending operations concluded by the Community under the MTFA mechanism. It also must report, once a year, to the Ecofin Council on the state of preparations for Stage III. This report includes an assessment of the progress towards convergence in the Community as well as the statutory requirements to be fulfilled for national central banks to become an integral part of the European System of Central Banks (ESCB), e.g. independence with the primary objective of promoting price stability and the prohibition on the provision of central bank credit to the public sector (European Monetary Institute 1995e, 1996d).

Decision process to launch Stage III

Stage II shall remain in effect until a decision is made to enter into Stage III, which, according to the Treaty, *may* occur on 1 January 1997 or *must* occur on 1 January 1999 at the latest, *if no other date has been set by the end of 1997*.

The decision to launch Stage III on 1 January 1997 would have required that a majority (i.e. eight) of the Member States satisfy for calendar year 1996 the convergence criteria, described below. As of mid-1995, it was clear that a majority of the Member States would not satisfy the public finance criteria (see Table 4.4). At that time, only five Member States – Denmark, Germany, Ireland, Luxembourg, and the United Kingdom – were forecast to satisfy the criteria, precluding the possibility of 1 January 1997 as the first date for the start of Stage III. Accordingly, the Ecofin Council *informally* agreed, on 19 June 1995, to shelve the date of 1997 in favour of an all-out push to launch the start of Stage III in 1999. Since then, the Council meeting in the composition of Heads of State or Government (see below), on the basis of recommendations from the Commission, the EMI and the Ecofin Council, formally confirmed in December 1996 that a majority of the Member States did not satisfy the convergence criteria to launch a monetary union in 1997. Thus, the procedure described below refers to the 1999 deadline, which allows the monetary union to start with only a minority of the Member States. Although the minimum number of Member States to launch a monetary union in 1999 is not specified in the Treaty, there seems to be a general consensus that a minimum of two large countries and of a few small countries is necessary for the formation of the initial single currency area. Since among the four large countries, the United Kingdom may not wish to participate in Stage III and Italy may not be able to join the first wave of countries, both Germany and France have to meet the convergence criteria to launch the monetary union in 1999.

Table 4.4 Convergence criteria – [Article 109J.1]

Member State	Inflation rate %, 1996 average^d	Long-term interest rate %, 1996 average^e	Budget balance, % of GDP				General govt gross debt, % of GDP				Member of ERM?^b
			1993	1995	1996	1997	1993	1995	1996	1997	
Belgium (B)	1.8	6.5	–7.5	–4.1	–3.4	–2.7	137.0	133.7	130.0	126.7	yes 22.02.1982
Denmark (DK)	1.9	7.2	–3.9	–1.6	–1.6	0.3	80.1	71.9^a	70.2	67.2	yes 22.02.1982
Germany (D)	1.2*	6.2	–3.5	–3.5	–3.8	–3.0	48.2	58.1	60.7	61.8	yes never
Greece (GR)	7.9	14.8	–14.2	–9.1	–7.4	–4.9	111.8	111.8	111.8	106.3	no
Spain (E)	3.6	8.7	–6.8	–6.6	–4.4	–3.0	60.5	65.7	69.6	68.1	yes 06.03.1995
France (F)	2.1	6.3	–5.6	–4.8	–4.2	–3.0	45.6	52.8	56.2	57.9	yes 07.04.1986
Ireland (IRL)	1.6^d	7.3	–2.4	–2.0	–0.9	–1.0	94.5	81.6	72.6	68.3	yes 01.02.1993
Italy (I)	4.0	9.4	–9.6	–7.1	–6.7	–3.2	119.3	124.9	123.7	122.4	yes^c
Luxembourg (L)	1.2*	6.3	1.7	1.5	1.8	1.1	6.2	6.0	6.4	6.5	yes 22.02.1982
Netherlands (NL)	1.5	6.2	–3.2	–4.0	–2.4	–2.3	80.8	79.7	78.5	76.2	yes never
Austria (A)	1.8	6.3	–4.2	–5.9	–3.9	–3.0	62.8	69.0	70.0	68.8	yes never
Portugal (P)	2.9	8.6	–6.9	–5.1	–4.1	–3.0	68.2	71.7	65.6	64.1	yes 14.05.1993
Finland (FIN)	1.5	7.1	–8.0	–5.2	–2.6	–1.9	57.3	59.2	58.7	59.2	yes never
Sweden (S)	0.8*	8.0	–12.3	–8.1	–3.6	–2.6	76.0	78.7	77.7	76.5	no
Britain (UK)	2.9^d	7.9	–7.8	–5.8	–4.4	–2.9	48.5	54.1	54.5	54.7	no

Criteria: Cols (1) and (2) based on average of 3 'best' Member States (*) of col. (1) ≤1.1+1.5 ≤6.8+2.0   deficit ratio ≤3.0   ≤60.0   In ERM; no 'own initiative' devaluation
≤2.6 ≤8.8

Notes:
(a) General government gross debt figures are not adjusted for the assets held by the Danish Social Pension Fund against sectors outside general government, and for government deposits at the Central Bank for the management of foreign exchange reserves. According to statements 5 and 6 relating to Council Regulation 3605/93 of 22 November 1993, the Council and the Commission agree that for Denmark, these items shall be specified in the presentation of general government gross debt. They totalled 10 percent of GDP in 1996. In addition, the data are not adjusted for the amounts outstanding in the government debt from the financing of public undertakings, which, according to statement 3 relating to that Council Regulation, will be the subject of a separate presentation for the Member States. In Denmark this item amounted to 6.2 percent of GDP in 1996.
(b) Date indicated refers to the last 'own initiative' devaluation in ERM; 'never' means no 'own initiative' devaluation of currency. According to the Commission report on convergence drafted at the end of 1996 (Commission 1996f:47), among the currencies that participated in the ERM over the last two years, none has been the subject of severe tensions.
(c) After withdrawing from the ERM in September 1992, the Italian lira re-entered the ERM in November 1996.

(d) Measured by consumer price indices calculated on a comparable basis, called the Harmonised Indices of Consumer Prices (HICPs). The HICPs will form the basis for the assessment of inflation convergence in early 1998 and will also be essential for the conduct of the single monetary policy in Stage III. HICP inflation rates for Ireland and the United Kingdom were not available for 1996. Therefore, inflation rates based on national CPI are shown for these two Member States.

(e) Annual average of the 10-year benchmark government bond yield.

As of mid-1997, only Denmark, Ireland, Luxembourg, the Netherlands and Finland were not the subject of an Ecofin Council decision under Article 104C.6 of the Treaty on European Union that an excessive deficit and/or debt ratio existed. These decisions were taken on the basis of an assessment of 1996 data.

Source: European Monetary Institute (1996d; 1997b); 1997 public finance ratios are forecasts from the Commission (1997).

During the first quarter of 1998, the Commission and the EMI will assess *all* the Member States to determine those that satisfy the convergence criteria for eligibility to pass to Stage III. These criteria are (see Table 4.4 for 1996 data and public finance ratio forecasts for 1997):

1   A high degree of price stability, which is defined as an average rate of inflation, observed over a period of one year before the examination (the data for 1997), that does not exceed by more than 1.5 percentage points that of, *at most*,[14] the three best performing Member States in terms of price stability.

2   The convergence of interest rates which is defined as a nominal long-term interest rate observed over a period of one year before the examination, that does not exceed by more than 2 percentage points the average nominal long-term interest rate of the same Member State(s) identified in (1) above. Long-term interest rate differentials reflect the financial market's assessment of the sustainable achievement of the convergence of monetary policies and public finance ratios. This criterion will provide additional information about the sustainability of criterion (1) above, and criteria (3) and (4) below.

3   The sustainability of the government financial position which is assessed through the regular surveillance procedure of public finance ratios described above and which did not result in an unfavourable Council decision. In September 1995, the Ecofin Council agreed that the final assessment of the deficit and debt ratios of each Member State in the run-up to the start of the initial monetary union in 1999 is to be based on the actual economic data of calendar year 1997 rather than forecasts, which may be subject to optimistic scenarios.

4   Participation in the ERM, which means that the Member State has respected the *normal* (emphasis by author) fluctuation margins without severe tensions for at least the last two years before the examination, and in particular, that the Member State has not devalued its currency's bilateral central rate against any other Member State's currency *on its own initiative*[15] (emphasis by author) for the same two-year period. On

5 December 1994, the Ecofin Council endorsed an opinion drawn up by the European Monetary Institute which considered it advisable to maintain the ERM arrangement of ±15 percent margins of fluctuation in effect since their introduction in August 1993. Although the Council studiously avoided declaring that these arrangements were 'normal', Council could retroactively declare, at some future date, that the wide bands are normal and legally satisfy this provision of the Maastricht Treaty (*Financial Times*, 6 December 1994: 1). It is generally agreed that with the introduction of the wide ERM bands, what matters more to meet this convergence criterion is not whether a currency remains within the wide bilateral bands but whether the currency has been 'stable' against the Deutsche mark and the other currencies of the future participating Member States of the single currency zone for approximately two years prior to the assessment of the convergence criteria. This will be measured by using the old ±2.25 percent bilateral bands.

The reports of the Commission and the EMI will also take into account the development of the ECU, the results of the integration of markets in goods, services, capital and labour, as well as the current account of the balance of payments and the unit labour costs of each Member State.

The Ecofin Council, on the basis of these reports and a specific recommendation from the Commission, will designate, by a qualified majority of *all* Member States, the Member States that fulfil the necessary conditions for the adoption of a single currency. However, the Council may *not* designate Denmark, which, by virtue of the TEU Protocol on Denmark, has been granted the right to notify the Council that it does not wish to participate in Stage III. In 1992, as one of the preconditions to hold a second Danish referendum for the ratification of the Treaty, Denmark exercised its right to that effect (Conclusions of the Presidency of the Edinburgh European Council *Bulletin of the European Communities*, 12/92:I.36). In addition, the Council may not, under certain conditions, designate the following Member States:

- The United Kingdom, which, by virtue of the TEU Protocol on the UK, has been granted an 'opt-out' of Stage III. Should the British Parliament decide that the United Kingdom will not join the single currency area, the Council may not designate the UK.
- Sweden, which by virtue of its accession negotiations in 1993–94, arrogated itself the right to introduce, at the relevant time, the question of the changeover from Stage II to Stage III to the Swedish Riksdag (Parliament). In the event that Sweden decides not to move to Stage III, the Council may not designate Sweden (Sweden 1994).

The Ecofin Council will in turn submit its recommendation to the *Council, meeting in the composition of the Heads of State or Government*,[16] who, on the basis of the Ecofin Council report and the opinion of the European Parliament, must, acting by qualified majority, confirm which Member States fulfil the necessary conditions for the adoption of a single currency. It is clear that the final decision regarding the composition of the Member States that will form the initial single currency area is not only a technical question but also a political one, taken at the highest political level.

Possible postponement of the start of Stage III

Although not explicitly stated in the Treaty, it is legally possible to postpone beyond 1999 the start of Stage III. On the basis of Article 109J.4 of the Maastricht Treaty, the Heads of State or Government would have to announce *before the end* of 1997 an ulterior date for the start of Stage III. If, by the end of 1997, it would appear, on the basis of preliminary data, that either France or Germany, or both, do not meet the convergence criteria (read 'public deficit' criterion), the Heads of State or Government might avail themselves of this opportunity instead of launching an initial monetary union in 1999 without a minimum of two large Member States, which are necessary to create a credible single currency area.

On the other hand, if the Heads of State or Government were to use a very flexible interpretation of the convergence criteria to 'wave in' either France or Germany, or both, to launch the initial monetary union, the German Bundestag may prevent German participation in the single currency area. According to the interpretation of German ratification of the Maastricht Treaty given by the German Federal Constitutional Court of Karlsruhe, the German Bundestag (lower house) has the right to make its own evaluation regarding the transition to the third stage of EMU and to

> resist any weakening of the stability criteria ... particularly in Article 6 of the [TEU] Protocol[17] on the convergence criteria [i.e. no dilution of the convergence criteria by the Council]. ... Notwithstanding the Council's scope for assessment, evaluation and forecasting, the text of the [TEU] Treaty does not allow it to depart from the basis for the decisions leading to the recommendations referred to in Article 109J(1) [the convergence criteria]. ... This provides an adequate guarantee that the convergence criteria cannot be weakened without German agreement, and thus without the German Bundestag having a decisive say in the matter. ... The German Bundestag can therefore give effect to its wish to make the introduction of the future monetary union dependent on strict stability criteria. ... This concept of the monetary union as a community of stability is the basis and the object of the German law giving assent to it. If the monetary union cannot, at the time of transition to the Third Stage, develop further and without interruption the level of stability then achieved in line with the agreed stabilisation mandate, it would not be in keeping with the concept of the Treaty.
>
> (Steinherr 1994: Appendix 3)

Given the German public's reluctance to substitute the Euro and a European central bank for the Deutsche mark and the Bundesbank, respectively, the Bundestag seems likely to take a restrictive stance when it examines whether the proposed Member States for a monetary union satisfy the budget deficit and debt requirements. The Bundestag may even be implicitly encouraged to do so in the event that the EMI report, submitted to the Council, indicates a lack of consensus to launch a monetary union in 1999, with a minority report written by the President of the Bundesbank. An unfavourable vote of the Bundestag would *legally* force Germany to postpone its participation in the initial monetary union, which in turn would effectively postpone to a later date the start of Stage III for the Community. A technical delay of nine months to a year, providing more time to meet the convergence criteria to launch the initial monetary union, would not be catastrophic – provided that the authorities clearly and convincingly argue the case. Paradoxically, a short and transparent delay may be supported by a majority of the Member States as it would permit some Member States (read: Italy, Spain and Portugal) to be part of the *initial* wave of countries forming the monetary union. The fewer the number of EU countries that remain outside the monetary union, the fewer the potential problems of the Exchange Rate Mechanism linking the 'outs' with the new Euro. Moreover, the politically sensitive problem of launching the initial monetary union without Italy, a founder-Member State of the Community, would be bypassed. However, a long and *sine die* postponement would effectively scuttle the process towards a monetary union under the provisions of the Maastricht Treaty.

STAGE III: SCHEDULED TO START ON 1 JANUARY 1999

Stage III marks the start of the European monetary union, initially composed of a limited number of Member States (the 'ins') who, as of the first day of Stage III, have a single currency and a single monetary policy. The Treaty provides for the eventual participation in the monetary union of *all* EU Member States. The non-participating Member States (the 'outs') have an obligation to meet, as soon as possible, the same convergence criteria in order to join the monetary union. By virtue of the participation of the central bank governors of the 'outs' in the European System of Central Banks and of the participation of all the Ministers of Finance in the Ecofin Council with regard to the continual multilateral surveillance procedure of the 'outs', monetary and fiscal policies between the 'outs' and the Euro currency area are to be well coordinated throughout Stage III.

The stability of the exchange rates between the currencies of the Member States outside the monetary union and the Euro is to be reinforced with the implementation of a new exchange rate mechanism. Moreover, throughout Stage III, the binding agreements, negotiated in the 'Stability and Growth Pact' on public finance deficit ratios that the 'ins' must meet, are to be enforced with sanctions, if necessary. Finally, during Stage III, the relatively long and gradual process for the changeover to the single currency begins for the participating Member States, with a deadline, at the latest, of mid-2002 to eliminate all references and uses of the national units of account. This timetable is described in Chapter 5.

On the first day of Stage III, a number of events take place. The Member States composing the monetary union must decide on conversion rates between their national units of account and the new single unit of account, the Euro, which replaces the ECU. The new European System of Central Banks and European Central Bank, which were established and replaced the EMI as soon as the Member States were designated in early 1998 to participate in the monetary union, become fully operational to implement the monetary and the exchange rate policies of the single currency area. The exchange rate policy is implemented with regard to the exchange rate regimes of the Euro vis-à-vis third currencies and of the Euro vis-à-vis the currencies of the 'outs'. All of these points are now elaborated in this section.

Conversion rates for the Euro

On the first day of Stage III, the Ecofin Council, acting with the unanimity of the Member States composing the monetary union will, on the basis of a proposal from the Commission and after consulting the ECB, set the '... conversion rates at which their currencies shall be irrevocably fixed, and at which irrevocably fixed rate the ECU will be exchanged for these national currencies ...' (Article 109L.4). Moreover, a Council regulation entering into force on 1 January 1999 will stipulate the continuity between the official ECU and the new single currency, the Euro, at the rate of 1 ECU = 1 Euro. At that point in time, the *official* ECU, defined as a basket of twelve currencies, disappears. The pledge that one official ECU equals one Euro means that public and private economic agents who hold prior to Stage III an ECU or an ECU-denominated contract based on the official definition of the ECU will be able to re-denominate that ECU or that ECU-denominated contract into a Euro, the new unit of account.

Using France and Germany as an example of two participating Member States, the Council, composed of the Ministers of the participating Member States, adopts a FF/Euro rate and a DM/Euro rate, which of course implies a FF/DM conversion rate. Although the Treaty on European Union is silent on the precise key to be used to fix the irreversible and irrevocable conversion rates, the Council will probably use one of the following formulas:

- conversion rates equal to the previous day's market-determined ECU rates which prevailed at a particular time of day on the foreign exchange markets;

- conversion rates equal to the daily *average* 'synthetic' or market ECU rates which prevailed over a previous time period;
- conversion rates equal to the ECU central rates;
- conversion rates equal to the previous day's 'synthetic' ECU rates calculated by the Commission, as was done when the ECU was substituted for the EUA in 1979 (see Chapter 2).

Only the last formula would be in line with the Treaty provision that '[t]his measure [adopting conversion rates] shall by itself not modify the external value of the ECU' (Article 109L.4). As described in Chapter 2, the 'external value of the ECU' is equal to the value of the ECU basket in its official uses. In concrete terms, the external value of the ECU against any currency such as the US dollar is its 'synthetic' ECU rate against the US dollar calculated by the Commission on each business day. And by using the US dollar rate against any currency composing the ECU basket, the Commission also automatically calculates the synthetic ECU rate against any component currency, such as the French franc, Deutsche mark, etc. Accordingly to be in line with the Treaty provision, the conversion rate of the ECU (Euro) against a participating currency, such as the French franc or the Deutsche mark on 1 January 1999, would have to be equal to the 'synthetic' ECU (Euro) rate against the French franc, or Deutsche mark, calculated on 31 December 1998. The market ECU rate will probably be different from the 'synthetic' rate for the reason now explained.

Throughout the period leading up to the start of Stage III, the increased uncertainty created by a 'regime change' may give rise to a reluctance on the part of economic agents to hold on to ECU-denominated assets. Two types of uncertainties related to a 'regime change' should be cited. The first one is related to the effective behaviour of the new ECB. Will the new ECB really be independent of the governments of the Member States? Could the German representatives sitting on the all-important Governing Council of the ECB be out-voted with the 'one man, one vote' principle for decision-making at the ECB? If the ECB decides to use the money supply as an intermediate operating target, will it have a reliable indicator with the new uncertainty created by the unreliability of the newly defined money supply figures? The second type of uncertainty is related to the inevitable litigation with respect to long-term financial contracts currently denominated in ECUs or the national currencies of the participating Member States. In particular, there are fears that issuers or investors in bonds, issued before the creation of the currency union, might invoke the 'change of circumstance' clauses of contracts, if the currency in which the bonds were dominated no longer exist. And even if the new regulations that will be introduced by the EU eliminate that uncertainty, how will they apply under New York or Japanese laws where many of these contracts were signed? For these reasons, the excess supply of ECUs on the foreign exchange markets will be translated in a spread between the market and synthetic ECU exchange rates, with the market ECU rate trading at a discount from its synthetic rate. If the Council were to consider that the market ECU exchange rates of 31 December 1998 do not properly reflect the underlying fundamentals of the new single currency, it might very well choose the 'synthetic' ECU rates (fourth formula) to set the conversion rates.

Another problem that the Council may consider when setting conversion rates is a last-minute, market-driven bilateral change between the currencies of the Member States designated to join the single currency area and the currencies of the Member States that do not initially participate in the monetary union. These variations in exchange rates would be reflected in the 'synthetic' or market ECU rates. To attenuate this effect, the Council could then use a time series average of 'synthetic' or market ECU rates (second formula) to set conversion rates. Although there are a number of tricky mathematical problems in the use of this formula to set conversion rates (see Nguyen 1995), the option is recommended by the German banking association (BdB), which suggests using the six or twelve months prior to the first day of Stage III for calculating the average ECU rates against the participating currencies.

The third formula, which is again not in line with the Treaty, has the advantage of precluding an implicit ERM realignment on the first day of Stage III. As explained in Chapter 2, an ERM realignment is a change in ECU central rates and *a fortiori* a change in bilateral central rates. Conversion rates that are different from the ECU central rates in force prior to start of Stage III would necessarily imply an ERM realignment.

Although there is no legal obligation according to the Treaty provisions, the private financial sector is recommending that the Council indicate clearly, and as soon as possible, the formula to be used to set the conversion rates (Ecu Banking Association 1995), so as to avoid any 'shock adjustment' for the financial markets on 1 January 1999. Mr Lamfalussy, the President of the EMI, proposed in mid-1996 that the formula to set the conversion rates should be announced at the time when the Member States of the monetary union are designated in early 1998 and that the formula should be based on the average market ECU rates prevailing in the three years before the monetary union starts in 1999. He also suggests greater weight be placed on the rates in 1996 and 1997 so as to minimize the impact of any movement in 1998 (*Financial Times*, 15 July 1996: 2). Others (e.g. Schlesinger 1997) have suggested that the central banks of the Member States designated in early 1998 to participate in the monetary union should set bilateral target rates to be reached at the end of 1998. These target rates would have a band of ±0.5 percent to be defended with unlimited intervention, if necessary.

'Stability and growth pact' for the 'ins'

From the start of Stage III, all Member States *have to avoid* excessive government deficits (Article 104C.1), not just *'endeavor to avoid* [emphasis by author] excessive government deficits' as required under Stage II (Article 109E.4). Moreover, according to the provisions of the Maastricht Treaty, if during Stage III a *participating* Member State persists in failing to implement the recommendations judged by the Council to be necessary to remedy the situation of excessive government deficits, the Ecofin Council, *composed of only the participating Member States* and acting by qualified majority excluding the votes of the representative of the Member State concerned, may:

- require the Member State to publish additional information before issuing bonds and securities, and/or
- recommend to the European Investment Bank to reconsider its lending policy towards the Member State concerned, and/or
- require the Member State to make a non-interest bearing deposit of an appropriate size with the Community until the excessive deficit has been corrected, and/or
- impose on the Member State fines of an appropriate size.

In late 1995, at the behest of Germany, the Commission and the Ecofin Council were asked to draft regulations that would clarify the implementation of the excessive deficit procedure for ensuring budgetary discipline of the 'ins' in Stage III. These draft regulations are to be adopted at the EU level in the second semester of 1997, even though full application would only concern the Member States participating in the single currency. National budgetary policies of the 'ins' in the third stage of EMU need to be set so as to create room for manoeuvre in adapting to exceptional and cyclical disturbances. This is necessary since the exchange rate instrument and the monetary policy instrument will no longer be available to a participating Member State to absorb a country-specific shock. The draft regulations (Commission 1996e and Annex I.II of the Presidency Conclusions of the Dublin European Council, 13/14 December 1996) propose that the appropriate way for Member States' (the 'ins') budgetary policies to ensure such a role is through pursuing medium-term budgetary objectives of close to balance or surplus. The 3 percent deficit to GDP reference value is therefore to be seen as an upper limit in normal circumstances. The application of these principles would involve a twin-track strategy: (i) a preventive, early-warning system for identifying and correcting budgetary slippages before they bring the deficit above the 3 percent ceiling and (ii) a dissuasive set of rules, with sufficient deterrent effect to put pressure on Member States to avoid excessive deficits – except under exceptional and temporary situations – or to take measures to correct them quickly if they do occur.

Preventive and dissuasive approach

Within the framework of the multilateral surveillance provision of the Maastricht Treaty, the Member States having adopted the single currency would have to submit 'stability programmes' setting out national medium-term budgetary objectives. Departures from the budgetary objectives of close to balance or surplus set in the stability programmes would prompt a warning from the Commission. This could lead to an Ecofin recommendation to the Member State concerned with a view to take the necessary measures so as to avoid the risk of breaching the 3 percent ceiling. The draft regulation proposes that the time span should not exceed ten months between the time the Member State reports its budgetary data to the Commission (in March of the year n referring to data of year n − 1) and the time the Ecofin Council decides to apply sanctions in the event that the Member State has not taken appropriate remedial action to correct the excessive deficit (January of year n + 1).

A non-interest-bearing deposit will be required whenever sanctions are triggered. A deposit would be transformed into a fine if, after two years, sufficient action to correct the excessive deficit has not been taken. The interest produced by deposits and the fines will be distributed among the Member States of the single currency area which have not run up excessive deficits. The scale of the deposits would include a fixed component, equal to 0.2 percent of GDP, and a variable component equal to 0.1 percent of GDP for each percentage point of the excess of the deficit over the three percent reference value, and would be subject to a ceiling of 0.5 percent of GDP. A Member State within the Euro zone which presents an excessive deficit for the second year running will be obliged to make an additional deposit, equal to 0.1 percent of GDP for each percentage point of the excess of the deficit over the reference value. However, in the second and subsequent years, the fixed component of the deposit (0.2 percent) will no longer apply.

'Exceptional and temporary' circumstances when the three percent deficit to GDP reference value can be automatically breached without triggering sanctions are defined as a Member State facing an unusual event (e.g. a natural disaster) beyond its control with significant impact on the public budget or a Member State facing an annual fall of real GDP of at least 2 percent over a twelve-month period. This has occurred only three times over the period 1970 to 1996 for the large EU Member States − once in Italy and twice in Britain. 'Exceptional circumstances' may also be invoked by a Member State, if its real GDP falls between 0.75 percent and 2.0 percent. However, the Ecofin Council will have to decide by a qualified majority of all the Member States (i.e. the 'outs' and the Member State concerned have the right to vote) whether such an exception is justified. A Member State should in principle never invoke the 'exceptional circumstance' clause if its real GDP falls by less than 0.75 percent.

Reasons for public finance penalties for the 'ins'

The conventional view is that with the prohibition of both central bank financing and mutual guarantee of government debt, a Member State participating in a monetary union with undisciplined budgetary behaviour is penalized by the market with higher interest rates on its government bonds to reflect the 'default risk'. This would by itself create pressures on a participating Member State to respect sound budgetary policies and obviate the need to impose penalties. For instance, let us assume that France is running a deficit to GDP ratio that is inconsistent with a stable debt-to-GDP ratio. Since the European Central Bank, Community institutions, and other Member States are not permitted to guarantee ('no central bank financing/no bail out') the government debt of France, there is no need to impose penalties on France as the market will automatically discipline the French government by imposing a default risk premium on its debt relative to the German government debt. France is disciplined by the market – not by Community-imposed penalties – to change its budgetary policies.

Recent experiences have challenged this conventional view and have demonstrated that the market mechanism comes into play much too late. The new argument is as follows:

First, although the market will ultimately discipline irresponsible government financial behaviour under a 'no bail-out' environment, the market cannot be relied on to *continuously* perform this task. Private credit rating agencies will allow the debt-to-GDP ratio to rise for many years before downgrading a government's debt. The sovereign debts of Canada and Sweden are recent examples.

Secondly, by the time the market mechanism begins to function, the country will have accumulated a public debt such that the debt-to-GDP ratio will now preclude the use of the automatic income stabilizing function of fiscal policy needed during a recession. With the combination of a high debt-to-GDP ratio and a real growth rate lower than the real rate of interest, the use of budget deficits as an automatic stabilizer will only exacerbate the problem of the *sustainability* of the government financial position. With the issue of sustainability in the forefront, the Member State is forced by the market to run primary surpluses (see Box 4.2). The government has lost the ability to use budgetary policy as a stabilization instrument. This has not only consequences for the Member State concerned, but also for the other Member States of the single currency zone, especially if the Member State concerned is large.

Instead of setting arbitrary indicators and penalties enforced by the Council, Eichengreen *et al.* (1995) propose the creation, in each Member State, of a national debt board, politically independent of the government with members appointed to long terms in office. The board would be charged with setting a binding ceiling on the annual increase in the public

Box 4.2 The arithmetic of some 'convergence criteria'

The public finance constraint

The standard expression of the intertemporal budget constraint is (ignoring seigniorage revenues):

(1) $dB/dt = -S + iB$

where B is the public debt, S is the primary surplus (i.e. the government budget balance less interest payments or what is known as the 'operating balance'), i is the nominal interest rate, d is the derivation operator, and t is time.

Rather than examining the absolute change of the public debt over time, the analysis is usually done in terms of the ratio to GDP, which provides a better indicator of the *capacity* of the economy to absorb a growing public debt. Thus, with some algebraic manipulation, equation (1) can be rewritten in terms of the ratio to GDP, as follows:

(2) $db/dt = -s + (r - y)b$

where b and s are the ratios of debt and primary surplus to GDP (in percent) respectively, r is the real interest rate and y is the growth rate of real GDP.

Equation (2) indicates that if the product of a given debt ratio and the difference between the real interest rate and the real growth rate exceeds the primary surplus, that debt ratio increases over time ($db/dt > 0$), which may be characterized as a non-sustainable fiscal position over the long run.

Assuming a real interest rate greater than the growth rate of real GDP and an initial debt ratio, equation (2) indicates that a primary surplus ratio is required to stabilize the debt ratio (i.e. $db/dt = 0$). For example, if $(r-y) = 0.02$ and $b = 60$ percent (the strict Maastricht criterion to be eligible for membership in the monetary union), a Member State must have a primary surplus ratio of 1.2 percent to maintain its debt ratio at the 60 percent level. Thus, the relevant budget deficit ratio criterion is whether the Member State is running a sufficient primary surplus ratio, and not the maximum 3 percent budget deficit ratio indicated in a Protocol to the Maastricht Treaty. Furthermore, for a given initial debt ratio greater than 60 percent, it is clear that the primary surplus ratio also determines whether the Member State is on a path to achieve the public debt ratio required by the Maastricht Treaty.

Equation (2) also indicates that if the real interest rate is less than real growth rate of GDP (a rare observation since the late 1970s), the debt ratio declines over time regardless of the initial debt ratio – and even with a primary deficit!

The long-term nominal interest rate spread

A Protocol to the Maastricht Treaty allows a 1.5 and a 2 percentage point spread between the inflation rates and between the long-term nominal interest rates, respectively, of the 'best',– or at most the average of the three 'best' – performing Member State and the 'worst' performing Member State designated to join the monetary union. These convergence criteria are to be assessed on the basis of macro-economic data available for the calendar year 1997.

The 1.5 percentage point difference in inflation rates allows some leeway for the differential impact that the same monetary policy may have on the inflation rates in two different countries. Even a monetary union like Canada or the US, has regional variations of the inflation rates. The 2 percentage point difference between the long-term nominal interest rates is to provide for a potential risk premium, reflected in the long-term nominal interest rate spread, and explained by:

- any *unexpected* variation of the exchange rate of the two currencies between the end of 1997 and the beginning of 1999 when the exchange rate is irreversibly and irrevocably set on 1 January 1999. Presumably, by the end of 1997, the long-run *expected* change of the exchange rate between two anticipated participating Member States is zero, which suggests that the long-term nominal interest rate spread would no longer reflect this variable;
- and/or any possible difference in the default risk on government sovereign debt of the two economies. Given the 'no mutual guarantee of public debt' clause of the Treaty, a difference in debt ratios may translate into different default risk on long-term government debt.

debt, with the power to enforce it. The boards could authorize budget deficits in recessions, but offset these with subsequent surpluses. Political bias towards excessive deficits would be eliminated. They argue that the EU Ecofin Council is not known for delivering impartial judgments on one another's compliance with EU regulations. National debt boards, by contrast, would improve the national budgetary procedures, which usually produce smaller deficits and smaller debts, and would rely on national enforcement, which is consistent with the Community principle of subsidiarity.

Monetary policy of the single currency area

From the start of Stage III, the single monetary policy of the Member States in the Euro currency area will be decided by the *Governing Council* of the

European Central Bank (ECB), an arm of the European System of Central Banks (ESCB), which is composed of the fifteen national central banks. During a transitional period and until such time as some Member States remain outside the single currency area, the *General Council* of the ECB, another arm of the ESCB, will coordinate the monetary policies of the 'outs' with the single monetary policy of the single currency area.

The ESCB and the ECB: organization and tasks

The European System of Central Banks (ESCB) is to begin functioning on the very first day of Stage III. This is possible since the EMI has to specify, by the end of 1996, the regulatory, organizational and logistical framework of the future ESCB/ECB. The final decisions regarding this framework are to be taken by the governing body of the ECB, which is appointed as soon as the Member States are designated in early 1998 to form the initial monetary union. Also, the ECB is to carry out a 'dress rehearsal' of monetary policy operations during 1998 to test its logistical structure.

The ESCB is composed of the national central banks of *all* the Member States and of the European Central Bank (ECB). The ESCB is governed by the decision-making body of the ECB, the Governing Council. During the transition period, during which time all the EU Member States have not joined the monetary union, another governing body of the ECB is temporarily established, the General Council of the ECB.

The Governing Council is composed of:

- an Executive Board, composed of a President, Vice-president, and up to four other members but not less than two[18] and appointed by unanimity, upon a recommendation of the Ecofin Council and consultation of the European Parliament and the EMI, of the Heads of State or Government of the *participating* Member States, and
- the Governors of the national central banks of the *participating* Member States.

Members of the Executive Board are to be chosen from among persons of recognized standing and professional experience in monetary or banking matters and are appointed for a non-renewable term of eight years. The statutes of *all* national central banks must comply with the condition that the term of office of a national central bank Governor must not be less than five years. These provisions are introduced to further guarantee, over and above an explicit provision (TEU Protocol on the Statute of the ESCB and of the ECB, Article 7), the independence of the Governing Council from all Community institutions and national governments.

The principal functions of the Governing Council of the ECB are as follows (Articles 105, 105A, 109K of the Treaty and Articles 3 and 43 of the Protocol on the Statute of the ESCB and of the ECB):

- To formulate, while the Executive Board implements, monetary policy for the participating Member States with the primary objective of price stability.[19]
- To issue, or authorize the issue by the national central banks, of banknotes within the monetary union.
- To promote the smooth operation of the payment systems.
- To manage and hold the official foreign exchange reserves of the participating Member States, as well as conducting foreign exchange *operations* of the monetary union. Foreign exchange *policy-making* of the monetary union with respect to the currencies of the 'outs' and to non-EU currencies remains the responsibility of the Ecofin Council (see below for more details).
- To undertake specific tasks concerning policies relating to the prudential supervision of credit institutions. Although each national government retains prudential supervision of credit institutions, the ECB may be given by the Council, acting unanimously on a proposal from the Commission and after receiving the assent of the European Parliament, specific tasks concerning policies relating to the prudential supervision of credit institutions.

Monetary policy decisions for the single currency area are taken by a simple majority with each member of the Governing Council having one vote. The Governing Council meets at least ten times a year.

The General Council of the ECB, composed of the President and Vice-president of the ECB and of the Governors of all the national central banks, is temporarily established and remains in place until such time that all Member States have joined the monetary union. During the transitional period, the General Council takes over the tasks of the EMI that still have to be performed in Stage III for the Member States outside the monetary union, such as the coordination of the monetary policy of each Member State outside the single currency area with the single monetary policy decided by the Governing Council of the ECB.

Single monetary policy: instruments and procedures

Currently, the use and specific features of the three major instruments of monetary policy – open market operations, standing credit facilities and reserve requirements on deposit liabilities of credit institutions[20] – vary considerably between the Member States (European Monetary Institute 1995a: 123–131). For example, the central banks of Belgium, Luxembourg, Denmark and Sweden do not impose reserve requirements on deposit liabilities of credit institutions. The United Kingdom requires only a reserve ratio of 0.35 percent, which is not even related to monetary policy functions. On the other hand, the Deutsche Bundesbank imposes a 2 and a 1.5 percent reserve ratio on sight liabilities and savings deposits, respectively, of credit institutions. The 'Protocol on the Statute of the ESCB and of the ECB' of the Maastricht Treaty contains two articles which are to be studied and elaborated by the EMI. These two articles deal with open market and credit operations of the monetary union (Article 18) and minimum reserves (Article 19). The EMI must study the questions of the instrument(s) to use, and of the degree of centralization, in the ECB's execution of the single monetary policy with a view to control efficiently its operational target, which is usually defined as a short-term interest rate, and to provide the private market a relatively precise signal of monetary policy intentions.

The EMI (European Monetary Institute 1997a) is proposing that the ECB use monetary policy instruments which include standing credit facilities, open-market operations, and possibly reserve requirements. Two standing facilities will be available to the credit institutions on their own initiative:

- The marginal lending facility, which will allow credit institutions to obtain overnight liquidity from the national central banks (NCBs) at a pre-specified interest rate against eligible assets (collateral). The interest rate on the marginal lending facility will provide a ceiling for the overnight market interest rate.
- The deposit facility, which will allow credit institutions to make overnight deposits at a pre-specified interest rate with the NCBs. The interest rate on the deposit facility will provide a floor for the overnight market interest rate.

The two standing facilities will be administered in a decentralized manner by the NCBs, but the terms and conditions of the facilities will be set by the ECB and will be identical throughout the Euro area.

The ECB will make use of open-market operations for the purpose of steering interest rates. The main open-market operation will be the weekly repurchase agreement ('repo') with a maturity of two weeks undertaken through the participating NCBs in the form of fixed or variable rate tenders. The rate in these weekly operations is expected to be the ECB 'headline' interest rate. The ECB will decide on the terms and conditions for the execution of the open-market operations. The bids will be submitted to the NCBs. The bids will be aggregated, and allocation decisions taken and announced by the ECB, but the deals will be done and settled with the NCBs.

The ECB may require credit institutions to hold minimum reserves on accounts with the NCBs. Should the ECB decide to employ a minimum reserve system to stabilize money market interest rates, all relevant institutions established in the Euro area would be legally subject to it, even branches in the Euro area of institutions with no registered office in the Euro area. Moreover, the terms and conditions of the minimum reserve system would be uniform throughout the Euro area.

With respect to the question of centralization vs decentralization of monetary policy operations, the Delors Report (1989b) suggested two possible models: the so-called decentralized or three-tier model composed of the ECB, the NCBs and the commercial banks and the centralized or two-tier model which bypasses the NCBs in the execution of the monetary policy (see Gros and Thygesen 1992, Kenen 1992, Sardelis 1993). For example, in the three-tier model, the ECB tries to control money creation indirectly, by imposing reserve requirements on the NCBs. In the centralized or two-tier system, the ECB exerts direct influence on the assets of the commercial banks and thus on money creation; the ECB bypasses the NCBs.

In the decentralized system, the ECB seeks to control the area-wide money supply by imposing reserve requirements on the NCBs. Each participating NCB would hold a part of its assets in an account with the ECB. The size of the account can be entirely determined by changes in reserve requirements. Higher reserve requirements on NCBs would imply a monetary contraction. Moreover, in this system, open-market operations are executed by the NCBs.

In the centralized system, the ECB tries to control money creation directly at the source by imposing reserve requirements on commercial banks. The open-market operations in this case are to be executed by the ECB with NCBs only allowed to play a secondary role in this procedure by collecting, for example, the bids from the domestic bidders. Articles 18 and 19 of the ESCB Protocol are ambiguous enough to allow either scenario to be chosen. On the basis of the operational framework described above, the EMI is proposing a framework which is more in line with a centralized system, albeit one that respects the principle of decentralization to the extent that it does not reduce operational efficiency.

Single monetary policy: strategy

The EMI must also study the question of which, if any, intermediate target the ECB should use to achieve the final target of monetary policy, namely price stability. The choice of a monetary aggregate as an intermediate objective of monetary policy supposes a stable or predictable relationship between the growth of the money supply and inflation and that, in turn, requires a stable or predictable demand function for money (see Davis 1990 for a general discussion of these issues). In general, national demand functions for money are not temporally stable whereas EU-wide money-demand equations tend to have better statistical properties in this regard (see, for example, Kremers and Lane 1990). These results may have some implications for the choice of an intermediate monetary target for the ECB.

Currently, a variety of monetary strategies is used in individual Member States. Within the ERM, most countries use an indirect strategy. For example, the Deutsche Bundesbank uses a monetary aggregate (M3) as the intermediate target while the Banque de France simultaneously targets a monetary aggregate (M3) and an exchange rate as the intermediate targets. The Banco de España directly targets inflation, but does not have a target money growth rate; instead, it monitors a range for the growth rate of the liquid assets held by the public (ALP). European Union Member States outside the ERM make use of an intermediate target or a direct inflation target (see Table 4.5 and European Monetary Institute 1995a: 128–129).

The EMI must also decide on which short-term interest rate, the operational target, the ECB will focus to implement day-to-day monetary policy so that local interest rate differentials will not send ambiguous policy signals to the financial markets regarding monetary policy. The EMI (European Monetary Institute 1997a: 14) is proposing the following general strategy of monetary policy to the ECB:

- the public announcement of a quantified definition of the final objective of price stability;
- the public announcement of a specific target (or targets) against which the performance of the ECB can be assessed on an ongoing basis by the general public;

Table 4.5 Monetary policy strategies in EU Member States, 1996

Member State	Strategy	1996 Monetary target/ guideline, percentage*	Inflation target/ guideline, annual percentage
Belgium–Luxembourg	XR		
Denmark	XR		
Germany	MT (M3)	4–7	≤2 (medium term)
Greece	XR, MT (M3)	6–9	
Spain	IT, XR, ALP	<8[a]	<3 (for 1997)
France	XR, MT (M3)	5	≤2 (medium term)
Ireland	XR		
Italy	MT (M2)	5	<3 (for 1997)
Netherlands	XR		
Austria	XR		
Portugal	XR		
Finland	IT		2 ('permanently')
Sweden	IT		1–3 (medium term)
United Kingdom	IT, MT (M0, M4)	0–4; 3–9[b]	1–4[c] <2.5 beyond 1997

XR = Exchange rate target.
IT = Inflation target.
MT = Monetary target (aggregate shown in parentheses)
*annual percentage changes, fourth quarter–fourth quarter:
(a) Monitors ALP (liquid assets held by the public), first quarter of 1996
(b) Monitors variables M0 and M4, measured from March to March.
(c) Refers to the end of the current Parliament (April 1997 at the latest).
Source: European Monetary Institute (1995a: 33, 128; 1996a: 31; 1997b: 46)

- within the set of indicators employed by the ECB, monetary aggregates should be assigned a prominent role, provided that the money demand is sufficiently stable in the long run;
- although the ECB should use all available information relevant to the final target of monetary policy, exchange rate developments should constitute less of a concern than is currently the case for many NCBs.

Exchange rate policies of the monetary union

By the start of Stage III, the exchange rate policies of the Euro vis-à-vis non-Community currencies, such as the US dollar and Japanese yen, and vis-à-vis the currencies of the 'outs' have to be formulated and adopted. The latter policies will be embraced in an exchange rate system dubbed ERM2. The broad framework of ERM2 has been outlined by the Ecofin Council and the EMI (Council of the European Union 1996a, 1996b; Annex I.I of the Presidency Conclusions, Dublin European Council, 13 and 14 December 1996; EMI 1997a: Annex 9). The details will have to be adopted in 1998 in an agreement between the European Central Bank and the national central banks of the 'outs'. Membership in ERM2, as with its predecessor ERM1, will remain voluntary for the Member States outside the Euro area.

The Euro vis-à-vis the currencies of the 'outs': ERM2

During Stage III, each Member State outside the single currency zone must continue to treat its exchange rate policy against the Euro and the other EU currencies as a matter of common interest (Article 109M.2). To that end, the Cannes European Council meeting of June 1995 requested that the Commission examine the exchange rate consequences of a small number of hard-core Member States forming the initial single currency monetary zone in 1999 with, at the same time, a few large Member States remaining outside the monetary zone (read: the United Kingdom, Italy and Spain). To avoid jeopardizing the EU single market with 'competitive devaluations' by the Member States outside the single currency area during the transitional phase of Stage III, France and Germany proposed, with the endorsement of all the other Member States except the United Kingdom,[21] the establishment of an 'Exchange Rate Mechanism 2'. 'Competitive devaluation', a term often used by France and Belgium, refers to nominal exchange rate variations, which do not reflect purchasing power parity and which consequently occur at the expense of the country whose currency is 'revalued' in real terms.

The proposed new system linking the Euro to the currencies of the non-participating Member States would have the following characteristics:

- The new exchange rate mechanism (ERM2) would be based on central rates, with margins of fluctuation, of non-participating currencies against the Euro. A standard fluctuation band would be established for these currencies around their central rates. Like the post-July 1993 ERM1, the standard band is expected to be relatively wide. Central rates and the standard wide band would be set by mutual agreement between the ECB, the Finance Ministers of the Euro area Member States, and the Finance Ministers and Governors of the central banks of the non-Euro area Member States, excluding those not participating in ERM2.

- ERM2 could include a 'multi-speed' exchange rate mechanism for currencies outside the Euro area. Currencies of Member States deemed close to meeting the Maastricht criteria for EMU – the 'pre-ins' – could trade in relative narrow bands against the Euro.
- In general, the central rates and bands of ERM2 would only be defined against the Euro. Unlike ERM1, there would be no multilateral parity grid to defend. This would imply that the implicit exchange rate band defined between two 'out' currencies would be twice as large as the exchange rate band defined with respect to the Euro. In ERM2, the Euro is the 'hub' and the other 'out currencies' are the 'spokes'. However, if appropriate, non-Euro area Member States could establish, on a bilateral basis, fluctuation bands between their currencies and intervention arrangements, with the aim of narrowing the excessively large band between two 'out' currencies.
- Unlike the original provisions of the EMS, ERM2 would be asymmetrical, meaning that policy adjustments to stabilize currencies would be primarily undertaken by the 'outs' so as not to undermine the objective of the monetary policy of the single currency area. In other words, the Euro would be the anchor of the system. Although both central banks would be expected to intervene at the bilateral margins of the Euro exchange rate band, neither the ECB nor the central bank of an 'out' Member State participating in ERM2 would be required to continue to support a weak currency if such a policy were to undermine its price stability objective. This means, for example, that the ECB would not be liable to lend unlimited quantities of Euros for intervention purposes to any central bank of a Member State outside the single currency bloc participating in ERM2 whenever the weak edge of its currency band with respect to the Euro is reached. The Bundesbank insists that the intervention rules to maintain the parities should not compromise the price stability objective of the ECB. Whenever fundamentals, combined with market forces, seem to indicate that a realignment of an 'out' currency against the Euro is required, it should be done in a timely fashion, devoid of political considerations. In practical terms, the procedure to examine a change of the central parities should involve, in a confidential manner, the ECB, the other central banks, and the Commission. The decision to change and set new parities against the Euro would require,

in the final step, the unanimous agreement of the Ecofin Council, excluding the Ministers of the Member States not participating in ERM2.

- The General Council of the ECB would be responsible for administering the new multilateral fund established to manage the intervention required under ERM2. As provided by the Maastricht Treaty, the mechanism for the creation of official ECUs against gold and dollars provided under the original EMS Agreement is scheduled to be unwound on the first day of Stage III, along with the settlement of all claims and liabilities arising from the VSTF and STMS mechanisms. The VSTF facility would be continued, following some appropriate adjustments. The initial duration, as well as the rules for extending maturities of VSTF financing operations would be retained. However, financing balances would be denominated and settled in the creditor's currency. ERM1 rules governing access to the VSTF facility for intramarginal intervention would be broadly continued. The Short-Term Monetary Support (STMS) mechanism should be discontinued.

- In order to ensure exchange rate stability between the Euro and the currency of each Member State remaining outside the monetary union, the convergence process and procedures in the context of the broad economic policy guidelines of Article 103 will be reinforced. This could be accomplished by obtaining a higher degree of political commitment from Member States on the implementation of their respective programmes and by emphasizing country-specific recommendations in the broad economic policy guidelines adopted by the Council.

The Euro vis-à-vis the dollar and yen

The Ecofin Council composed of the Member States *participating* in the Euro area, with a recommendation from either the ECB or the Commission, is given the responsibility to formulate the exchange rate policy of the Euro against non-EU currencies. This policy must be taken with the full participation of, and agreement with, the ECB and must be consistent with the objective of price stability. Formal international agreements on an exchange rate system of the Euro require unanimity of the Ecofin Council composed of the participating Member States. Decisions to adjust the central rates of the Euro against non-EU currencies within the agreed-upon exchange rate system are taken by a qualified majority of the Ecofin Council composed of the participating Member States. In the absence of a formal exchange rate system of the Euro against non-EU currencies, the Ecofin Council, composed of the participating Member States, acts by a qualified majority to formulate general orientations for the exchange rate policy.

How the 'outs' join the 'ins'

The EMU section of the Maastricht Treaty does not assume that all Member States will satisfy the convergence criteria at the designated deadline to launch the monetary union. However, the general principle underlying the creation of a monetary union is that all the Member States are supposed to be on the road towards a monetary union while allowing 'multi-speed' tracks. Accordingly, those Member States that cannot (or do not wish to) enter the single monetary zone in the first wave must be assessed at least once every two years, or more frequently at their request, to determine whether they meet the Maastricht convergence criteria, which may not be modified for the second and subsequent wave of Member States. The inflation and long-term interest rate of a Member State outside the monetary zone are to converge on the inflation and long-term interest rate, respectively, prevailing in the monetary union. Although participation of the 'outs' in the future ERM2 is to be non-compulsory, exchange rate stability against the Euro will still be required in the two years prior to joining the monetary union. Then on the basis of the recommendations from the Commission, the ECB and the Ecofin Council, the Heads of State or Government of *all* Member States decide by a qualified majority to designate the Member State to join the monetary union. Finally, the Ecofin Council, after consulting the ECB and acting with the unanimity of the Member States already in the monetary union and the Member State concerned, adopts the rate at which the Euro shall be substituted for the currency of the Member State concerned.

EVALUATION OF THE MAASTRICHT PROCESS TOWARDS A MONETARY UNION

Whether the Maastricht rules governing fiscal rectitude on the part of the Member States and price stability of the monetary union as of Stage III are desirable depends on the benefits and costs of these two macroeconomic goals. These benefits and costs can be analysed with or without Maastricht and were discussed at the beginning of this chapter under the indirect benefits derived from the creation of a single currency area. The issues which are unique to Maastricht deal with the EMU transition scenario to a monetary union. Is the requirement that the nominal convergence criteria be met prior to entry into the monetary union necessary?

Box 4.3 The budget of the European Union

The European Union budget is composed of three envelopes: the General budget of the EC and Euratom, the European Development Fund (EDF) specifically intended to assist some seventy African,

Caribbean and Pacific countries which signed the Lomé Convention with the Union, and the European Coal and Steel Community (ECSC). In 1996, the total Union (EU15) budget expenditures of ECU84,548 million were broken down as follows (Commission 1995c):

	Percent
EDF	2.8
ECSC.	0.3
General budget	
Agriculture (the Guarantee Section of the European Agricultural Guidance and Guarantee Fund, EAGGF	48.8
Structural operations (the European Regional Development Fund, the European Social Fund, the Guidance Section of the EAGGF, the Cohesion Fund).	31.1
Research	3.7
Other Internal Policies (transport, education, culture, energy, environment, consumer protection, internal market and industry)	3.1
External action, other than EDF (contributions to the development of the Third World and to the economic reconstruction of the new democracies in Central and Eastern Europe)	5.4
Administration	4.8

Two-thirds of the expenditures of the Union budget is for tasks which the Member States would have to assume themselves if the Union were not there (agriculture, research, regional development, foreign aid).

The General budget of the European Union is financed by means of revenue which it receives as of right. The growth of these 'own resources' is limited by a ceiling set by the Member States at 1.20 percent and 1.27 percent of the Union's gross national product in 1994 and 1999, respectively. This revenue comprises customs duties and agricultural 'levies' which are charges collected on products imported from outside the Union (18.1 percent of total revenue in 1996). Added to this is an amount calculated by reference to the value-added tax (VAT) base determined in accordance with common rules (42.2 percent of total revenue) and a resource based on GNP, which is called the 'fourth resource'. Each of the Member States contributes to this fourth resource (39 percent of total revenue) according to its prosperity. The VAT and GNP resources come from the tax revenue of the Member States and are not collected directly by the Union from the taxpayer.

At the Edinburgh European Council meeting in December 1992, the Heads of State or Government agreed on a comprehensive package of measures for the financing of the European Community in the years 1993–99. The basis for these measures was formed by the proposals drawn up by the Commission immediately after the ceremonial signing of the Maastricht Treaty in February 1992 (Delors II package). In order to secure the resources needed to meet both new and existing commitments, the ceiling on the Community's own resources was raised. Until the end of 1992, the Community could claim up to 1.2 percent of the Community's GNP, compared to an average of 30 percent for the budget of Member States' national governments. Under the new financing plan, this figure remained unchanged until the end of 1994 but as from 1995 it is gradually raised to reach 1.27 percent in 1999. In 1996, the top four contributing Member States to the Community budget were: Germany which provided 30 percent of the revenues for the General budget; France, 17.7 percent; Italy, 12.3 percent and the United Kingdom, 10.8 percent. The Union budget financial flows to a Member State and from a Member State are in principle easy to measure. On that basis, Germany, as a percentage of its GDP, is the main net contributor to the Union budget, and Ireland, Portugal and Greece, as a percentage of each of their GDP, appear as the main net beneficiaries of the Union budget. In terms of total ECUs, the ranking of the *net* contributors are: Germany, Britain, the Netherlands, France, Sweden, Austria, Italy, Belgium, Finland and Luxembourg. The ranking for the *net* recipients are: Spain, Greece, Portugal, Ireland and Denmark. However, these figures do not reflect the redistributive effects of the Union budget and have been the subject of controversy (see Ardy 1988).

The Commission, the Council of Ministers, and the European Parliament are all involved in the adoption and execution of the General budget. Since 1975, the European Parliament (EP) and the Council share budgetary powers, with the EP having the right of two readings. The second reading is mainly concerned with the level of non-compulsory expenditure (compulsory expenditure relates to commitments derived from the internal and external obligations of the EU which are established by the EU Treaties or by secondary legislation adopted in accordance with the Treaties). Under the Treaty of Rome, the EU budget is circumscribed by a strict prohibition on borrowing and subsequent amendments have only served to relax the restriction on borrowing for a limited range of specific purposes – to support the balance of payments and to promote infrastructure investment within the EC.

If so, how should the convergence criteria, and in particular the fiscal consolidation requirements, be interpreted to determine whether a Member State has met them? Should real convergence criteria be considered before entry into the monetary union?

Why impose the nominal convergence criteria as a precondition to entry into the monetary union?

A fundamental criticism of the Maastricht process towards a monetary union is the requirement that each Member State must satisfy the nominal convergence criteria as a precondition for joining the monetary union. De Grauwe (1995) has argued that linking the start of the monetary union on fulfilling the Maastricht nominal convergence requirements is not necessary and risks splitting the European Union politically and economically. He suggests that all convergence requirements be dropped as preconditions, but that all the rules defined in the Treaty, such as the price stability objective of the European central bank and fiscal rectitude ratios be retained once the monetary union is launched. What is needed is an *institutional framework* that guarantees the process towards price stability and fiscal consolidation once the monetary union is established. Stage II can be abbreviated to a time period needed to prepare the technical and logistical work for the establishment of the European central bank. While De Grauwe accepts the argument that a country like Italy should reduce its government debt-to-GDP ratio, the goal becomes more difficult to achieve outside the monetary union. Countries outside the monetary union have to keep their real interest rates higher than those inside it because of the risk of devaluation. This increases the debt burden and makes it harder to reduce the budget deficit. Moreover, dividing the European Union between the 'ins' and 'outs' may reverse the process towards economic integration to the extent that increased volatility between the Euro and the currencies of the 'outs' may reduce trade and investment flows.

The usual arguments in favour of satisfying the Maastricht nominal convergence criteria as a pre-condition to entry into the monetary union are as follows:

● Since these criteria will be 'de rigueur' for the monetary union, the authorities and general public of Member States must pass an 'entrance exam' to determine whether they have understood, acquired and accepted the proper 'culture' of monetary and fiscal stability. The rationale of this argument is based on the premise that a successful monetary union must be composed of partners that have converged in terms of 'economic culture'. There must not be fundamental differences between the Member States of a monetary union in their views regarding monetary and fiscal stability.

- One or two large countries entering the monetary union without having met the convergence criteria may create turmoil on the financial markets. This explanation is often put forward by Germany, arguing that a significant portfolio shift from Deutsche mark-denominated assets to non-EU denominated assets may raise the interest rate for the new monetary union. The new Euro-denominated assets may require a higher interest rate to cover for the risk premium perceived by the financial markets. To avoid this possibility, the new single currency must be perceived as 'hard' as the Deutsche mark. For this to occur, the participating Member States must have satisfied the nominal convergence criteria *before* entering the single currency area.
- The convergence criteria are required as pre-conditions to entering the monetary union to preclude an 'end-game problem'. An end-game problem occurs whenever the participants in a given institutional regime have an incentive to change their relative position (income or wealth) just before the pre-announced date of the change-over to a new institutional regime (Fratianni *et al.* 1992). A country that knows that it will be part of a monetary union at some later date may have an incentive to increase its money supply for one last time just prior to entry into the monetary union. An immediate devaluation of its currency may occur just before the fixing of the irrevocable and irreversible exchange rates vis-à-vis its partners and thus gain a competitive advantage over its partners since future inflation will no longer be determined by national policies. This type of end-game problem is virtually eliminated by the EMU provisions of the Maastricht Treaty, which requires, as a pre-condition to entry, an inflation rate converging to the inflation rate of the Member State with the lowest rate (or to the inflation rate of the average of the three Member States with the lowest rates) and exchange rate stability.

Are the nominal convergence criteria reasonably defined?

The formal inflation convergence criterion, defined as a maximum inflation differential of 1.5 percentage points between the inflation reference value and the inflation rate of any Member State, implies a convergence of monetary policies between the Member States that are candidates for the monetary union. The convergence must be towards the best, or at most, the average of the three best-performing Member States in terms of price stability. The 1.5 percentage point difference in inflation rates allows some leeway for the differential impact that the same monetary policy may have on the inflation rates in two different countries.

This criterion, coupled with the formal condition that a Member State's long-term nominal interest rate must converge, with a maximum 2 percentage point difference, towards the interest rate of the same best, or at most, the average interest rate of the same three best-performing

Member States in terms of price stability (hereafter referred to as 'the best Member State'), implies that the financial markets must perceive, as of the start of 1997, stability of the exchange rate of the Member State's currency with respect to the currency of the 'best Member State'. Otherwise, the spread between long-term nominal interest rates would not converge. According to standard economic theory for two open economies, the nominal interest rate spread between the two countries reflect the *expected* inflation spread plus a risk premium. Since, in the final run-up to the creation of the initial monetary union, the *expected* inflation spread between the two countries is effectively zero with the future implementation of a single monetary policy, the maximum two percentage point spread of nominal interest rates reflects the maximum potential exchange rate risk premium in the final run-up to the start of the monetary union, at which time the irreversible conversion rates are set for the currencies forming the monetary union.

The Maastricht criterion, drafted in 1991, that a Member State's currency must have participated in the narrow ±2.25 percent fluctuation band, with no severe tensions and no 'own initiative' devaluation in the previous two years, was to be an additional and explicit indicator of exchange rate stability for the prospective candidate to the monetary union. In light of the widening of the ERM bands of August 1993 and of a recommendation made by the EMI in 1994 to maintain the wide bands, it appears that the Ecofin Council will not strictly apply the two-year requirement of membership in the ERM to satisfy the entrance requirements to the monetary union. Instead, the Council will use the former ERM narrow fluctuation band against the Deutsche mark, over some undefined previous period of time, as a measure of exchange rate stability. Moreover, the nominal exchange rate stability condition is in general redundant with the combination of the interest rate convergence condition, inflation rate convergence condition and the fiscal consolidation condition.

Public finance criteria

The Maastricht public finance criteria are considered to be the Achilles' heel in the transition path to the monetary union. If the monetary union is postponed or abandoned, the non-fulfilment of these criteria will be invoked. Since the Treaty allows a strict or flexible interpretation of the deficit and debt ratios to satisfy the 'entrance requirements' to the single currency area, the final interpretation given by the Heads of State or Government of the public finance criteria will determine whether the monetary union is launched in 1999 and which Member States compose the initial monetary union. The final interpretation of these criteria must also be taken with the realization that if the public finance criteria are too diluted, the Bundestag has the power to prevent Germany from participating in the single currency area.

On the basis of the comments made by German officials, Germany is insisting that a strict interpretation of the Maastricht public finance ratios must be taken in early 1998 to designate the participating Member States of the initial monetary union.[22] This German strategy in the run-up to the creation of the single currency area serves two purposes. First, it provides incentives to countries like Germany, France, Belgium, the Netherlands and Austria, which do not strictly qualify on the basis of projected public finance data but which are nonetheless realistic candidates for the first wave of countries to form a monetary union, to make the necessary efforts to meet the public finance requirements of the Treaty. Secondly, it reassures the German public that the Maastricht convergence criteria are not just an 'irgendeine idée' without any real meaning. It provides reassurances to the Germans that they will not be replacing a strong DM with a weak Euro. This, in turn, provides to the German government the public support necessary to keep the Maastricht EMU project on track.

Economic arguments in favour of a flexible interpretation of the public finance criteria

As indicated at the beginning of this chapter, the major argument against a persistent public deficit is that it crowds out private productive investment with the negative, long-run macroeconomic welfare consequences on the level of capital stock in the long run. The Ricardian equivalence theorem[23] suggests the relevant variable to consider is the national saving ratio. A country with a high public deficit ratio combined with a high private saving ratio does not suffer the usual negative welfare consequences of a persistent public deficit. Dissaving by the public sector is offset, one for one, by private saving, precluding the usual negative effects of persistent public deficits. It is usually argued that Italy, the country with one of the largest public deficit ratios, is also the one which generates one of the highest private saving relative to GDP. This type of consideration, not envisaged by the Maastricht Treaty, would suggest the need for a flexible interpretation of the 3 percent threshold for the public deficit ratio criterion.

A provision of the Treaty tries to take into account the welfare impact of public deficits on productive investment by assessing the size of the deficit relative to government investment expenditures: the assessment '. . . shall also take into account whether the government deficit exceeds government investment expenditure . . .' (Article 104C.3). Presumably, a deficit used to finance government investment expenditures is not the same as a deficit used to finance government consumption expenditures.

Moreover, the fiscal situation is partly determined by the business cycle position of the country. During a recession or a period of very slow growth, the public deficit ratio rises, which may distort the underlying tendency. Thus, the actual public deficit ratio should be interpreted in light of the structural one. The structural budget balance reflects what government revenues and expenditures would be if output was at its potential level. Assuming that structural estimates are reasonably reliable, one can use them to assess the nature and the extent of fiscal deterioration over a period of time. A Treaty provision permits the assessment of the public deficit ratio to take into account the difference between the cyclical and structural concepts (Article 104C.2a). Objections to the use of the structural deficit ratio could be made by arguing that its measurement is subject to arbitrariness since it depends on the estimate of the potential level of output.

A strict interpretation of the public debt ratio criterion is even more controversial than a strict interpretation of the public deficit ratio criterion. The former ratio combines a stock (the public debt) with a flow (GDP). At any point in time, the public debt ratio reflects more the past history of the public deficit than its current and future evolution. Starting from a given debt/GDP ratio, convergence towards a lower ratio depends upon the relationship among the primary budget balance ratio, the real rate of interest and real growth rate of GDP (for details, see Box 4.2). In short, what matters more to attain a particular debt/GDP ratio is determined not by past fiscal history, but by the current and future deficit/surplus flow path, along with the GDP growth path and real interest rates. The Treaty allows these considerations to be taken into account when examining the debt-to-GDP ratio of a Member State. A Member State may have a debt-to-GDP ratio above the 60 percent threshold provided that '... the ratio ... is sufficiently diminishing and approaching the reference value at a satisfactory pace' (Article 104C.2b). Ireland is a case in point. With a 1993 ratio of 97.3 percent, which was estimated to decline to 81.3 and 77.3 percent in 1996 and 1997, respectively, the Council decided in mid-1996 that the ratio was diminishing and approaching the reference value at a satisfactory pace. Denmark is another case in point. With a 1993 public debt/GDP ratio of 80.1 percent, which was estimated to decline to 71.0 and 66.7 percent in 1996 and 1997, respectively, and with a public deficit ratio of 1.4 percent in 1995, the Council decided in mid-1996 that Denmark satisfied the Maastricht public finance ratios. It is clear from these two examples that the Council will use a flexible interpretation of the debt/GDP threshold ratio to assess in early 1998 the Member States which meet that criterion. In this context, Belgium will be the most problematic Member State for the Heads of State or Government in early 1998 when they meet to designate the Member States that will compose the initial monetary union. All indications point to the fact that Belgium will not even satisfy a flexible interpretation of the public finance ratios, with a 138 percent debt/GDP ratio in 1993 expected to decline to only 127 percent by 1997. This is by far the highest ratio of any Member State, including Italy and Greece, which is not even considered for membership in the first wave of Member States participating in a monetary union. Yet Belgium is closely associated with Luxembourg and the Netherlands by virtue of the Belgo-Luxembourg Economic Union (BLEU), signed in 1921 and renewed every decade since 1971, and the Benelux regional union, signed in 1948 and included a monetary union as one of its objectives. Moreover, since the early 1990s, Belgium has attempted to maintain its currency in a very narrow band against the Deutsche mark, even in the face of the widened ERM band. It would be difficult to allow the Netherlands and Luxembourg into the monetary union without the third leg of the historical tripod. In the final analysis, the European Council could appeal to Article 233 of the Treaty of Rome, which specifically recognizes the existence of the regional union of Belgium–Netherlands–Luxembourg.

Real convergence

The convergence criteria that Member States are expected to meet before entering into the monetary union are nominal macroeconomic indicators related to monetary stability, such as a low inflation rate determined by the (three) best-performing Member State(s), a sustainable public debt–GDP ratio either not exceeding or approaching a specific ceiling, and nominal exchange rate stability. The convergence criteria do not deal with the issue of real macroeconomic variables such as the convergence towards an 'equilibrium' real exchange rate before the formation of a monetary union.[24] If two Member States A and B, with complete economic and financial integration in the goods, services and capital markets, have satisfied all the nominal convergence criteria, but State A has an unemployment rate which is twice the unemployment rate of State B, one could reasonably argue that States A and B should not irrevocably lock their nominal exchange rate. If relative real unit labour costs are not flexible or labour is not mobile between the two Member States, or both, the difference in unemployment rates will persist with a single currency and a single monetary policy combined with binding fiscal policy rules. Although real wages (total of direct and non-wage cost of labour) differ between Member States – with Portugal, Greece and Spain at the low end of the spectrum and Germany, Belgium and the Netherlands at the high end – real wages in the EU tend to be very sticky compared with the US case (Emerson *et al.* 1990). Under these circumstances, the irrevocably fixed nominal exchange rate between the two countries is not an equilibrium real exchange rate.

For the Member States which constitute the probable, first-wave candidates for the monetary union, the problem is not so much the differences in unemployment rates between those Member States as the generally high rate of unemployment. With the exception of Luxembourg (2.9 percent forecast for 1997), Austria (5.1 percent) and the Netherlands (7.0 percent), the 1997 unemployment rates for those Member States forecast by the

Commission are close to or above double-digit values: Belgium, 9.8 percent; Germany, 9.4 percent; France, 11.7 percent; Ireland, 12.8 percent; and Finland, 15 percent. France and Germany, who both constitute the core of the future monetary union, highlight the problem in the EU. These two countries have converging unemployment rates, albeit towards a high level. The arguments that real wages in France are too high for full employment and that a devaluation of the French franc is a way to reduce those high real wages also apply to Germany. A devaluation of the French franc against the Deutsche mark would be considered a 'beggar-thy-neighbour' solution to the unemployment problems of France.

The Commission and the Council believe that the persistent high rates of unemployment in Europe are due to long-run structural labour market problems, which cannot be solved by macroeconomic policies which deviate from the Maastricht nominal convergence criteria. Such a strategy would only be a short-run solution to a long-run structural problem, which requires labour market reforms (see Box 4.1) and policies to reinforce the competitiveness of small and medium-size enterprises as a potentially important sector for generating growth and employment opportunities.

5   From the ECU to the Euro[1]

INTRODUCTION

From 1979 to the start of the monetary union, when the official ECU will disappear on the first day of Stage III, a distinction is made between the *official* and the *private* ECU. The status and functions of the official ECU are derived from Community legal texts, including the Treaty on European Union. The official ECU is primarily used as the numéraire for debit and credit operations and as a settlement reserve asset – which is only a mirror image of dollar and gold reserve assets – between central banks of the EU and the European Monetary Cooperation Fund in connection with marginal and intramarginal ERM interventions. The status and functions of the private ECU are primarily derived from private contracts between parties who use the ECU as a financial or commercial instrument, such as a loan, bank deposit, bond or invoice denominated and perhaps even settled in private ECUs. Some of these parties may be sovereign governments or international institutions that issue ECU bonds to the private sector. With the decision to launch an economic and monetary union with a single currency, Community institutions and some national governments have made an effort to encourage the use of the private ECU.

This chapter examines some aspects of the official ECU and the private ECU, as well as the changeover scenario to the single currency, the Euro.

THE OFFICIAL ECU

Prior to the coming into force of the Treaty on European Union on 1 November 1993, the official ECU had a legal status derived from various Community texts which essentially gave it its official functions as a *unit of account* and *an official monetary asset*. The principle references[2] in this regard are:

- Paragraph 2.1 of the European Council Resolution of 5 December 1978 on the establishment of the European Monetary System, which states that the EMS will have at its centre a currency unit, the ECU, which, at the outset, will be identical in value and composition with the European Unit of Account (EUA),[3] created on 21 April 1975 under the Lomé Convention (Lomé Convention 250/75/EEC).

- Paragraph 2.2 of the same European Council Resolution, which states that the ECU is the numéraire for the Exchange Rate Mechanism in order to define an ECU central rate for each currency and to define the divergence indicator, as explained in Chapter 2.
- Council Regulations (EEC) Nos. 3180/78 and 3181/78 of 18 December 1978, which change the unit of account used by the European Monetary Cooperation Fund (EMCF) and create an official reserve asset of ECU from dollars and gold. The definition of the new unit of account was adjusted twice: once in 1984 and once in 1989 (Council Regulations 2626/84/EEC and 1971/89/EEC). The official ECU accounts may be used as a means of settlement between the monetary authorities of the Community under the Very Short-Term Financing facility of the EMCF, as explained in Chapter 2.
- The Single European Act (1986), which enshrines for the first time in a Community treaty (Article 102A) a *reference* to the ECU. It becomes a part of the 'acquis communautaire'.

The Treaty on European Union changes the status of the official ECU to the extent that the composition of the basket of currencies defining an official ECU is frozen (Article 109G) on the basis of the last modification made in September 1989. Accordingly, the *legal definition* of an official ECU is now entrenched in a Community treaty, not in a Council regulation. Article 109G removes some of the uncertainty with respect to the legal nature and composition of the official ECU, which may no longer be changed.

Prior to the coming into force of the Maastricht Treaty, the ECU basket was open. Its currency composition could be changed in order to introduce the currency of a new Member State and/or to adjust the weight of two or more currencies in the ECU basket (see Chapter 2). Although changing the currency composition of the ECU basket does not by itself change the value of the ECU basket on the day of the change of the composition of the basket, reducing the weight of strong currencies and increasing the weight of weak currencies in the basket, as was always the case, means that the value of an open ECU basket will evolve differently over time from a closed ECU basket. In the latter basket, the market is guaranteed that the currency that is revalued (devalued) has an increasing (decreasing) weight in the basket. The freezing of the composition of the ECU basket will result in a gradual hardening of the ECU during the convergence period of Stage II since the weights of the devalued currencies decrease and those of the revalued currencies rise.

On the first day of Stage III, the official ECU will have again a change of status. The official ECU, hitherto defined as a closed basket of twelve currencies, disappears. The mechanism for the creation of ECUs against gold and US dollars is unwound. All the claims and liabilities arising from the VSTF and STMS facilities are settled. The Euro, defined as a currency (unit of account, medium of exchange, monetary asset) in its own right, issued by the European Central Bank and whose value will no longer be based on a weighted average of twelve currencies, appears. Of course, there will be a legal and economic continuity in the transition from the official ECU to the Euro, the single currency of the monetary union. This continuity is guaranteed by official declarations made at the Ecofin Council meeting of 27 November 1995 and at the Madrid European Council meeting of December 1995. Since then, these declarations, which guarantee that one official ECU is to be exchanged for one Euro (1:1 conversion rate), have been introduced in legal Community texts (see below). By extension, any private contract (asset or liability) denominated in ECUs and based on the official definition of an ECU, will be guaranteed a 'nominal continuity' with the Euro.

THE PRIVATE ECU

The use of the private ECU may be enhanced or diminished by virtue of the legal framework in which it operates. This is determined by Community and/or national laws (see Box 5.1). In some Member States (Germany, Greece, Ireland, Luxembourg), the fact that courts cannot use the ECU in their judgments places the private ECU at a disadvantage relative to the national currency. In Germany, the private ECU is not even legally considered a foreign currency or an instrument of legal payment, conditions which make it extremely difficult, if not impossible, to develop the use of the private ECU. In France and the Netherlands, prices may not be displayed in a foreign currency, which includes the ECU. A list of all the legal obstacles to the use of the private ECU in each Member State is found in a Commission White Paper presented to the Council (Commission of the European Communities 1992), with updates in Vissol (1994). France is an example of a Member State that has recently tried to enhance the legal status of the private ECU. On 16 July 1992, France adopted a law which allows all 'obligations' in the sense of the Civil Code to be drawn and paid in ECU if the private contracting parties agree. More importantly, such contracts will be enforced by the French legal system (Moulin 1992). France, as well as the United Kingdom and Italy, has also tried to remove uncertainty regarding the continuity of ECU-denominated debt in the period leading up to the introduction of the future single currency, the Euro. The French Treasury announced in late 1995 that a one-to-one continuity vis-à-vis the future single currency (Euro) would apply to its outstanding and future ECU-denominated government securities. This measure should encourage investors to hold sovereign ECU-denominated debt of France. The United Kingdom and Italy ('Decreti ministeriali' re CTEs) took similar measures. Moreover,

Box 5.1 The current status of the private ECU in Member States

Austria: ECU is recognized legally as a 'freely convertible foreign currency' since 26 June 1986 (administrative measure of the Oester-reichischen Nationalbank).

Belgium: ECU is recognized legally as a foreign currency since March 1982 (administrative measure); official quotation on the foreign exchange market as of 3 September 1984.

Denmark: ECU is recognized *de facto* as a foreign currency; official quotation on the foreign exchange market as of 17 March 1984.

Finland: ECU is recognized legally as a foreign currency since 1987; official quotation on foreign exchange market since 1987.

France: ECU is recognized legally as a foreign currency since 21 May 1982 (administrative measure); official quotation on the foreign exchange market since 4 June 1984.

Germany: ECU, according to interpretation of Monetary Law of 1948, is recognized legally only as a unit of account, notwithstanding Bundesbank Communication No. 1002/90 that provides the necessary authorization for a number of commitments to be denominated either in ECU or in SDR.

Greece: ECU is legally recognized as a foreign currency since 14 July 1984 (administrative measure); before that date, it was recognized *de facto* as a foreign currency; official quotation on the foreign exchange market since 24 January 1983.

Ireland: ECU is recognized *de facto* as a foreign currency.

Italy: ECU is recognized legally as a foreign currency since 17 July 1981 (ministerial decree); official quotation on foreign exchange market since May 1984; before that, the ECU theoretical exchange rate was officially calculated.

Luxembourg: same as Belgium.

Netherlands: ECU is recognized *de facto* as a foreign currency; official quotation on foreign exchange market since 5 July 1985.

Portugal: ECU is recognized legally as a foreign currency since 1990 (government order).

Spain: ECU is recognized legally as a foreign currency since 1987 (administrative measure).

Sweden: ECU is recognized *de facto* as a foreign currency.

UK: ECU is recognized *de facto* as a foreign currency.

since 1996 the Banque de France accepts ECU-denominated commercial paper as collateral for its open-market operations. In Germany, the Frankfurter Wertpapierbörse introduced in 1994 the quotation of ECU bonds and settlement in ECUs via special accounts in three German commercial banks. Heretofore, ECU bonds had to be quoted and settled in Deutsche marks.

To enhance the status of the private ECU, the Commission, soon after Stage II began, adopted a Recommendation and an Explanatory Note. They are as follows:

- Recommendation (94/284/EC, 19 April 1994) 'concerning the legal treatment of the ECU and of contracts denominated in ECU in view of the introduction of the single European currency'. This recommendation has two parts. The first part aims at removing the legal obstacles to the use of the private ECU in each Member State and at strengthening the legal protection of the ECU during Stage II. This means, *inter alia*, that in all Member States the ECU should be given the legal status of a foreign currency, and not of a mere unit of account, without any discrimination vis-à-vis the other foreign currencies. The second part of the Recommendation deals with the continuity of contracts denominated in ECUs. In order to reduce uncertainty, the Commission also recommends to private parties that all references to the ECU in contracts, in whatever form (ECU, écu, E.C.U. or other), should be clearly indicated as references to the ECU as defined in the Treaty, namely to a closed basket of twelve currencies.
- 'An explanatory note concerning new clauses in the prospectuses of loans and bonds of the European Communities'. The note deals with two sorts of different clauses. In bond and loan documentation which are denominated in one or more currencies of the Member States, a 'monetary union' clause is inserted. This clause anticipates the replacing of the currency of contract by the new single currency. At that point in time, payment of principal and interest can be legally effected in Euro. Consequently, the replacement of the currency of contract cannot be considered as a breach of contract, nor can it result in changes to the terms and conditions of the loan or bond documentation, such as the coupon interest rate. In contracts denominated in ECU, the clauses defining the value of the ECU are slightly modified. First, reference is made to the freezing of the currency composition of the ECU and the fixing of its value against participating currencies at the starting date of Stage III. Secondly, a new paragraph is inserted in the bond and loan documentation guaranteeing the continuity of the payment obligations in ECU throughout the process leading to the monetary union. Although the scope of the note is limited to loans and bonds involving the European Community itself as lender or borrower, it is clear that the Commission wishes to give an example to the parties in private transactions.

Retail use of the private ECU

Since the creation of the official ECU in 1979, the use of the private ECU at the retail level has been practically non-existent. The single most important reason is the lack of ECU notes and coins (fiat money) that are necessary to develop a retail medium of exchange. As no sovereign state or central bank issues ECUs (recalling that even official ECUs 'created' by the EMCF, or the EMI since 1994, are only temporary swaps of gold and dollars), there is no country where the ECU is legal tender, which partly explains the absence of ECU notes and coins. Although private ECU chequing accounts may be obtained from certain banks in all Member States, except Germany and Greece, so far these cheques are not accepted in national clearing systems alongside cheques denominated in national currencies. This increases the transaction cost of using ECU cheques at the retail level. For cross-border retail payments, Eurocheque SA, a private organization, started in January 1991 clearing ECU Eurocheques at the same cost and with the same guarantees as the other Eurocheques it handles. Visa issues a card, backed by an ECU account, which can be used to settle ECU denominated bills.

Financial use of the private ECU

The private ECU exists in the form of *financial* instruments, such as commercial paper, medium-term notes, public and private bonds, derivatives (ECU currency swaps, ECU interest rate futures and options), commercial bank loans, interbank deposits and foreign exchange contracts (spot and forward). The total stock of the financial instruments outstanding, excluding the foreign exchange and derivative markets, almost doubled from 1989 to 1992 (Table 5.1). From the peak reached in September 1992 of nearly ECU200,000 million, the estimated overall size of the ECU financial markets declined by 13 percent for the period ending September 1995. This, in part, is a consequence of uncertainty over aspects of EMU, created by the 1992–93 ERM turmoil and by the legal issues surrounding the conversion of ECU private contracts once the official ECU disappears.

This private ECU financial market is a vast, world-wide market on which primary and secondary ECU financial instruments are traded. It also includes ECU transactions on the foreign exchange markets and on organized derivative markets (Table 5.1). Spot and forward ECUs are traded against all major currencies on foreign exchange markets. Supply and demand determine the *market* ECU exchange rate (see Box 5.2). In 1993, the average daily turnover of the ECU against other currencies was approximately ECU40,000 million. The MATIF (Marché à Terme International de France) in Paris trades ECU Long Interest Rate Futures, introduced in October 1990, and corresponding ECU bond options, introduced in

Table 5.1 ECU financial markets (amounts outstanding at end-period in thousand million ECUs)

	1989	1991 Q3	1992 Q3	1993 Q3	1994 Q3	1995 Q3
Bonds, of which	65.2	111.4	130.3	124.5	125.4	119.1
● international		72.3	86.3	78.2	69.1	62.5
● domestic		39.1	44.0	46.3	56.3	56.6
(National) Treasury bills	6.7	7.9	6.9	8.3	4.7	3.5
Commercial paper and notes	4.0	9.5	8.6	6.5	6.4	8.2
Estimated bank lending[a]	39.9	60.7	67.5	66.6	59.9	56.9
Estimated total market size[b]	100.8	169.5	193.3	185.9	176.4	167.7
Bank assets,[c] of which:	124.1	175.7	198.0	196.0	178.3	163.6
● vis-à-vis non-banks	31.2	46.1	61.6	61.0	55.5	52.0
Bank liabilities,[d] of which:	112.1	180.9	200.7	191.9	175.0	157.6
● vis-à-vis non-banks	14.4	28.7	34.9	30.9	27.1	23.2
Memorandum item: Central banks' holdings of private ECUs[e]	17.0	28.8	18.9	19.1	24.0	23.5
Foreign exchange market[f]	4.0	n.a.	n.a.	40.0	n.a.	n.a.
Derivatives (outstanding contracts)						
● MATIF	—	6,837	19,866	13,183	8,592	8,406
● LIFFE	904	4,615	10,329	26,590	27,628	19,997

Notes:
(a) Final lending and lending to banks outside the BIS reporting area.
(b) ECU15,000 million are deducted in 1989 and ECU20,000 million are deducted in all other years for estimated double counting. There is an overlap between the securities and banking markets owing to the role of banks as issuers and holders of ECU securities.
(c) Mainly loans but also holdings of securities.
(d) Mainly deposits but also securities issued by banks.
(e) Held primarily to service governments' ECU-denominated debt.
(f) Average daily turnover.
Source: EMI (1996b: 3) and BIS.

1991; the LIFFE (London International Financial Futures and Options Exchange) in London trades ECU Three-Month Interest Rate Futures, introduced in October 1989. In January 1986, FINEX in New York began trading ECU/US$ Exchange Rate Futures. Trading on this exchange was suspended at the beginning of 1993. The European Option Exchange (Amsterdam) and the Philadelphia Stock Exchange trade options on the spot ECU/US$ exchange rate since December 1985 and February 1986, respectively. A good indicator of the growth of the ECU financial market is given by the average daily turnover of ECU clearing operations via the Ecu Banking Association (EBA) clearing system since most ECU transactions (financial and commercial) go through this system. In 1989, the value of these transactions was ECU21,200 million per day. By 1995, it was ECU46,800 million per day (European Monetary Institute 1996b).

Box 5.2 Private ECU terminology

(Market) ECU is a unit of account/medium of exchange/store of value, equivalent to a 'bundle' of the twelve currencies *tied together* in the quantities defined in the official ECU. The market ECU is traded and exchanged as a single unit (one 'bundle').

Theoretical ECU is a basket (portfolio) composed of the twelve currencies in the amounts defined in the official ECU. This is also referred to as the 'synthetic ECU'.

(Market) ECU exchange rate is the market-determined value of the ECU against a particular currency. Since the mid-1980s, the private ECU is traded on the spot and forward foreign exchange markets against all major currencies, with an average daily turnover of 40,000 million ECUs in 1993.

Theoretical ECU exchange rate is the *calculated* exchange rate of the theoretical ECU, using the same methodology as the one applied by the Commission and described in Chapter 2.

Difference between market and theoretical exchange rates of the ECU: If the *market ECU exchange rate* (relative to any currency) deviates significantly from its *theoretical ECU exchange rate*, arbitrage takes place. Arbitragists would take positions in the private ECU against a basket of component currencies so as to profit from the elimination of large differences. Suppose, for example, that the market ECU trades at a significant discount relative to its 'synthetic' rate. Then, to profit from this situation, the arbitragists would 'create' market ECUs by tying together the twelve component currencies. The behaviour of these 'basket makers' would eventually eliminate the discount on the market ECU.

However, if the risk of holding a market ECU is greater than the risk of holding a basket of the twelve currencies defining an ECU, then a significant gap may appear between the market ECU exchange rate and the theoretical ECU exchange rate without triggering arbitrage operations. This was the case, for example, during the 1992–93 period of the ERM turmoil. In September 1992, the negative spread between the ECU market exchange rate and the ECU theoretical exchange rate reached 200 basis points (see graph 5.2 in box 5.3). This means that the ECU was trading against the US dollar at a 2 percent discount relative to its theoretical exchange rate against the US dollar. After returning to a level close to zero, in July 1993 the negative spread reached 160 basis points. Throughout 1994, the divergence remained in the range of ±20 basis points. However, from April

1995 onwards, the negative spread widened markedly and durably to reach 250 basis points in late 1995 and 300 basis points in early 1996 (see graph 5.1 below). Several factors, such as liquidity risk of the market ECU, may explain the emergence of the negative exchange rate spread. One of them appears to have been the uncertainty among market participants about the EMU process and the continuity of contracts denominated in ECUs, which led to increased perceptions of risk in holding private market ECUs. By the fourth quarter of 1996, the legal clarification of the continuity of ECU-denominated contracts resulted in the return to the usual 20 basis points divergence between the market ECU and the theoretical ECU exchange rates.

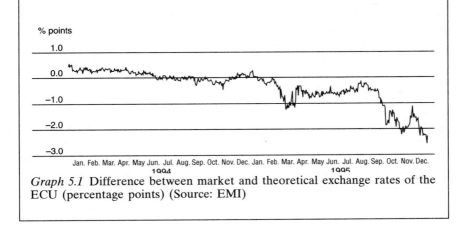

Graph 5.1 Difference between market and theoretical exchange rates of the ECU (percentage points) (Source: EMI)

Issuers and types of ECU securities

There are three principal categories of issuers of ECU-denominated securities, namely *supranational*, *sovereign* and *private* issuers, which may be decomposed as follows:

- international and supranational institutions and organizations such as EU institutions (European Investment Bank, European Coal and Steel Community, EURATOM, European Community), the World Bank, the Council of Europe and specialized institutions of the United Nations;
- EU Member States such as the United Kingdom, Italy, France, Greece, Portugal and Spain;
- non-EU States such as New Zealand;
- the private sector composed of EU and non-EU private borrowers such as commercial banks (Bayerische Hypobank) and private companies (General Electric).

are two types of long-term ECU bonds: the *domestic bond* and the
ional bond. The domestic bond[4] is only issued in the national
. of the borrower and subject to the regulations of that state. The
international bond is issued simultaneously in a number of countries (not
restricted to European states) and is subject to a far lesser degree of
regulation than the domestic bond. The ECU-denominated international
bonds represented 0.5, 4.8, 6.7 and 0.9 percent of all the gross new international bonds issued in 1981, 1985, 1992 and 1995, respectively (Bank
for International Settlements 1994b; European Monetary Institute 1996b).
The outstanding amounts of ECU-denominated international bonds at
the end of 1995 was ECU60,100 million, which represented 3.6 percent
of the stock of all international bonds. This placed the ECU international
bond in seventh position, behind the US dollar, the Japanese yen, the
Deutsche mark, the Swiss franc, the pound sterling and the French
franc. The ECU international bonds do not include ECU-denominated
bonds issued by the governments of France, Italy, Spain, Greece (ECU-
linked), the United Kingdom and Portugal. These bonds are designated
as 'domestic (sovereign) ECU bond' issues. Following are the principal
domestic (sovereign) ECU securities (bonds, notes and bills):

- *UK T-Notes:* three-year Treasury Notes, introduced in 1992.
- *UK T-Bills*: Treasury bills with maturities of one, three and six months,
  introduced in October 1987. The stocks outstanding at the end of 1989
  and at the end of April 1995 were ECU2,800 million and ECU3,498
  million, respectively.
- *Italian Treasury Certificates (CTEs):* Treasury certificates with maturities ranging from four to eight years, introduced in 1982. The very first
  public ECU bond issue was by the Italian telecommunications state
  corporation (STET) in March 1981, in the amount of ECU35 million.
- *Italian BTEs:* one-year Treasury Bills, introduced in October 1987. The
  amounts outstanding decreased from ECU7,400 million at the end of
  1989 to ECU3,100 million at the end of March 1994 and to zero thereafter, as CTEs replaced BTEs.
- *French Fungible Treasury Bonds (OATs):* fungible Treasury Bonds with
  maturities ranging from five to thirty years, introduced in 1989, and
  financing 15 percent of French public deficit. A fungible bond is a bond
  not individually designated by a serial number as belonging to a particular owner. The owner has title to, say, ten bonds of a particular issue,
  but not to ten specific bonds with designated serial numbers.
- *French BTFs*: short-term Treasury bills, introduced in 1996.
- *Greek ECU-linked Bonds (ELBs)*: ECU-linked Bonds with maturities
  ranging from one to five years, introduced in 1986 and temporarily
  discontinued in 1995.

Among the total new ECU domestic bonds issued in 1995, around 80
percent were issued by governments in their respective domestic capital

markets. At the end of 1995, the largest outstanding amount of ECU domestic bonds (public and private issuers) was in France with ECU24,900 million, followed by Italy with ECU24,000 million and the UK with ECU6,500 million.

ECU-denominated bank loans and deposits

Commercial banks grant loans and, to a lesser extent, open deposits denominated in ECUs. Although Belgian–Luxembourg banks were the first to do so in response to a demand by EC institutions to open ECU-denominated bank accounts, these operations are now done by banks throughout the world but still primarily concentrated in Member States of the European Union. The first negotiable ECU certificate of deposit (a type of bank deposit) was issued by Lloyds Bank on 25 February 1981. By 1992, this market was estimated at ECU6,000 to ECU7,000 million. In 1990, the ECU accounted for over 8 percent of new bank loans to non-financial companies, compared with just 0.3 percent in 1982. Outstanding bank loans denominated in ECUs to non-financial companies jumped from ECU27,000 million at the end of 1988 to ECU52,000 million in 1995. Syndicated ECU bank loans have maturities from five to ten years.

Another development of some significance in the private ECU market is the growth since 1987 of ECU deposits held by central banks in commercial banks. European central banks have been placing part of their reserves in the form of private ECUs to carry out transactions with respect to government debt issued in ECUs. Scandinavian central banks (Norway, Sweden and Finland), which until 1992 had tied their currencies to the ECU, used their private ECU balances to intervene directly with ECUs on the foreign exchange market. The Bank for International Settlements (1992: 20) estimates that ECU liabilities of commercial banks vis-à-vis official monetary institutions surged from ECU1,000 million at the end of 1987 to ECU30,000 million at the end of September 1991. By the end of the fourth quarter of 1995, these deposits had declined to ECU23,100 million (European Monetary Institute 1996b).

Commercial use of the private ECU

The use of the private ECU in cross-border, intra-EU commercial transactions is very limited. Moreover, the data are unreliable. In 1995, the use of the private ECU as a *commercial* instrument for cross-border settlement purposes was estimated to be in a range from a high of 1.6 percent of the total value of Portuguese exports (ECU285 million) to a low 0.2 percent of the total value of German exports (ECU750 million) (European Monetary Institute 1996b: table 8). The private ECU for commercial transactions is used mainly for intra-EU external transactions. The proportion of current account transactions denominated in ECU is higher than the numbers cited above. This is due in part to transfer payments made in ECUs by the EU in the framework of the Structural Funds and to private financial transfers (interest flows) linked to cross-border ECU-denominated assets and liabilities.

In an attempt to improve statistics on the commerical use of the ECU, the Commission launched in 1994 a survey, undertaken with the participation of fourteen Ecu Banking Association clearing banks from seven different countries, to estimate commercial ECU payments. These were estimated to be in the range of ECU50,000 to ECU75,000 million or approximately 6 to 11 percent of intra-EU trade between the twelve Member States. This is in sharp contrast to the estimates based on balance-of-payments data noted above, which for 1994 were estimated at ECU6,500 million or approximately 1 percent of intra-EU trade of the twelve Member States (Commission of the European Communities 1995d: 12; Vissol 1994).

Other commercial uses of the private ECU

Other uses of the private ECU in the commercial field are in intragroup settlements. Several multinationals record the transactions between their subsidiaries in ECUs. Price lists for intracompany transactions are fixed and netted in ECUs. Saint-Gobain (France) was the first multinational to have denominated its internal transactions in ECUs. Alcatel (France) has used the ECU for all internal settlements since 1990. The ECU is also used for clearing and settlements between different organizations that are part of the same clearing house, such as IATA and the European Railways. IATA has used the ECU for clearing payments between the different airline companies since July 1991. It claims that the ECU is stable and neutral, i.e. that none of the countries has an advantage above the others (see Commission of the European Communities 1993: 33). Finally, the ECU is used for accounting and reporting. In 1990, forty-seven different large companies in the European Union published their annual reports in ECUs, as well as in their own national currencies since most countries require compulsory accounts calculated in national currency. Avis (UK) produces its annual reports and accounts in ECUs, which simplifies comparisons of results between a number of countries by virtually eliminating the foreign exchange distortions (see Commission of the European Communities 1993: 10).

Use of the ECU in the EU budget

Since January 1988, the ECU has been used not only as a unit of account but also as a means of payment for particular transactions emanating from the General Budget of the European Communities. Since September 1990, transfers resulting from the Structural Funds (see Box 4.3) are carried out in ECUs. The Commission pays experts, consultants and most suppliers and funds external aid programmes, research and cooperation with third countries in ECUs. Taking this into account, in total around 44 percent of expenditures arising from the execution of the Community General Budget were effected in ECUs in 1995.

Reasons for using the private ECU

The private ECU is used as an investment strategy, as an invoicing strategy and as a strategy by public institutions to increase the liquidity of the private ECU financial markets.

As an investment strategy

As explained in Box 5.3, the interest rate on an ECU financial instrument is a weighted average of the twelve interest rates prevailing on the currencies composing the ECU basket. Following the well-known general principles of traditional portfolio theory, an ECU-denominated financial instrument offers a higher than expected rate of return for the same risk, or a lower risk for the same expected rate of return, than any financial instrument denominated in one of the component currencies of the ECU.[5] ECU-denominated securities enable investors to obtain a favourable risk/return trade-off at a savings in transaction costs compared to a tailor-made portfolio composed of securities denominated in the twelve component currencies. Jorion (1986) and Masera (1986) have studied the portfolio diversification effect of ECU securities.

A study (*Ecu Newsletter*, February 1986) of three-month Eurocurrency interest rates for the period 1980–85 shows a lower variability (risk) of three-month ECU interest rates compared with the variability of its component Eurocurrency interest rates. The Commission (Deidda 1993) has recently undertaken a study of the relative volatility of the ECU interest rate. This study, covering the period June 1992 to April 1993, concluded that the ECU is a currency with a high and stable yield. Compared with the other currencies' interest rates, ECU interest rates are (i) usually higher than those with a lower level of volatility (risk) and (ii) lower than others whose volatility is much higher. This suggests the diversification opportunities of using ECU-denominated financial instruments.

As an invoicing strategy in corporate decisions

Empirical analyses (*Ecu Newsletter* July 1985 for the period 1980–85, and Deidda 1993 for the period June 1992 to April 1993) show that from the viewpoint of any component currency of the ECU basket, the variability of that currency against the ECU is smaller than the variability of that same currency against many of the other component currencies.

Box 5.3 The market vs theoretical ECU interest rates

The interest rate (yield) on an ECU financial instrument is market determined, but because of potential arbitrage operations, cannot deviate significantly from the weighted average of the twelve interest rates (Eurocurrency interest rates corresponding to the twelve currencies composing the ECU basket) prevailing on comparable financial instruments with the same risk, maturity, terms, etc. This calculated ECU interest rate is known as the *theoretical* ECU interest rate. It is calculated as the sum of the product of the *forward* weight of each component currency and the corresponding Eurocurrency interest rate. For example, if the Deutsche mark represents a forward weight of 30 percent in the ECU basket of twelve currencies, then the Euro–DM interest rate represents 30 percent of the weight of the twelve Eurocurrency interest rates determining the theoretical ECU interest rate.

Since the ECU *spot* rate is usually different from the ECU *forward* rate, the spot weight of any component currency in the ECU basket is different from its forward weight. Therefore, the *forward weight* of each component currency is used to calculate the theoretical ECU interest rate. The basis for using the forward weight instead of the spot weight is the relationship in international finance known as the 'covered interest rate parity', which links the forward exchange rate, the spot exchange rate and the Eurocurrency interest rates (Levich 1987).

Because of the bullish sentiment after the initialling of the Maastricht agreement in December 1991, the market yields on five-year ECU financial instruments were from 50 to 75 basis points (100 basis points = 1 percentage point) below their theoretical yields in early 1992. The abrupt reappraisal of the role of the official ECU, not to mention its future existence, following the Danish rejection of the Maastricht Treaty on 2 June 1992 had a major impact on the private ECU market. The increasing risk of holding ECU-denominated instruments in the latter half of 1992 pushed the market yields of those same five-year ECU bonds 50 basis points above their theoretical yields. The private market was factoring in the ECU market interest rate the possibility that the European Monetary System with its official ECU could disappear along with the legal underpinning provided to the private ECU contracts. Most long-term private ECU contracts (bonds) have a 'doomsday' clause indicating the consequences of the disappearance of the official ECU:

> With respect to each due date for the payment of interest or the reimbursement of principal [on an ECU bond] on which the ECU

is used neither with the European Monetary System nor for the settlement of transactions by public institutions of or within the EC, the Fiscal Agent shall choose a component currency of the ECU in which all payments due on that maturity date with respect to bonds or coupons are to be made.

Another clause explains how the exchange rate will be calculated if the official ECU should disappear.

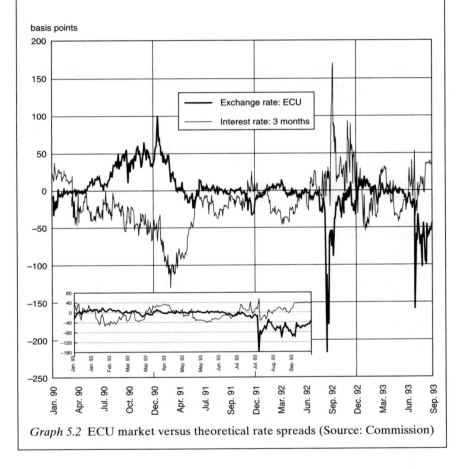

Graph 5.2 ECU market versus theoretical rate spreads (Source: Commission)

For example, for the period June 1992–April 1993, the variability of the Deutsche mark against the ECU was smaller than the variability of the Deutsche mark against either the Irish punt, British pound, Spanish peseta or Italian lira. There are many other such examples, especially from the viewpoint of the Italian lira or the Irish punt or the British pound.

Accordingly, an importer who may be unwilling to accept an invoice denominated in the exporter's currency, may accept being invoiced in ECUs. Similarly, an exporter who may be unwilling to invoice in the importer's currency, may be willing to invoice in ECUs. Moreover, over the periods 1979–85 and June 1992 to April 1993, the variability of every major European currency against the ECU was significantly smaller than the variability of each of those European currencies against the dollar (*Ecu Newsletter* July 1985 and Deidda 1993). Consequently the risk to Europeans of invoicing in ECUs for the purpose of cross-border commercial activities is considerably smaller than the risk of invoicing in dollars.

As a strategy by public institutions to encourage the use of private ECUs

Through their active borrowing policies via the issue of ECU-denominated bonds, the EC supranational bodies and EU sovereign States have provided the ECU markets with benchmarks, which are used for pricing private issues. These institutions, by issuing ECU-denominated debt instruments, have strengthened the liquidity of the markets, further encouraging investors to issue and acquire financial assets denominated in ECUs.

The private ECU clearing system

With respect to the financial use of the private ECU, the ECU was from the beginning used as a unit of account and a settlement currency. The latter function may explain how banks were 'forced' to transfer ECUs within the financial system. If the buyer of an ECU-denominated bond has to pay for the bond in ECUs, he must convert part of his national currency account into an ECU account. Similarly, if the issuer of the bond is obligated to redeem the bond at maturity in ECUs, he also needs an ECU account. Thus, banks eventually need a clearing system for ECU accounts. Most clearing systems are run by the central bank, but as the ECU market has no central bank, the commercial banks had to set up their own ECU clearing system. In the early 1980s, the Kredietbank (Brussels) took the initiative to assemble the major banks and to arrange for a clearing agreement. Starting from a very limited number, this group was progressively extended to seven members, which included Lloyd's of London. The group was called the MESA (Mutual Ecu Settlement Accounts). The member banks opened 'mutual' ECU accounts to record both credit and debit entries between MESA banks. The final settlement of the balances, which were centralised on a rotating basis in one of the member banks, could be done in either of two ways: (i) a net ECU-debtor bank was automatically granted credit by the net ECU-creditor banks up to a ceiling of ECU20 million, or beyond that figure by mutual agreement, or (ii) the net debtor banks had to provide the component currencies of an ECU.

By the mid-1980s, at the initiative of the Commission, a new more comprehensive clearing and settlement system was established. In 1985, the Ecu Banking Association (EBA), composed of eighteen commercial banks, and the European Investment Bank negotiated an agreement with SWIFT (Society for Worldwide Interbank Financial Telecommunications) and the BIS (Bank for International Settlements) to launch in 1986 an Ecu Clearing and Settlement System (Rambure 1987; Lelart 1988; BIS 1993: 498–501). The EBA is a body formed under French law with head-quarters in Paris. Membership is open to commercial banks which have their head office or a branch in one of the EU countries and which demonstrate sufficient interest in the development of ECU transactions. The system essentially functions as follows:

● the BIS, as agent of the clearing banks, opens and operates clearing accounts in their names;
● each clearing bank also opens an ECU sight account in the books of the BIS;
● every working day, the clearing banks are able to send each other payment orders in ECUs through the netting centre provided by the SWIFT network;
● to square the residual balances, the BIS, having established that all debtor clearing balances are covered by credit balances on the respective banks' ECU sight accounts, carries out the settlement operations; that is, clearing banks in a debtor position obtain the funds from the clearing banks in a creditor position.

Since 1988, the system operates on a same-day settlement basis. Today, the EBA's current ninety members represent all countries of the European Union as well as other European countries, Australia, Japan and the United States. As of early 1996, forty-seven member banks have the status of Clearing Bank. The average daily turnover of the EBA was ECU50,100 million in 1994. It is important to emphasize that although the BIS participates as an agent in the operations of the ECU clearing mechanism, it does not play the usual role of a central bank to the extent that it may not cover net debtor ECU positions of banks (i.e. net debtor banks which do not have sufficient funds in their BIS sight accounts), except since 1987 within very limited amounts and duration. This is in contrast to the role a national central bank is allowed to play with respect to the clearing and settlement mechanism in the domestic currency. There is no institution to ultimately guarantee liquidity or credit risks of the private ECU within the banking system. The private ECU is a currency without its own central bank. In late 1991, the Banque de France and the Bank of England signed agreements with the EBA in order to reduce some of the liquidity risks inherent in the private ECU settlement system. Under certain conditions, these two central banks allow their member banks to use their private ECU deposits held at the central bank as a guarantee against any ECU borrowings that EBA clearing banks may have to undertake with another bank to settle a debtor position.

CHANGEOVER SCENARIOS TO THE SINGLE EUROPEAN CURRENCY

As mentioned in Chapter 4, on 19 June 1995 the Ecofin Council, under the presidency of France, informally agreed that Stage III would not start on 1 January 1997. After considering the recommendations of the Commission, of the European Monetary Institute and of the Ecofin Council, this was officially confirmed by the Heads of State or Government in December 1996. Accordingly, Stage III is scheduled to start on 1 January 1999, the last possible date according to the provisions of the Treaty on European Union, unless the Heads of State or Government announce an ulterior date before the end of 1997. On the first day of Stage III, the conversion rates between each national currency of the Member States participating in the monetary union and the Euro are to be announced, along with the 'rapid' introduction of the Euro as the single currency. The Maastricht Treaty leaves the door open to the possibility that the scriptural Euro and the national currency of each participating Member State of the monetary union could co-exist side by side for a period of time with the proviso that the national currency is to be only a mirror image of the Euro. In France, for example, the scriptural Euro and the French franc could co-exist as units of account, media of exchange and stores of value. The physical introduction of Euro *notes and coins*[6] could conceivably appear only years later. These open issues prompted the private financial sector (Maas 1995a, 1995b) to pressure EU officials to draft and adopt an official blueprint for the changeover scenario to the single European currency. This reference scenario would guide in an orderly fashion the private sector throughout Stage II with a view to plan and implement the technical changes required for the new environment of Stage III. On the basis of a widely discussed Commission Green Paper (Commission of the European Communities 1995b) and an EMI document (European Monetary Institute 1995d), the Heads of State or Government adopted at the Madrid European Council meeting of December 1995 the official reference scenario for the changeover to the single currency.

Scenario proposed by the Commission

In its Green Paper entitled 'One Currency for Europe: Green Paper on the Practical Arrangements for the Introduction of the Single Currency', released on 31 May 1995, the Commission favoured what it called the 'mounting wave' scenario instead of the 'Big Bang' approach. In the latter scenario, all means of payment, including national banknotes and coins, are converted into Euros within a short period of time ranging from one week to two months (Commission 1994). For technical and psychological reasons, the 'Big Bang' approach is not feasible and therefore not credible. The 'mounting wave' scenario would build up, soon after the start of Stage III, a 'critical mass' of Euro transactions equivalent to 90 percent of all the monetary transactions in the single currency area and would allow Euro banknotes and coins to be introduced some three years later.

The Commission divided the changeover scenario into three time periods, denoted A, B and C (see Table 5.2). Period A begins as soon as the Heads of State or Government designate the participating Member States of the single currency area. In the event that Stage III begins on 1 January 1999, the decision should be announced at the end of 1997 since approximately a period of *twelve months* is required for the finalization and implementation of the organizational, logistical and regulatory framework that will enable the ESCB to start conducting the single monetary policy from the first day of Stage III. During this time period, the *production* of Euro banknotes and coins is to begin and EU directives are to be translated into national laws so as to provide the necessary legal national framework for the single currency. Period B begins on 1 January 1999 when the conversion rates between the national currencies of the participating Member States and the Euro are announced. During the *three-year* duration of this time period, both the Euro (only scriptural) and the national currency (scriptural and fiat) are used in each participating Member State of the single monetary zone. Then, on 1 January 2002, the beginning of Period C begins at which time the use of, and reference to, the national currency (scriptural and fiat) entirely disappear. Over a time period of a few weeks, the national banknotes and coins are replaced with Euro banknotes and coins.

According to the Commission, the 'delayed Big Bang' scenario favoured by Germany, whereby the Euro conversion rates are announced in 1999 but the *use* of the Euro is delayed until 2002 (Period C) with the introduction of the Euro banknotes and coins, does not create a 'credible environment' for the introduction of the single currency and does not respect the terms of the Treaty. With the 'mounting wave' approach, Euro transactions between the central bank and commercial banks, as well as wholesale transactions on the financial markets and on the foreign exchange markets, would start immediately at the beginning of Stage III (Period B). This would avoid the risk of economic agents operating on these markets of quoting conversion rates between the national currencies of the participating Member States different from those announced at the beginning of Period B. Thus, at the 'wholesale' level, the financial sector, the corporate sector and public bodies would begin to operate in Euros immediately after the start of Stage III (Period B), with the proviso that their 'retail' activities would have to accommodate the use of the national currency as a unit of account, as a medium of exchange, and as a store of value.

Table 5.2 Commission proposal of time sequence for the changeover to the single currency*

Period A Start: end of 1997* Duration: one year	Period B Start: 01/01/1999 Duration: three years	Period C Start: 01/01/2002* Duration: a few weeks
At the start of period: ● List of participating Member States ● Confirmation of starting date of Stage III ● Announcement of the date for the beginning of Period C ● Establishment of ESCB and ECB ● Start of the production of Euro banknotes and coins	*At the start of period:* ● Conversion rates fixed ● Euro becomes currency in its own right ● Monetary and exchange rate policies executed in Euros ● Interbank and capital markets (short-term and long-term instruments) and exchange markets in Euros ● New public debt issued in Euros ● Wholesale payment systems in Euros ● Corporations liable for taxes in Euros	*At the start of period:* ● Introduction of Euro banknotes and coins ● End of changeover of banking system to Euros (retail clearing done in Euros) ● Complete changeover for public and private agents ● Exclusive use of the Euro
Throughout the period: ● Transposing EU directives into national legislation to provide necessary legal framework for the Euro: continuity of contracts, laws regarding payment of taxes in Euros ● Establishment in each country of a national steering structure to guide the introduction of the single currency	*Throughout the period:* ● Progressive changeover of the banking and financial sectors ● Public and private operators other than banks proceed with the changeover circumstances permitting; principle of subsidiarity respected ● Display of prices in national currency and Euro	

*The author substituted the name Euro for Ecu.
Source: Commission of the European Communities 1995b: 32

Scenario proposed by the EMI

The scenario for the changeover to the single currency adopted by the Heads of State or Government in December 1995 at the Madrid European Council meeting is essentially the one recommended by the European Monetary Institute (1995d), which undertook extensive consultations with the private banking community. The adopted scenario (see Table 5.3) rejects the 'mounting wave' scenario recommended by the Commission,

Table 5.3 Adopted reference scenario for the changeover to the single currency

Period A *Start: early 1998* *End: December 1998*	*Period B* *Start: 01/01/1999* *End: December 2001*	*Period C* *Start: 01/01/2002, at the latest* *End: 01/07/2002, at the latest*
● Decision by the Heads of State or Government on the countries participating in the Euro area ● Adopt legislation with respect to the establishment of the ESCB and the introduction of the Euro ● Render ESCB operational (setting up the ECB and testing monetary policy framework) ● Start the production of Euro banknotes and coins ● Launch a wide-ranging public information campaign	● As of day one, irrevocable fixing of conversion rates and entry into force of legislation related to the introduction of the Euro in non-cash form (legal status, continuity of contracts, rounding) ● As of day one, execution of monetary and exchange policy in Euro by the ESCB ● Operation of TARGET payment system ● Issue new tradeable public debt maturing after 2002 in Euro ● Monitor progress in the changeover developments in the banking and finance industry ● ESCB and public authorities assist the whole of the economy in an orderly changeover; prepare changeover of the public administration.	● Start circulation of the Euro banknotes and coins and withdrawal of national banknotes and coins ● Implement the complete changeover of the public administration ● On last day, cancel the legal tender status of national banknotes and coins

Source: Conclusions of the Presidency of the Madrid European Council meeting, December 1995, in the European Union *Bulletin* (12/95).

which, according to the EMI, would create significant competitive distortions between small and large banks. From the start of Stage III, set for 1 January 1999, private economic agents – banks, companies, financial markets, consumers, retail outlets – are free to use the Euro; on the other hand, they are not obliged to do so before the deadline set for the completion of the changeover. This principle has been dubbed 'no compulsion, no prohibition' on the use of the Euro. The deadline to adopt the Euro starts on 1 January 2002[7] with the introduction of Euro banknotes and coins, and ends on 1 July 2002 with the national banknotes and coins losing their legal tender status. The private sector agents are allowed to develop their own mechanisms of adjustment to the changeover. This would avoid placing the smaller credit institutions at an economic disadvantage to the larger ones, which would have the resources to run a dual payment/accounting system composed of the national unit of account for their 'retail' operations and the Euro for their wholesale money market and foreign exchange operations and for their clearing and settlement operations.

Settlement/clearing systems and conversion facilities

Following the start of Stage III and until the completion of the changeover to the single currency, two scriptural monetary units will be used in each of the participating Member States: the national one and the Euro. Moreover, a wide range of settlement/clearing systems will exist at the start of Stage III in the participating Member States. Some of them process mainly large amounts typically dealing with payments stemming from the interbank money and foreign exchange markets. Other process mainly small amounts linked to retail transactions. Some are organized by the national authorities, others are privately run. The infrastructure of all of them is quite different except for the fact that they all use one monetary unit, the respective national currency, in their system, and final settlements are ultimately routed to the national central bank in most cases.

During Stage II of the EMU, the European Monetary Institute has a mandate to study and recommend the type of clearing/settlement system necessary to ensure rapid, final settlement at minimum risk and cost at the EU level. Accordingly, the system has to be designed to take into account that at some future date the Euro, the currency of the European Central Bank, will be introduced in co-existence with the national currencies of the participating Member States and the national currencies of the non-participating Member States. The task of the EMI is to continue the work undertaken by the Ad Hoc Working Group on EC Payment Systems, established at the request of the Committee of Governors of the central banks of the Member States of the EEC (1992a). The Working Group endorses what is called 'real-time gross settlement' systems (RTGS) for all Member States. This system attempts to reduce the systemic ('chain-reactions') risks created by delayed settlement of netted positions. Under RTGS, fund transfer orders are settled as soon as they have been sent, provided that the sending bank has sufficient cover in its account with the central bank or settlement agent. The individual transfers (one by one, or what is known as 'gross', and in real-time) are thus unconditional and irrevocable.[8]

From the start of Stage III, the System of European Central Banks will have the task of managing and regulating the clearing and settlement systems of the Member States within and outside the monetary union. The EMI (European Monetary Institute 1995c) proposes an EU clearing/settlement system, called TARGET (Trans-European Automated Real-time Gross settlement Express Transfer). This payment system is to be composed of one RTGS system in each of the Member States participating in the single currency area and an Interlinking mechanism to connect the various national RTGS systems of the participating Member States. Under certain conditions, RTGS systems of non-participating countries may also be connected to TARGET. A major unresolved issue is whether EU banks operating outside the monetary union should have access to the Euro intraday liquidity facilities of TARGET on the same terms as banks in the monetary union. If the UK does not initially participate in the monetary union, will banks operating in London be able to obtain liquidity in Euros from the ECB for clearing purposes during the day on the same terms as banks operating in Frankfurt or Paris? If banks in the UK had access to TARGET on the same terms as EMU banks, they could offer clearing facilities in Euros across Europe as cheaply and quickly. In this case, customers outside the EU would probably enter the Euro area mainly through London, which would reap the profits. However, restricting access to TARGET by imposing discriminatory terms on the 'out' Member States may be a breach of the free movement of capital by erecting barriers through a payment system.

Right from the start, the Interlinking system will operate in the Euro and the national RTGS systems will be capable of operating in both units, the national one and the Euro. In most cases, the national central bank will provide the conversion facilities to the small credit institutions which experience difficulties in organizing conversion capabilities for the processing of cross-border payments channelled through the Interlinking system of TARGET. Although alternative payment systems will be allowed, payments related to the implementation of the single monetary policy will have to be processed through TARGET.

Monetary policy and foreign exchange operations in Euros

At the start of Stage III, the ESCB is to execute its single monetary policy in Euros, not in the national currency units of the participating Member States. Similarly, the ESCB is to encourage the use of the Euro on the foreign exchange markets by executing and settling in Euros all of its foreign exchange operations. To enable the smaller credit institutions that will not have changed over to the Euro during the three-year transitional period to nevertheless participate in the refinancing and payment system facilities of the ECB, the EMI is suggesting that each participating national central bank could provide conversion services. This would avoid placing the smaller banks at a competitive disadvantage relative to the larger banks.

Continuity of ECU and national currency contracts

At the Dublin European Council meeting of December 1996, agreement was achieved on the content of a European Regulation regarding the legal underpinnings of the Euro. This proposed Regulation (Commission 1996d and Bank of England 1996), adopted on 7 July 1997 by the Ecofin Council composed of all the Member States, is designed to eliminate the market uncertainty with regard to the continuity of ECU and national currency contracts when the monetary union is launched. Moreover, the Regulation is to apply across the entire EU, even in Member States which do not initially participate in the single currency area. The objectives of the Regulation are:

- to confirm that, with effect from the first day of the establishment of the monetary union, references to the ECU in contracts and other legal instruments are replaced by references to the Euro at the rate of one Euro for one ECU;
- to confirm the continuity of contracts which are denominated in national currencies and in ECU;
- to determine the degree of precision at which conversion rates will be irrevocably fixed on the first day of the monetary union and to establish rounding rules.

The Regulation clearly indicates that substitution of the Euro for the national unit of account does not of itself alter the continuity of contracts; amounts expressed in national currency are converted into Euro at the rate of conversion laid down by the Council. In the case of fixed interest rate securities and loans, this substitution does not of itself alter the nominal interest rate payable by the debtor unless otherwise provided in the contract. This is to prevent any attempts, by either the lender or the borrower, to change the coupon interest rate when the contract is redenominated in Euros. Currently, interest rate spreads exist between some Member States that are candidates for the initial single currency area. The banks were afraid that current long-term borrowers in currencies with high interest rates would attempt to renegotiate their contracts (e.g. mortgages) to take advantage of the lower interest rates on Euro-denominated contracts (Maas 1995a). In the case of contracts denominated by reference to the official ECU basket of the European Community, substitution by the Euro is at the 1:1 rate. References in a legal instrument to the ECU without references to the official definition of the ECU shall be presumed to be based on the official ECU, unless the legal document clearly stipulates otherwise. This provision of the Regulation eliminates the potential legal complications with ECU-denominated contracts which may not refer clearly to the definition of the official ECU. Without an unambiguous EU Regulation, the parties to these contracts could invoke the principle of 'frustration', 'Wegfall der Geschäftsgrundlage', or 'théorie de l'imprévision', which would render the contract null and void.

The Regulation specifies that there will be a fixed conversion rate between the Euro and each participating currency. These conversion rates (defined for one Euro) will be expressed to six significant figures. Calculations with 'inverse rates' will not be permissible; for large sums, the use of 'inverse rates' would produce inaccurate results. Conversion between two national denominations will follow a three-step procedure: (i) convert from the first national denomination into the Euro; (ii) convert the result of step (i) into the second national denomination; (iii) round the result to the nearest sub-unit of the second denomination.

Another proposed Regulation, to be adopted in early 1998 by unanimity of *participating* Member States, dealing with an elaboration of the principle of 'no compulsion/no prohibition' during the transition period has been agreed. Unless the parties to a transaction have agreed otherwise, any amount denominated either in the Euro unit or in the national currency unit of a given participating Member State and payable within that Member State by crediting an account of the creditor, can be paid by the debtor either in the Euro unit or in that national currency unit. The amount will be credited to the account of the creditor in the denomination of his account, with any conversion being effected at the conversion rates. In other words, according to the provision, the debtor may choose the denomination in which he discharges the debt, but the creditor would be credited with his own choice of denomination. This provision also serves to enhance the fungibility between the Euro and the national currency unit in a participating Member State during the three-year transition period.

Public debt of participating Member States

From 1 January 1999, new tradeable public debt with a maturity date after 1 January 2002 is to be issued in Euro by the participating Member States. Purchasers of such debt instruments, if they so desire, will be able to pay the equivalent amount in national currency throughout the transitional period and will likewise be able to have the interest credited to them in national currency. Short-term public debt and non-tradeable public debt may still be issued in the national currency. By 1 July 2002, at the latest, the entire stock of public debt denominated in the former national currencies is to be redeemable only in the single currency.

The redenomination of the existing stock of public debt must be done by each participating Member State, at the latest, by 1 January 2002. France, Belgium, Austria, Spain and Italy announced that they plan to redenominate their existing stock of public debt into the Euro as of 1 January 1999. This should increase the liquidity of Euro-denominated debt as soon as EMU is launched. The generalization of the use of the Euro for public sector operations, such as the collection of taxes and the payment of pensions, will occur in all participating Member States at the latest when the Euro banknotes and coins are fully introduced.

Risks of a lengthy Period B

There are some drawbacks to lock conversion rates between the currencies of the participating Member States without moving rapidly thereafter to a single unit of account and medium of exchange with its own banknotes and coins. There is always a probability greater than zero that the market may attempt for various reasons to place a premium (discount) on the official conversion rates as one currency becomes preferred (undesirable) to the other. A case in point is the situation between the Belgian and Luxembourg francs. Although the exchange rate between these two currencies is 1:1 since 1921 when the Belgo-Luxembourg Economic Union was set up and although there is effectively only one monetary authority for the two countries, a 'discount' is sometimes observed on the Belgian franc in the form of Luxembourgeois retailers insisting on payment in Luxembourg francs during periods of significant uncertainty; i.e., as in 1982 when there was an expectation that the parity of the Belgian franc would be devalued vis-à-vis other Community currencies and that at the same time the Luxembourg franc might be decoupled from the Belgian franc. In fact, after 1982, Luxembourg passed laws to require banks to maintain matched positions in Belgian and Luxembourg francs, just in case the Belgo-Luxembourg currency union should suddenly break up or would not be renewed every decade, as required since 1971 (Connolly 1995: 327).

In short, should one of the participating Member States face a significant asymmetric shock during Period B, it is unclear whether financial markets would really be convinced that official conversion rates were permanently and irrevocably fixed. For example, suppose France, a participating Member State of the Euro-currency union, were to receive an asymmetric shock during Period B. The uncertainty may motivate economic agents to substitute assets denominated in the Euro subdivision called the French franc into the assets denominated in the other subdivision called the Deutsche mark. The private foreign exchange market may begin to quote spot conversion rates between the French franc and the Deutsche mark different from the official conversion rates. Speculative forward exchange contracts may be traded and interest rates on French franc and Deutsche mark assets/liabilities may be decoupled. The 'mounting wave' scenario proposed by the Commission Green Paper tried to reduce this risk by creating soon after the start of Period B a critical mass of transactions in Euros. To prevent a spread between the private and official conversion rates, intervention by the ECB would be required. The ECB would be forced to engage in market transactions denominated in French francs and Deutsche marks, both of which were replaced from the start of period B by the Euro for all ECB operations. This intervention should not create a problem to the ECB monetary authority insofar as no change in the Euro money supply would occur as a result of the substitution of Deutsche marks for French francs. Although no legal action would be available to the ECB or to the ministers to enforce any conversion rate other than the official rate for private dealings between participating currencies or between a participating currency and the Euro, the Community could discourage such behaviour by legislating that business contracts that flout the official conversion rates during Period B would not be upheld in a European law court. Or, the Community could legislate that anybody who owes a debt during Period B should be able to repay it in either the Euro or the participating national currency, regardless of the wishes of the lender, unless special legal provisions had been drawn up in advance. This latter measure would eliminate some incentives for foreign exchange transactions between the Euro and the participating currencies in the event that the market expected the Euro exchange rates against those currencies to deviate from the official conversion rates.

Another drawback of the adopted changeover scenario is the difficulty that could arise during Period B with the combination of fixed conversion rates between each participating national currency and the Euro on the one hand, and identical interest rates on bank deposits denominated in these different units, on the other hand. The issue is whether banks should charge transaction fees between deposits denominated in the national currency and the Euro.[9] The Commission recommended in its Green Paper no such conversion fees since bank accounts denominated in the national currency of a Member State participating in the monetary zone and in Euros are to be perfect substitutes (Commission of the European Communities 1995b: 35, para. 47). In fact, to ensure a legal equivalence betweeen the Euro and the national currency units during the transition period, the proposed legal text on the provisions relating to the introduction of the Euro (see above) stipulates that the national currency units are only *subdivisions* of the Euro, but does not imply that payments involving conversion must be free of charge. From the beginning of Period B, large banks may have to offer services of similar quality in two different units of account, the national currency and the Euro. Moreover, in some large commercial outlets, dual pricing may begin to appear during Period B. There is a risk of a generalized demand for multiple currency services during the three years of Period B. This would suggest that some of the welfare gains of introducing a single currency would not be realized immediately.

CONCLUSION

At the Dublin Summit of December 1996, the Heads of State or Government of the fifteen Member States, following the procedures described in Chapter 4, decided, after having considered the recommendations of the Commission, the European Monetary Institute and the Ecofin Council, that a majority of the Member States did not satisfy the Maastricht convergence criteria and, as a consequence, Stage III of the Economic and Monetary Union could not be launched in 1997. They confirmed that the procedure laid down in Article 109J.4 of the Maastricht

Treaty will be applied as early as possible in 1998, with a view to the commencement of the third stage of EMU on 1 January 1999. At the beginning of 1997, the EMI (1997a) published the regulatory, organisational and logistical framework proposal for the ESCB, with an elaboration of the monetary operations and procedures for the single currency area to be released in late 1997. As of July 1997, the EMI is to begin testing the national central bank links with the new EU clearing and settlement system, TARGET. In the spring of 1998 the Commission and EMI are to finalize their reports on convergence, on the basis of actual data for calendar year 1997 and forecasted data for 1998, and to prepare recommendations on which Member States fulfil the conditions for entry to EMU. Then, during the first weekend of May 1998, under the presidency of the United Kingdom at a meeting in London, the appropriate recommendations will be made by the Ecofin Council, followed by a decision of the Heads of State or Government on whether EMU should begin and, if so, which Member States will be in the first wave. Although the strict Maastricht public finance (deficit and debt) criteria will be difficult to achieve for most Member States in the calendar year 1997, it is not unrealistic to assume that the initial monetary union will be composed of at least eight Member States – France, Germany, the Benelux countries, Ireland, Austria and Finland. On the basis of estimates made by the Commission (1997) in early 1997, it appears that Spain and Portugal could be included in the first wave of Member States participating in the monetary union. Even if by the end of 1997 some of these countries will still be some distance from the required debt to GDP ratio,[10] they, unlike Italy, will have proved to be serious in their commitment to achieve sustainable fiscal stability, to the satisfaction of Germany for a successful launch of the initial monetary union. Further reductions of the debt ratio for the 'ins' will take place after EMU starts, within the framework of the 'Stability and Growth pact'.

Thirty years after The Hague Summit of December 1969 when the Heads of State or Government of the six founding Member States committed themselves to such a goal, the monetary union is expected – short of a major international or European shock – to be finally launched. The formidable amount of work already accomplished towards reaching an economic and monetary union and the political will behind the EMU project compensate for the less than convincing economic arguments in favour of it. For Germany, a monetary union is seen as a sacrifice in return for moves towards greater political integration. EMU is seen as an essential part of the movement towards the wider political integration that Chancellor Kohl desires to reassure European nations that Germany is well anchored in the current and future Europe. For France, a monetary union is seen as a way to dilute the pre-eminence of the Bundesbank in setting monetary policy for the rest of Europe and as a way, by means of the new Euro, to challenge the leading role of the US dollar as the international currency. And for almost all EU continental countries, if EMU were to founder, the whole question of the future of European integration would be in doubt. The EU ex-UK would face a shattering crisis of identity and direction. The United Kingdom, on the other hand, would be relieved and might even experience a temporary period of *Schadenfreude*. Whether EMU is necessary or sufficient for greater political integration is the subject of a paper by Issing (1996), a member of the Bundesbank. The President of the Bundesbank, Mr Tietmeyer, recently warned that monetary union in Europe could fail if it was not backed by increased political integration. He questioned whether an independent European central bank would be able to maintain stable monetary policies if it came into permanent conflict with politicians, such as finance ministers, and public opinion: '[Political union] should be a corset for a lasting orientation towards stability and for the will to stick together, also in difficult times.' (*Financial Times*, 4/5 November 1995: 2)

The long European debate between the 'monetarists' and 'economists' on how to achieve a monetary union is no longer the issue. With the progress made towards achieving the single market and with the multilateral surveillance towards the achievement of the nominal convergence criteria based on economic performance, the ground has shifted. Given the decision to launch a monetary union with an independent central European bank by 1999, the debate is on the necessity to create further integration by way of establishing a European 'political roof' to ensure that the monetary union retains legitimacy. Some, like Mr Kenneth Clarke, the former UK chancellor, argue that 'it is a mistake to believe that monetary union needs to be a huge step on the path to a federal union' (*Financial Times*, 9 April 1996). Others, like Delors, are 'neofunctionalists'. Just as Monnet and Schuman believed that cooperation in particular economic areas, with a minimum of institutional apparatus, leads to 'spillover effects' in the political arena with new supranational institutions, neofunctionalists believe that a successful monetary union requires new supranational institutions in other areas, such as a European economic government in fiscal and employment policies. For instance, divergences in unemployment rates due to national differences in indirect taxes on labour and to national differences of labour laws may compromise grass-root support for the single monetary policy decided by the ECB.

Since mid-1996, financial markets appear to be convinced that an initial monetary union centred on France and Germany will be launched in 1999,[11] or soon thereafter. The long-term interest rate spread between these two countries has all but disappeared. With the exception of the Irish punt, all of the ERM currencies are within their narrowly defined ERM bands. With market expectation that the Ecofin Council will use the 1987 bilateral central rate of the French franc-Deutsche mark to fix the conversion rate of these two currencies in 1999, the French franc is gradually approaching its 1987 bilateral central rate with the Deutsche mark. The financial sector, most notably in France and Germany, in cooperation with the EMI and the Commission, is preparing itself for the technical changeover to a new regime with the single currency (Hannoun 1996 and German Banking Association 1996). By the end of 1996, the legal framework to clarify the transition from the ECU and the national currencies to the Euro has been adopted by the European Council. The public finance rules, with the procedures for their enforcement, for the 'ins' have been agreed and need only be drafted in a legal text. The general framework of ERM2 with respect to the exchange rate regime between the Euro and the other EU currencies has also been agreed and the legal details need only be drafted once the ECB is established in May/ June 1998.

Short of a major recession in Europe and/or significant foreign exchange volatility between the core Member States of the EU in the period leading up to early 1998 when the Member States are to be designated to form the first wave of countries composing the monetary union, the initial monetary union is expected to be launched on schedule. At about the same time that the EU will have 'deepened' the economic and monetary integration between the 'hard core' Member States, the revised Maastricht Treaty, negotiated at the intergovernmental conference of 1996–97, is expected to come into force. The EU will also be in the process of negotiating accession treaties with the Central European states to 'widen' the union. From the very start of the post-war period, the road of European monetary, economic and political integration has always been difficult with numerous setbacks over the years – the rejection by France of the European Defence Community in 1954, de Gaulle's chauvinism and his 'empty chair' policy in the 1960s, the oil price shocks of the 1970s accompanied by the collapse of the Bretton Woods gold–dollar standard, the 1992–93 currency turmoil during the ratification process of the Maastricht Treaty, and the ambiguous position of Britain in the march towards European integration ranging from hesitancy in the 1970s and intransigence in the 1980s to outright obstruction of Council legislation during the 'mad-cow' crisis of the Major government. But by 1999 or shortly thereafter, the 'acquis communautaire' will appear to have increased substantially as modern-day Europe enters the new millennium.

Questions

CHAPTER 1

1.1 'The international economic environment of the 1970s sabotaged the plans of the Community to achieve in stages an economic and monetary union by 1980.' Discuss.

1.2 Compare the 1971 Ecofin Decision on strengthening the coordination of short-term economic policies of the Member States with the Ecofin Decision taken in 1974 when the Ministers had to 'temporarily' abandon the timetable to achieve an EMU.

1.3 What is the essential difference between the 'monetarists' and the 'economists' to achieve a monetary union? In the context of these two schools, how would you characterize the definitive version of the Werner Report?

1.4 Why have Continental Europeans been keen on establishing fixed exchange rate regimes?

1.5 Explain the difference between the 'maximum instantaneous fluctuation' of a currency around its parity and the 'maximum temporal fluctuation' of a currency, given a fixed parity.

1.6 For the following time periods, state the maximum instantaneous fluctuation and maximum temporal fluctuation between two European currencies participating in the following exchange rate systems:

- 1958 to end of 1971 (EMA and Bretton Woods);
- December 1971 to April 1972 (Smithsonian Agreement);
- April 1972 to March 1973 (Smithsonian Agreement with Basle Agreement of 1972);
- March 1973 to December 1978 (Basle Agreement of 1972, only).

1.7 A major North American textbook in international finance describes the 'snake in the tunnel' as follows:

Thus, following the Smithsonian agreement, the EEC decided on narrower bands of plus or minus 1.125 percent for community members.

Because of the visual appearance of a time graph giving changes in the value of EEC currencies with respect to the US dollar, the arrangement was referred to as the 'snake in the tunnel' ... the tunnel was formed by non-EEC currencies, which moved in the larger Smithsonian band of plus or minus 2.25 percent.

Explain the error in this statement.

CHAPTER 2

2.1 Using the following table, answer the following questions:

Table EU currencies and composition of the ECU basket

Currency	ECU central rates: 6 March 1995	Theoretical ECU rates: 31 Oct. 1996	1989 composition of ECU basket
BFR	39.3960	38.6941	3.301
DKR	7.28580	7.39636	0.1976
DM	1.91007	1.92661	0.6242
DRA	292.867	302.667	1.440
ESC	195.792	194.838	1.393
FF	6.40608	6.50246	1.332
FMK	5.80661	5.76963	—
HFL	2.15214	2.15989	0.2198
IRL	0.792214	0.781208	0.00855
LFR	39.3960	38.6941	0.130
LIT*	2,106.15	1,929.33	151.8
ÖS	13.4383	13.5563	—
PTA	162.493	162.342	6.885
SKR	—	8.3460	—
UKL	0.786652	0.782167	0.08784

* LIT re-entered the ERM on 25 November 1996.

(a) Assuming that each currency participating in the ERM on 31 October 1996 had a ±2.25 percent band around its bilateral central rates, calculate the bilateral central rate, floor and ceiling of each participating currency against the DM; i.e., BFR/DM, DKR/DM, ... FF/DM, ... PTA/DM.

(b) Which currencies lie outside the narrowly defined ERM bands on 31 October 1996? Still assuming the existence of narrow bands, what would have been the obligations of each central bank in those circumstances?

(c) Still assuming the ±2.25 percent band for the participating ERM currencies, which currencies have reached their 'threshold of maximum divergence' on 31 October 1996? Show calculations without adjusting for the facts that DRA, LIT, and UKL do not participate in the ERM and that the actual band for the participating currencies is ±15 percent.

(d) List in descending relative strength the ERM currencies on 31 October 1996. How did you define the 'strength' of a currency?

(e) Give the reason for each cell that has a blank entry.

(f) In the above table, DRA, LIT and UKL do not participate in the ERM. What is the purpose of designating a notional ECU central rate for these currencies? Why does the SKR not have a notional ECU central rate?

(g) Give the formula for calculating the theoretical ECU rate of the US dollar (US$/ECU).

(h) How were the ECU central rates of 6 March 1995 set? With the re-introduction of the Italian lira in the ERM on 25 November 1996, all the ECU central rates of 6 March 1995 were changed. Why? Yet, all the bilateral central rates of the currencies participating in the ERM prior to 25 November 1996 remained the same. How can that be possible? When the Finnish markka was introduced in the ERM on 14 October 1996, the ECU central rates that had been established on 6 March 1995 were not changed. What is different in the case of the FMK?

(i) How was the composition of the ECU basket set in September 1989? Did the EU authorities use the same procedures in 1989 as they had in 1979 and 1984? Why or why not?

2.2

(i) Under the terms and conditions of the amended EMS agreement between Central Banks of the Member States participating in the ERM, known as the Basle/Nyborg Agreement (1987):

- What are the legal obligations of the central banks with respect to marginal interventions whenever two currencies reach their bilateral edge?
- What are the limits (if any) on loans granted by the central bank with the strong currency to the central bank with the weak currency, for marginal interventions and what are the terms for renewals and reimbursements of those loans?

(ii) Answer the same questions with respect to intramarginal interventions.

(iii) Compare your answers of (i) and (ii) with the terms and conditions available under the Basle Agreement of 1972 (including amendment of July 1975) between Central Banks of the Member States, known as the 'snake'.

2.3 Under the provisions of the VSTF facility of the EMS, what is the unit of account for loans and reimbursements (including interest)? What are the consequences of using a unit of account different from the medium of exchange (e.g. a national currency, such as the DM) for loans and repayments?

2.4 Assuming that the French franc is on its weak edge against the DM and that the Banque de France does not hold any DMs in its reserves, is there a material difference between intervention undertaken by the Banque de France in Paris and intervention undertaken by the Bundesbank in Frankfurt to support the French franc, under the terms of the EMS? Explain.

2.5 What was the purpose of defining a 'threshold of maximum divergence' of the ECU in the EMS? How was this to reinforce the 1974 Ecofin Convergence Decision on economic policies between Member States? Why were participating Member States only presumed, and not legally required, to take the necessary measures whenever the threshold was attained?

2.6 Under the original terms of the EMS, what was the maximum instantaneous spread between any two ERM currencies around their bilateral central rate? What was the maximum temporal spread of an ERM currency against any other ERM currency? Did the architects of the ERM just transpose the Smithsonian Agreement (amendment to the original Bretton Woods Agreement) to the European case? Explain your answer.

CHAPTER 3

3.1 Explain the static benefits and costs derived from the formation of a customs union. Why did the UK estimate the costs of joining a customs union composed of the original six Member States of the Community in the mid-1950s to be greater than the benefits and instead argue in favour of a large European Free-Trade Area?

What are the dynamic benefits derived from the formation of a customs union?

3.2 'The objective of the Treaty of Rome establishing the EEC was much more than just the elimination of tariffs and quotas between Member States with the establishment of a common external tariff against third countries.' Discuss.

3.3 What were the objectives of the Single European Act of 1986? To what extent are they a repetition of the objectives included in the Treaty of Rome?

CHAPTER 4

4.1 Without introducing any amendment to the Treaty on European Union, describe two legal ways the EU can postpone the date of 1 January 1999 for launching the single currency area.

4.2 In late 1996, a Swedish government Commission on EMU concluded that 'it is not possible to draw unambiguous conclusions regarding participation in the monetary union' in 1999. This group of economists argued:

- That participation in the monetary union will mean that Sweden relinquishes the possibility of pursuing an independent monetary and exchange rate policy. This entails a *cost* if Sweden is subjected to domestic economic shocks that call for different monetary policies than in the rest of the union. Macroeconomic shocks to the Swedish economy have exhibited a relatively low degree of covariance with shocks in other EU countries.
- That *nominal* wages are not likely to be sufficiently flexible to compensate for the loss of monetary policy independence.
- That there is a substantial risk associated with the fiscal policy rules in the Maastricht Treaty and in the planned stability pact for countries with low public debt.
- That although there are no reasons to believe that unemployment should be influenced by participation in the monetary union in the long run, the probability of large *variation* in employment will increase if Sweden participates in the monetary union. Thus with a high current level of unemployment, Sweden should wait before joining the monetary union.

Elaborate and explain each point. What other factors may explain the fact that Finland has decided to join the monetary union with the first wave of countries in 1999?

4.3 Explain the difference between the nominal convergence criteria of the Maastricht Treaty that Member States must satisfy for entry into a monetary union and real convergence criteria between Member States. Why does the Treaty only require that Member States must satisfy the nominal criteria?

4.4

(a) 'Studies indicate that there is very little mobility of labour between Member States. Hence, the loss of the nominal exchange rate variable under the EMU scenario of the Maastricht Treaty will create persistent unemployment in a Member State which receives an asymmetric shock.' Discuss.
(b) 'Studies show that intra-country labour mobility in Member States is not greater than inter-country labour mobility between Member States. Therefore, the monetary union should not create unemployment problems greater than the ones existing at the present time'. Discuss.

4.5 Is a single currency necessary to realize fully the Community objectives of the single market (SEA)? Explain.

4.6 What is the indirect evidence among the core Member States to support the argument that external shocks are more likely to be symmetric than asymmetric? What are the implications of this evidence regarding the costs of launching a single currency?

4.7 If a Member State participating in the monetary union were to receive a negative asymmetric shock, could a variation in the real exchange rate be possible to stabilize that economy? Explain how the real exchange rate could change between Member States participating in a monetary union. Cite another adjustment mechanism available to the Member State participating in the monetary union. Does the 'Stability and Growth Pact' take this possibility into account?

4.8 One of the nominal convergence criteria allows a spread of 1.5 percentage points between the inflation rate of a candidate to the monetary union and the average inflation rate of the three best performing Member States while another convergence criterion allows a 2 percentage point spread between the long-term interest rate of that Member State and the average of the long-term interest rate of those same three Member States. Explain the rationale for the 0.5 percentage point difference in these two spreads.

4.9 'If the pace of the reduction of the debt-to-GDP ratio towards the 60 percent threshold level is more important than the actual ratio for the evaluation of whether a Member State satisfies the public debt criteria to join the monetary union, then what matters is the Member State's public primary surplus-to-GDP ratio and not the 3% threshold level of the public deficit-to-GDP ratio.' Discuss.

4.10 What are the welfare benefits of achieving a low level of inflation or price stability? Why does the Commission argue that one of the benefits flowing from the creation of a monetary union is the guarantee of the maintenance of price stability? Why should the ECB be more successful in achieving this goal than a national central bank?

4.11 What is meant by a 'non-sustainable path of public deficits'. What are the macroeconomic costs of running a budgetary policy that leads to such a path? How does the Maastricht Treaty deal with such a problem? How does the Stability and Growth Pact deal with such a problem once a Member State participates in the monetary union?

4.12 Some economists argue that the nominal convergence criteria spelled out in the Maastrict Treaty are redundant. Explain.

CHAPTER 5

5.1 Using the table given in problem 2.1, answer the following questions:

(i) On 31 October 1996, the market ECU rate against the French franc was 6.478 French francs per ECU. What could explain the difference between this rate and the theoretical ECU rate against the French franc shown in the table (6.50246)?

(ii) On 31 October 1996, the market ECU rate against the DM was 1.919. Is the percentage difference between the theoretical and market ECU rates against the DM approximately the same as the one found in (i) above?

(iii) On 4 April 1996, the market FF/ECU rate was 6.34 while its theoretical rate was 6.46. What is the percentage spread between the theoretical and market rates? What could account for the turnaround between April and the end of October?

5.2 Explain the advantages, the disadvantages, and the major advocates of the following changeover scenarios between the national currencies and the Euro:

● the 'Big Bang' scenario;
● the 'delayed Big Bang' scenario;
● the 'mounting wave' scenario;
● the 'no compulsion, no prohibition' scenario.

5.3 Explain the reason for the TEU requirement that *all* national central banks (except the Bank of England, unless the UK decides to join Stage III of EMU) must become independent monetary institutions *before* the ECB/ESCB is established in mid-1998.

5.4

(a) How does the Treaty on European Union guarantee the monetary principle of 'nominal continuity' on 1 January 1999?

(b) Consider an old 1990 contract denominated in ECUs, with a par value of ECU10,000 maturing in 2008 and with the ECU defined as the 1989 basket of twelve currencies. Is the par value of that contract equal to 10,000 Euros in 2008 or could the creditor insist that its value be recalculated on the basis of the 1989 composition of the ECU basket with the conversion rates of each of these currencies against the Euro? Could this value be different from 10,000 Euros? Why? Is the Treaty clear on this question? Is there any legal uncertainty surrounding this question? If the Heads of State or Government had not changed the name of the new single currency from ECU to Euro, would the same legal uncertainty remain regarding this example? Explain. Has the Council settled this question by adopting the legal framework for the Euro?

5.5 The Treaty on European Union is vague on how the conversion rates are to be set between the Euro [ECU] and the national currencies that will participate in the single currency area.

Article 109L.4 just states '... This measure shall by itself not modify the external value of the ECU [Euro].' Mention at least three different formulas to set these conversion rates and explain their advantages/disadvantages. In each case, specify whether the formula is consistent with the Treaty language.

5.6 From the beginning of 1998, suppose the following scenario were to unfold with certainty:

(a) Only France, Germany, the Benelux countries, Ireland, Austria and Finland have been designated to launch on 1 January 1999 an irreversible single currency area, with all the convergence criteria clearly fulfilled.

(b) Italy, Spain and Portugal have been given informal guarantees that they will be allowed to join the initial monetary union in the year 2000, provided that they continue to respect the nominal Maastricht convergence criteria.

(c) On 1 January 1999, the closed ECU basket defined as the composition of twelve currencies will disappear with the new single currency (Euro) equal to one theoretical ECU.

(d) No asymmetric shocks will occur in the EU Member States between now and 1999; no ERM realignments will occur between now and 1999.

(e) Under ERM2, the Euro central rates of the currencies of Italy and the Iberian Member States will be equal to their current ECU central rates, with very narrow bands of fluctuation.

(f) The conversion rates between the FF, DM, ÖS, IRL, BFR, LFR, HFL, FMK and the Euro will be equal to their current ECU central rates.

Now answer the following questions:

(i) What would immediately happen to the interest rates between France and Germany? To the exchange rate between the French franc and the Deutsche mark?

(ii) Would the interest rates between Italy, Spain, Portugal and Germany immediately converge? Explain.

(iii) What would immediately occur to the spread between the market ECU exchange rate and theoretical ECU exchange rate? Explain.

(iv) What is the purpose of giving informal guarantees to Italy and the two Iberian Member States to become participating members of EMU in 2000 instead of allowing them to enter in 1999 with the first wave of the eight Member States?

Notes

INTRODUCTION: '. . . AN EVER CLOSER UNION'

1 An expression found in the preamble to the Treaties of Rome (1957) and repeated in the preamble to the Treaty on European Union (1992).

2 Charlemagne, recognized as an exceptional administrator who founded monasteries and schools, imposed in 794, after the military campaigns, a monetary union. Article 5 of the proceedings of the Council of Frankfurt reads as follows:

> As regards denarii [originally, an ancient roman coin] . . . you should be fully aware of our decree that everywhere, in every city and every trading-place, the new denarii are also to be legal tender and to be accepted by everybody. And if they bear the monogram of our name and are of pure silver and full weight, should anyone reject them, in any place, in any transaction of purchase or sale, he is to pay 15 solidi [roughly the price of a cartload of wheat].
>
> (From the *Economist*, August 14th 1993:44)

Other historical European monetary unions are described in Thiveaud (1989) and Olszak (1996).

3 The Oaths of Strasbourg are important in Continental European history to the extent that they formalize for the first time the official use of two different languages. The Oaths are available in both Vulgar Latin and Old High German in Nithard (1926: 102–108), who was a Carolingian historian whose mother was the daughter of Charlemagne. The original manuscript can be seen in the Bibliothèque Nationale (Paris).

4 **Jean Monnet** (1888–1979), originator of the Schuman Plan, was the first President of the High Authority (forerunner of the Commission) of the ECSC.

   Robert Schuman (1886–1963), born in Luxembourg and French Foreign Affairs Minister, is associated with the Schuman Plan proposed on 9 May 1950, the day which is now celebrated within the Union institutions as a holiday (Europe Day).

   Konrad Adenauer (1876–1967), Chancellor of the Federal Republic of Germany from 1949 to 1963, was an enthusiastic supporter of the Schuman Plan to integrate Europe within a federal structure.

   Alcide de Gasperi (1881–1954), Italian Prime Minister in the post-Second World War period, was a supporter of the federalist movement towards European integration led by Monnet and Schuman. In 1954, de Gasperi was elected President of the Common Assembly (forerunner of the European Parliament) of the ECSC.

5 In the preamble to the Treaty of Paris (1951) establishing the European Coal and Steel Community (ECSC). The complete citation is:

RESOLVED to substitute for age-old rivalries the merging of their essential interest; to create, by establishing an economic community, the basis for a broader and deeper community among peoples long divided by bloody conflicts; and to lay the foundations for institutions which will give direction to a destiny henceforward shared.

6　See Pisani-Ferry (1995) for a further elaboration of this point in the context of the construction of a Europe with a 'variable geometry'.

7　In January/February 1988, Ministers Balladur (1988) of France, Amato (1988) of Italy, and Genscher (1988) of Germany called for a strengthening of the EMS and the establishment of a European central bank.

8　By the beginning of 1997, the Greek Parliament had still not ratified this Convention.

9　For a concise history of the WEU, based on excerpts from published articles and original documents, see Dumoulin (1995).

10　With the victory of a Labour government in late 1996, Malta has withdrawn its application for EU membership.

1　EUROPEAN ECONOMIC AND MONETARY COOPERATION: 1958–78

1　In fact, in 1959 the IMF authorized margins of 2 percent on either side of each bilateral parity for cross-rates (the exchange rate between two non-US dollar currencies).

2　This is an average rate. For example, for the Italian lira, the margins were set at ±0.72 percent; for the Deutsche mark, at ±0.82 percent.

3　For a visual presentation of these concepts, see Nivollet (1980).

4　The suspension of the dollar's convertibility into gold transformed the international monetary system from an exchange rate system where the dollar was pegged and convertible to gold, and all other currencies were pegged to the dollar (thus, the so-called 'gold–dollar standard') into an exchange rate system pegged to the dollar.

5　On 18 December 1971, an agreement was reached at the Smithsonian Institution in Washington, DC on a realignment of exchange rates that included a commitment by the US authorities to recommend to Congress a 7.9 percent devaluation of the dollar – equivalent to raising the US official gold price from \$35 to \$38 per fine ounce. In addition, four other countries – Belgium, Germany, Japan and the Netherlands – agreed to revalue their currencies vis-à-vis gold by amounts ranging from 2.8 percent for the Belgian–Luxembourg franc and the Dutch guilder to 4.6 percent for the Deutsche mark and 7.7 percent for the yen. France and the United Kingdom simply accepted the proposed dollar devaluation, while Italy and Sweden proposed to devalue their currencies by 1 percent against gold. Switzerland decided to limit the further appreciation of the Swiss franc against the dollar to 6.4 percent. The Canadian dollar continued to float. As the United States was unable to devalue the dollar until Congressional action was taken, other countries intending to change their official gold parities did not do so at once. Instead they declared 'central' rates for their currencies against the dollar, equivalent to the proposed new parities, while countries maintaining their gold parities adopted 'middle' rates against the dollar.

6　However, the Benelux Member States (Belgium, Luxembourg and the Netherlands) had decided, as of August 1971, to maintain the fluctuations between their currencies within the 1.5 percent range on either side of their bilateral parity that had existed before the guilder began to float in May 1971. This meant intervening, i.e. buying one another's currency to the extent necessary in order to prevent the rate between the guilder and the Belgian–Luxembourg franc from moving at any given moment ('instantaneous spread') more than 1.5 percent away from the rate of 13.81 Belgian–Lux. francs to the guilder. This implied a maximum 'temporal spread' of 3 percent between these two currencies.

7   This system is described, with its origins, in Ansiaux (1972), Banque nationale de Belgique (1972), and Ansiaux et Dessart (1975).
8   Except for Italy which negotiated a temporary dispensation whereby the lira could be maintained within the 'snake' margins by carrying out interventions in dollars. This dispensation was in effect from June 1972 to December 1972.

2   EUROPEAN MONETARY SYSTEM (EMS): 1979–90

1   The EMCF used the EMUA as the unit of account from 1973 to 1978, and thereafter, the ECU.
2   Special Drawing Right (SDR): an international reserve asset initially created *ex nihilo* by the IMF in 1970. Initially and until 1 July 1974, the value of the SDR was set at 1 SDR = 0.88867088 gram of fine gold or 35 SDR = 1 ounce of fine gold.
3   We write 'in principle' because the methodology used by the Commission to calculate the quantity of each currency in the EUA basket is somewhat more indirect than the one indicated in the text. It uses the average value of the SDR relative to the Belgian franc over the period 28 March to 27 June 1974, along with the average exchange rate of each currency relative to the Belgian franc over the same period. For example, for the period 28 March–27 June 1974, the average value of the SDR = 45.8564 Belgian francs. The average exchange rate of the Belgian franc/French franc during the same period is 7.8440 Belgian francs. Therefore, the EUA basket should contain

$$0.195 \times (45.8564 \div 7.844) = 1.13998 \text{ French francs}$$

This number is different from the 1.15 French francs actually put in the basket. Two other minor adjustments are necessary to obtain the actual number of 1.15 French francs. See Lelart (1994:37) for details.
4   Following a decision of the Ecofin Council, the Commission calculated the EUA/ECU rates on the basis of the market exchange rates observed on 12 March 1979 at 11 a.m., not 2:30 p.m.
5   Since October 1988. Prior to that time period, the Commission used the exchange rates observed at 2:30 p.m., Brussels time.
6   As discussed in Chapter 5, by 1989 the outstanding value of bonds and interbank deposits denominated in ECUs became relatively important. Since the ECU interest rate on these assets (liabilities) is a weighted average of the interest rates prevailing on the corresponding assets denominated in currencies composing the ECU basket, it became important to determine the new composition of the ECU basket by limiting the distortions created on the private ECU market. This explains the *procedural* difference, described in note (b) of Table 2.2, followed by the Council in changing the composition of the ECU basket in 1989 vs 1984.
7   It should be emphasized that there are no physical transfers of gold and US dollars from the national central banks to the EMCF. They are simply bookkeeping entries.

8 For reasons given below, even those Community currencies not participating in the ERM have a 'notional' ECU central rate and therefore 'notional' bilateral central rates. Notional ECU central rates are also modified on the occasion of each currency realignment. The notional ECU central rate of the British pound was also modified outside of a parity realignment on three occasions in the 1980s (17 May 1983, 15 September 1985 and 21 September 1989) and on 8 October 1990 when Britain joined the ERM.

9 Even if the amount of funds available under the VSTF facility is said to be unlimited, this is not literally true, as explained in Chapter 4 with regard to the 1992 ERM crisis.

10 Since 15 May 1995, the European Monetary Institute, the precursor to the European central bank, took over the task performed by the BIS.

11 Since the Commission only calculates the ECU rate in terms of any currency once a day at 2:15 p.m., Brussels time, the Agreement of 13 March 1979 between the central banks of the Member States of the EEC laying down the operating procedures for the European Monetary System provides in Article 4 that '... for purposes of the operation of the indicator of divergence the ... value of the ECU in each currency shall be calculated by a uniform method as frequently as necessary [i.e., more than once a day, if necessary] and at least on the occasion of each daily concertation session among central banks.'

12 To determine whether the 'threshold of maximum divergence' of the ith currency in the narrow band is crossed, the ECU rate of the ith currency is adjusted for two reasons: (1) some currencies, such as the British pound, the Italian lira, the Spanish peseta, and the Portuguese escudo, have at various times been allowed to fluctuate in the wide band of ±6 percent and (2) some currencies, such as the British pound, the Italian lira, and the Greek drachma, do not participate in the ERM, but are part of the ECU basket. The adjusted ECU rate for the ith currency is calculated by assuming that any ECU currency in the wide band bilaterally deviating by more than ±2.25 percent is on the ±2.25 percent margin. The same assumption is made for any currency in the ECU basket not participating in the ERM but which has deviated from its notional bilateral central rates by more than ±2.25 percent against one or more currencies. These adjustments are made to neutralize the effects created by the fact that certain currencies in the ECU basket are granted 'special privileges'.

13 See previous note. In this case, the only required adjustment relates to the non-ERM currencies composing the ECU basket and which are deviating by more than ±6 percent from their notional bilateral central rates.

14 In this case (see above note), the only required adjustment relates to the non-ERM currencies composing the ECU basket and which are deviating by more than ±15 percent from their notional bilateral central rates.

3   FROM A CUSTOMS UNION TO THE SINGLE MARKET

1 The Single European Act (1986) refers to the goal of achieving a monetary union directly in the Preamble and indirectly in Article 102A.2:

● Preamble: 'Whereas at their Conference in Paris from 19 to 21 October 1972 the Heads of State or of Government approved the objective of the progressive realization of Economic and Monetary Union.'
● Article 102A.2: 'Insofar as further development in the field of economic and monetary policy necessitates institutional changes [e.g. establishing a European central bank], the provisions of Article 236 [re amendments to the Treaty] shall be applicable.'

4 THE MAASTRICHT ROAD TO A MONETARY UNION: 1989–99

1 Provided that short-term unemployment does not lead to long-term unemployable individuals, or what is known as 'hysteresis'.
2 Provided that there does not exist a perfect positive correlation between public deficits and private saving.
3 The Treaty on European Union (TEU) or 'Maastricht Treaty' (1992) is a long and complex document composed of 7 Titles (or divisions) with some 17 Protocols and 33 Declarations. Title I deals with the Common Provisions (Articles A–F: principles, institutional framework); Title II, sometimes referred to as the 'first pillar', deals with 86 provisions amending the Treaty of Rome establishing the European Economic Community (1957) and the Single European Act (1986); Title III deals with the provisions amending the Treaty establishing the European Coal and Steel Community (1951), which expires in 2002; Title IV deals with the provisions amending the Treaty establishing the European Atomic Energy Community (1957); Title V, sometimes referred to as the 'second pillar', deals with the provisions on a common foreign and security policy; Title VI, sometimes referred to as the 'third pillar', deals with provisions for cooperation in the fields of justice and home affairs; and finally, Title VII deals with the Final provisions (ratification, amending provisions, accession procedures).
4 For a snapshot view of various national positions taken by Member States in early 1991, see France 1991. In that progress report, presented to the French Senate, it is noteworthy to highlight three points:

- The German government, with the support of the Deutsche Bundesbank, wanted to introduce in the EMU section a provision that would have excluded realignments of ERM currencies from the start of Stage II (January 1994). Since this proposal could not 'pass', it introduced currency stability as one of the convergence criteria to meet for entry into Stage III.
- The German government, with the support of the Deutsche Bundesbank, wanted the decision to move to Stage III (the start of the monetary union) to be taken by unanimity. As explained below, the decision is to be taken by a qualified majority. However, on the basis of a ruling by the German federal constitutional court during the German ratification process of the Maastricht Treaty, the German Bundestag may, under certain circumstances, legislate that Germany may not join Stage III (see below).
- France, along with the Commission, wanted the European system of central banks, the European central bank, to be established at the start of Stage II. Germany wanted – and obtained – the European central bank to be established just a few months prior to the start of Stage III and to be operational only from the start of Stage III.

As indicated in Kenen (1995b: 1), other EMU drafts and in particular the Netherlands Draft of 28 October 1991, are cited by Gros and Thygesen (1992); Bini-Smaghi *et al.* (1994); and Italianer (1993).
5 Although numerous modifications and additions were made to the Delors Report in the Maastricht Treaty, the broad outline of the Report was retained. A summary of the Delors Report can be found in Ungerer *et al.* (1990: 40–42).
6 In accordance with Council Directive 88/361/EEC of 24 June 1988 for the implementation of Article 67 of the Treaty of Rome and as indicated in Chapter 3, Greece, Spain, Ireland and Portugal were granted a derogation with respect to the liberalization of capital movements. Moreover, this Directive contained procedures under which Member States could take

protective measures restricting certain capital movements between Member States and between Member States and third countries. These were permitted only when foreign exchange markets were exposed to short-term capital movements of exceptional magnitude, leading to serious disturbances in a Member State's monetary and exchange rate policies. The protective measures could not apply for more than six months. Effective 1 January 1994, in accordance with Article 73A of the Treaty on European Union and coinciding with the start of Stage II, these safeguard measures were repealed. However, they were retained in a modified procedure with respect to third countries.

7 Preamble to the Single European Act (1986): '. . . Whereas at their Conference in Paris from 19 to 21 October 1972 the Heads of State or of Government approved the objective of the progressive realization of economic and monetary union' (*Bulletin of the European Communities*: Supplement 2/86).

8 See the Introduction for more details.

9 For an entertaining but politically incorrect blow-by-blow account of the role and motivations of all the official decision-makers during this ERM crisis period, see Connolly's (1995) chapter 6, entitled 'Pricking the Bubble'. Connolly was, until the publication of his highly critical book of the ERM and EMU, head of the Commission unit responsible for monitoring and servicing the EMS.

10 Other proposals, such as a 'dash' to EMU, were suggested. These proposals are mentioned in Kenen (1995b: 164f.).

11 Pursuant to Article 104C(6) and on the basis of a Commission recommendation, the Council decided in September 1994 that excessive deficits existed in the following Member States: Belgium, Denmark, Germany, Greece, Spain, France, Italy, the Netherlands, Portugal and the United Kingdom, i.e. in all of the Member States of EUR12 with the exception of Luxembourg and Ireland. Then, on 7 November 1994 the Council, pursuant to Article 104C(7), adopted recommendations addressed to each of the above Member States urging them to take the appropriate measures to bring to an end the situation of an excessive public deficit (*Bulletin of the European Union*: 11/1994). The recommendations were not made public. By mid-1995, the three new Member States of the Union (Austria, Finland and Sweden) were added to the list of countries with an excessive deficit while Germany and Denmark were removed from that list. In mid-1996, Germany was placed back on the list of Member States with an excessive deficit.

12 Except by using the threat of cutting off access to the Cohesion Fund. At an Ecofin Council meeting of 10 July 1995, EU finance ministers, on a recommendation from the European Commission, *warned* Greece, Portugal and Spain that they risk losing access to the EU Cohesion Fund unless they curb their public deficits. The ministers wished to demonstrate that the Maastricht convergence criteria had 'teeth'. The Cohesion Fund is the seven-year (1993–99) ECU15,100 million aid programme set up in 1992 to help the four poorest EU Member States. The aid is mainly intended to fund environmental and transport infrastructure projects. The strengthening of economic and social cohesion is a necessary precondition for the establishment of economic and monetary union. Since the public deficit criterion means that these countries are going to have to impose very strict budgetary discipline, while at the same time bring their prosperity up to the Community average more swiftly, Brussels decided to finance public investment projects of these four Member States, provided they complied with the convergence programme.

13 A. Lamfalussy was the first President of the EMI for the period January 1994 to July 1997. W. Duisenberg, the former Governor of the De Nederlandsche Bank, was appointed to replace him effective July 1997.

14   As the Bundesbank and the German government like to emphasize, the inflation and interest rate criteria could be based on the single best-performing
Member State, e.g. Mr Tietmeyer, president of the Bundesbank: 'A currency
union must be oriented towards the best. It must strive for the gold medal,
not the bronze medal.' Or Mr Waigel, the finance minister: 'The [German]
citizen will receive a [new] currency that is at least as strong as the D-
mark'(*Financial Times*, 6 April 1995: 1).

15   The expression 'on its own initiative', which appears in Article 3 of the
Protocol on the convergence criteria referred to in Article 109J(1), may be
important at the time the final decision is taken as to which Member States
satisfy the 'convergence criteria'. In general, a realignment of bilateral central
rates in the EMS is undertaken following the request of one or more Member
States. The realignment must be unanimously approved by the Council
(Ecofin). For example, at the last realignment of 6 March 1995, requested by
Spain, Portugal was forced to accept a devaluation of the escudo against the
DM and the other 'hard' currencies in the ERM in the wake of the peseta
devaluation. Under the Maastricht Treaty, Portugal could reasonably argue
that this devaluation was not 'on its own initiative'.

16   The *Council meeting in the composition of Heads of State or Government* is
different from the European Council which brings together the Heads of State
or Government *and* the President of the Commission to 'provide the Union
with the necessary impetus for its development ...' (Article D of the
Maastricht Treaty). The European Council has no legal decision-making
power.

17   That Article reads as follows:

> The Council shall, acting unanimously on a proposal from the Commission
> and after consulting the European Parliament, the EMI or the ECB as the
> case may be, and the Committee referred to in Article 109c [the Monetary
> Committee], adopt appropriate provisions to lay down the details of the
> convergence criteria referred to in Article 109j of this Treaty, which shall
> then replace this Protocol.

18   Accordingly, up to two seats may not be filled at the time the initial monetary union is launched. This provision is stipulated to allow a large Member
State (e.g. Italy or Spain), who might be unable to join the first wave of countries composing the monetary union, to reserve a seat for itself on the
Executive Board when it joins the monetary union one or two years later.

19   The TEU and its Protocols do not define 'price stability'. In the literature, a
distinction is usually made between the goal of 'stable prices' and that of 'zero
inflation'. The unofficial Deutsche Bundesbank goal of 'price stability' is
defined as a target inflation rate of less than or equal to 2 percent. The EMI
(1995a: 35) defines price stability 'as the achievement of an inflation rate that
no longer distorts the saving and investment decisions of private agents'.

20   For the reader who may not be familiar with these monetary policy intru-
ments, the following summary, taken from the European Monetary Institute
(1995a: 123), is provided:

> Under systems of *compulsory reserves*, banks are required to keep a
> minimum amount of reserves in deposit accounts with the central bank,
> which may or may not be remunerated; these minimum reserves are usually
> calculated as a percentage of the banks' monetary liabilities. *Standing facil-
> ities* represent standing offers by central banks to engage in certain types
> of operations (discount, refinancing, acceptance of deposits) at the initiative
> of commercial banks, but at conditions pre-announced by the central bank;

access to these facilities by individual commercial banks may be subject to quotas. *Open market operations* are transactions carried out by the central bank at its own initiative with private market participants either to inject liquidity into or to absorb liquidity from the market; they may consist in either outright or reversed transactions, and may involve different types of financial assets (public debt, private paper, central bank paper and foreign exchange).

21 After the withdrawal of the pound sterling from the ERM in September 1992, the Conservative government in the United Kingdom argued that the pound sterling would never again participate in a currency band. The government argued that it is more important to have a monetary policy with a view to achieve an inflation rate within a defined target band before joining – if the United Kingdom so decides – the monetary union.

22 In 1995, a joint communiqué released by the German Finance Minister, Mr Theo Waigel, and the then French Finance Minister, Mr Edmond Alphandéry, stated that both Member States pledged to 'oppose vigorously any attempt aimed at bending these [fiscal] criteria' by other EU states (*Financial Times*, 22 March 1995: 14). Mr Wolfgang Schäuble, CDU/CSU member of the Bundestag and second-in-command to the German Chancellor Helmut Kohl, acknowledged publicly in March 1995 that the way the Maastricht convergence criteria are defined is somewhat ambiguous but added 'We are for a strict interpretation but not an excessive one' (*Financial Times*, 21 March 1995: 14). Since then, official declarations have underlined the need to respect strictly both the criteria and the timetable of the Treaty. At the European Council meeting of June 1995 held in Cannes, the Heads of State or Government declared that Stage III would begin, at the latest, on 1 January 1999. At an informal meeting in Valencia on 30 September 1995, the fifteen Ministers of Finance put much emphasis on the confirmation of the 1 January 1999, at the latest, as the date for the entry into force of Stage III and on the need for a strict interpretation of the convergence criteria to decide the Member States that will qualify to form the initial monetary union. The ministerial declaration was made in order to put to rest the suggestion by the then Italian Prime Minister, Mr Dini, that the start of Stage III should be delayed to allow Italy, a founding Member State of the European Union, to be among the first wave of states to form the monetary union. The tough German draft budget for 1997, with a then-planned deficit of 2.5 percent of GDP, placed France and others on the spot to target a 1997 deficit which meets the strict Maastricht criterion (*Financial Times*, 15 July 1996: 2). Moreover, at an Ecofin Council meeting of 3 June 1996 in the context of the annual excessive deficit procedure (Article 104C.6), the German Minister of Finance was the only one to vote against the recommendation of the Commission to declare that Denmark's public debt ratio of 71.9 percent in 1995 was approaching the 60 percent target at a satisfactory pace. Since the decision is taken by qualified majority, Denmark was declared to satisfy the Maastricht public finance ratios for calendar year 1995. But the German vote was not lost on how Germany might interpret the more important 1997 data in early 1998 when the Member States will be designated for the monetary union. Referring to the Maastricht convergence criteria and timetable, Klaus Kinkel, Germany's foreign affairs minister, declared in September 1996 that 'wobblers, delayers and vacillators should have no chance [to be among the first wave of countries forming the monetary union]' (*Financial Times*, 23 September 1996: 8). In mid-1997, with an expected shortfall of some DM18,000 million in tax revenues and higher than expected unemployment benefit expenditures for calendar year 1997, the

German government intends to use the surplus generated from a market revaluation of its gold and dollar reserves to hit the strict Maastricht public finance ratios of three percent for the deficit ratio and of sixty percent for the debt ratio (*Financial Times*, 16 May 1997: 1 and 17/18 May 1997: 1).

23 The Ricardian equivalence theorem states that the public sector's financing mix (taxes vs borrowing) for a given level of public expenditures will not change the level of *national* (public + private) saving. This suggests that the capital stock and output will not vary with the financing mix.

24 For examples of this recent literature on real convergence, see Eichengreen (1992), De Grauwe and Vanhaverbeke (1993) and De Grauwe (1994).

5   FROM THE ECU TO THE EURO

1 Although the ECU is specifically mentioned in the Treaty on European Union as the single currency of the monetary union, Germany launched in mid-1995 a campaign to change the name of the future single currency. From the German point of view, the ECU is synonymous with a 'weak' currency since the ECU declined by about 40 percent against the DM over the period 1979–95 (*Financial Times*, 25 May 1995: 1). Mr Waigel, the German minister of finance, suggested the name 'Euro' for the single currency, with the possibility that each Member State participating in the single currency area could add on one face of the banknotes the former name of its currency, e.g. Euro-franc, Euromark (*Le Monde*, 13 June 1995: 10). At the Madrid European Council meeting of December 1995, the Heads of State or Government agreed to name the single currency simply the 'Euro'.

2 The complete list may be found in a Commission 'Proposal for a Council Regulation (EC) on the consolidation of the existing Community legislation on the definition of the ECU following the entry into force of the Treaty on European Union' (COM(94) 140 final), submitted on 21 April 1994 to the Council and later adopted by the Council on 22 December 1994 (Regulation 3320/94/EC). The aim of this proposal is to give a definitional ruling for the ECU that would replace the wide variety of existing texts. Consequently, this proposal does not add anything new to the legislation in effect, but is a mere consolidation of the existing rules.

3 Although it is common knowledge that the choice of the term 'ECU' was based on the English acronym 'European Currency Unit' and on the French medieval coin, the Écu (Droulers 1990 and Belaubre 1986), it should be noted that the word 'ECU' in Community texts is not considered an acronym to be translated. By contrast, the EUA was an acronym translated into other Community languages: UCE in French and Italian; ERE in German, Dutch and Danish. At the Madrid European Council meeting of December 1995, the Heads of State or Government decided that the name 'ECU', which also appears in the Maastricht Treaty as the name of the future single currency, is only to be considered a generic term. This allowed them to adopt a new name, the 'Euro', for the single currency without amending the Treaty.

4 An 'ECU domestic bond' may be considered a misnomer as the ECU is not the legal tender of any country. However, the BIS defines such a category for certain ECU bonds issued in France, Greece, Italy, Spain, the United Kingdom and other EU states.

5 In this statement, risk is only defined in terms of 'interest rate risk'. A complete portfolio analysis combines interest rate risk and exchange rate risk. However, this requires the introduction of investors' consumption preferences for goods and services of the various countries.

6 The European Monetary Institute (1995a and 1996a) is given the responsibility of studying the technical questions relating to the design, manufacture and distribution of Euro banknotes. There is already an agreement between the EMI and the Ecofin Council to have seven different denominations of Euro banknotes: 5 ($\approx$\$5.75), 10, 20, 50, 100, 200 and 500 Euros. At the Dublin European Council meeting of December 1996, the EMI presented the features to be included in the design of the banknotes. Each denomination will depict one of seven different historical European architectural styles of gateways and windows on the obverse face and of bridges on the reverse face. The historical periods are Classical Greek, Roman, Gothic, Renaissance, Baroque, Rococo and Post-Modern (cf. Bank of England 1996: 63). The numerical denomination, the name of the currency (including the Greek variant), and the initials of the ECB in the five language variants will also be included on the banknote. Two options on the appearance of the Euro banknotes are retained: banknotes without any national differentiation and banknotes which include a limited national feature, occupying no more than 20 percent of the reverse face, but which are otherwise identical. The Governing Council of the ECB, which can only be established after the participating Member States of the monetary union have been designated, must decide on this latter remaining question. There is still no consensus on the production allocation of the banknotes between Member States. The question of the design and production of Euro coins (Eurocents) is examined by a group composed of members of each national Treasury department, which has jurisdiction in this matter. This group has decided that all coins will have one common side and one national side. The Mint Directors have also decided there will be coins with denominations of 1 ($\approx$1.15 US cent), 2, 5, 10, 20 and 50 cents and 1 and 2 Euros.

7 The banks and the retail sector have stressed that the precise date on which Euro banknotes and coins are introduced is very important for an orderly transition. The worst time would be at the beginning of 2002. The summer and autumn of 2001 are possible alternative dates depending on the availability of sufficient banknotes.

8 For more details, see Bank for International Settlements (1994b: Chapter VIII) and European Monetary Institute (1995c and 1996c).

9 The Green Paper (Commission of the European Communities 1995b: 61, para. 121) specifically mentions administrative fees for converting banknotes from one participating Member State to those of another. Assuming that France and Germany are part of the initial monetary zone, it is clear from the Green Paper that during the transition period French franc banknotes would not be legal tender on the German territory and vice versa.

10 Belgium is a case in point. With a projected debt to GDP ratio of 127 percent in 1997, more than two times greater than the Maastricht ceiling and the highest ratio among the fifteen EU Member States, it is sometimes questioned how the Heads of State or Government will be able to justify the acceptability of Belgium in the first wave of countries composing the monetary union and the rejection of Italy with a projected debt to GDP ratio of 123 percent. One possible explanation is that Belgium, unlike Italy, will have satisfied the Maastricht criterion of a public deficit to GDP ratio that is 'sustainably convergent'. The Belgian government was given the power to adopt its 1997 budget by decree to attain a public deficit of not more than three percent of GDP and the Commission forecasted in April 1997 that this ratio will decline to 2.3 percent for calendar year 1998. By contrast, the Italian government's deficit for 1997 was estimated by the Commission to be 3.2 percent of GDP, and more importantly, the Commission forecasted a public deficit to GDP ratio of 3.9 percent for 1998 on the basis of unchanged policies by the Italian government. Another

reason that may be invoked will be that the Belgian public debt cannot be a destabilizing factor in the new monetary union, given the relative size of Belgium's GDP, which is equivalent to about one-fifth of Italy's GDP.

11 Since late 1996, the *Financial Times* publishes each week, the 'J.P. Morgan Calculator' on the probabilities which the markets place on a country joining the single currency area. These probabilities are calculated from the interest rate swaps market. Investors use this market when they are receiving interest payments on an investment at a floating rate, but would prefer payments at a fixed rate, or vice versa. Following monetary union the 'swap rate' which investors pay to switch from floating to fixed rate payments will be the same for investments made in all the participating currencies because they will have been subsumed in the Euro. The probability which the markets place on France joining Germany in EMU (assuming that the monetary union is launched) can therefore be calculated by looking at the current difference between the French franc and Deutsche mark swap rate, and comparing it to the difference which one would expect to see if EMU were postponed indefinitely. This can be estimated by looking at the typical differences between swap rates for non-EMU currencies.

References

NOTES:

A summary of the Communications, Declarations, Resolutions, Directives, Regulations, Decisions of the Community [Union] may be found in the European Commission periodical entitled *Bulletin of the European Union [Communities]* (ten issues per year, plus supplements). The *Official Journal of the European Communities*, Series 'C' or 'L' (Luxembourg) carries the complete text.

The Treaties of the European Union may be found in an official publication entitled *European Union: Selected instruments taken from the Treaties*, Book I, Volume I: 'Treaty on European Union and Treaty establishing the European Community' (Luxembourg, 1995). It is customary to indicate in parentheses the year of the signature – not the year of ratification or of coming into force – of a treaty or its amendment. This practice is followed in this book. Another practice used here is to list publications of the Commission under the letter 'C', and not 'E', since the expression 'European Commission' is – officially – a misnomer.

Eurostat (Statistical Office of the European Communities, Luxembourg) publishes a wealth of statistics, which include general statistics, economy and finance, intra-community and external trade, population and social conditions, etc. These are now available in a comprehensive, user-friendly tool in the form of its Yearbook CD-ROM (ECU60). Details to order are provided on the Internet address http://europa.eu.int/eurostat.html

Amato, G. (1988) 'Un motore per lo Sme', *Il Sole 24 Ore* (Milan), 25 February.
Ansiaux, Baron (1972) 'Le Rétrécissement des marges de fluctuation entre les monnaies de la C.E.E. – Aspects et modalités techniques', *Revue Banque*, avril, no. 306: 321–330.
Ansiaux, Baron et Dessart, M. (1975) *Dossier pour L'Histoire de L'Europe Monétaire, 1958–1973*, Louvain: Vander.
Ardy, B. (1988) 'The national incidence of the European Community budget', *Journal of Common Market Studies*, Vol. 26, no. 4: 401–429.
Artus, P. and Lenoir, K. (1995) 'La monnaie unique: Les conséquences pour les marchés et les taux', *Revue Banque*, no. 559, mai: 32–35.
Balassa, B. (1961) *The Theory of Economic Integration*, Homewood, Ill.: Richard Irwin.
Ball, L. and Mankiw, N.G. (1995) 'What do budget deficits do?', National Bureau of Economic Research Working Paper 5263, Cambridge, Mass.
Balladur, E. (1988) 'Mémorandum sur la construction monétaire européenne', *ECU*, No. 3, March.

Bank for International Settlements (1992) 'Recent developments in the ECU financial markets' in *International Banking and Financial Market Developments*, February: 16–25, Basle.

Bank for International Settlements (1993) *Payment Systems in the Group of Ten Countries*, Prepared by the Committee on Payment and Settlement Systems of the central banks of the Group of Ten Countries, December, Basle.

Bank for International Settlements (1994a) *International Banking and Financial Market Developments*, May, Basle.

Bank for International Settlements (1994b) *64th Annual Report*, 13 June, Basle.

Bank of England (1996) *Practical Issues Arising from the Introduction of the Euro*, issue no. 3, 16 December, London.

Banking Federation of the European Union (1995) *Survey on the Introduction of the Single Currency: A First Contribution on the Practical Aspects*, March.

Banque nationale de Belgique (1972) 'Les marges de fluctuation entre monnaies Communautaires', *Bulletin d'information*, juillet-août: XI-XLI, Bruxelles [Article is not signed].

Belaubre, J. (1986) *Histoire numismatique et monétaire de la France médiévale (de la période carolingienne à Charles VIII)*, Paris: Le Léopard d'or.

Beuter, R. (1994) 'Germany and the ratification of the Maastricht Treaty' in F. Laursen and S. Vanhoonacker (eds) *The Ratification of the Maastricht Treaty*, pp. 87–112, Netherlands: Martinus Nijhoff Publishers for the European Institute of Public Administration.

Bini-Smaghi, L., Padoa-Schioppa, T. and Papadia, F. (1994) *The Transition to EMU in the Maastricht Treaty*, Essays in International Finance 194, Princeton: International Finance Section, Princeton University.

Bini-Smaghi, L. and Vori, S. (1993) 'Rating the EU as an optimal currency area', *Banca d'Italia Temi di Discussione*, no. 187, January.

Bossuat, G. (1994) *Les Fondateurs de l'Europe*, Paris: Éditions Bélin.

Central banks of the Member States of the European Economic Community (1972) 'Agreement of 10 April 1972 between the central banks of the Member States of the European Economic Community establishing a system for the narrowing of the margins of fluctuation between the currencies of the European Economic Community' [Basle Agreement also signed by the central banks of Denmark, Ireland and the United Kingdom], Basle, 10 April. This Agreement was amended on 8 July 1975.

Central banks of the Member States of the European Economic Community (1979) 'Agreement between the central banks of the Member States of the European Economic Committee laying down the operating procedures for the European Monetary System', Basle, 13 March. This Agreement was amended on 10 June 1985 and again on 10 November 1987 [Basle/Nyborg Agreement]. The complete amended text is reproduced in the *Compendium of Community Monetary Texts* compiled by the Monetary Committee, op. cit.

Chirac, J. (1995) 'Pour une Europe forte', *Revue des Affaires Européennes* (Paris), no. 1: 27–33.

Church, C.H. and Phinnemore, D. (1994) *European Union and European Community: A Handbook and Commentary on the Post-Maastricht Treaties*, London: Harvester Wheatsheaf.

Churchill, W.S. (1946) 'The tragedy of Europe' in R.R. James (ed.) *Winston S. Churchill: His Complete Speeches, 1897–1963*, Vol. VII, London: Chelsea House Publishers, 1974.

Colasanti, F. (1994) 'Economic policy co-ordinations in Stage II of Economic and Monetary Union', *ECU*, no. 27, II: 17–22.

Collignon, S. with Bofinger, P., Johnson, C., and de Maigret, B. (1994) *Europe's Monetary Future: Policy Options*, London: Pinter Publishers.

Collins, S. (1988) 'Inflation and the European Monetary System', in F. Giavazzi, S. Micossi and M. Miller (eds) *The European Monetary System*, Cambridge: Cambridge University Press.

Commission of the European Communities [Year] *ECU Markets Review*, Brussels: Directorate-General for Economic and Financial Affairs (DG II-D2-ECU), various issues.

Commission of the European Communities (1969) 'Memorandum on the coordination of economic and monetary policies [Barre Plan]' in *Bulletin of the European Communities*, Supplement, no. 3, Luxembourg: Office for Official Publications of the European Communities.

Commission of the European Communities (1970) 'A plan for the phases establishment of an economic and monetary union [Second Barre Plan]' in *Bulletin of the European Communities*, Supplement, no. 3, Luxembourg: Office for Official Publications of the European Communities.

Commission of the European Communities (1978) *Communication on the calculation of the equivalents of the ECU and of the European unit of account published by the Commission*, 28 December, Brussels. Also published in the *Official Journal of the European Communities*.

Commission of the European Communities (1979) 'European Monetary System: comments and documents' in *European Economy*, July, no. 3, Luxembourg: Office for Official Publications of the European Communities.

Commission of the European Communities (1982) 'Documents relating to the European Monetary System' in *European Economy*, July, no. 12, Luxembourg: Office for Official Publications of the European Communities.

Commission of the European Communities (1985) 'Completing the internal market', *White Paper* from the Commission to the European Council, Luxembourg: Office for Official Publications of the European Communities.

Commission of the European Communities (1987) *Green Paper* on the development of the common market for telecommunications services and equipment, Luxembourg: Office for Official Publications of the European Communities.

Commission of the European Communities (1988) 'The economics of 1992 – an assessment of the potential economic effects of completing the internal market of the European Community' in *European Economy*, March, no. 35, Luxembourg: Office for Official Publications of the European Communities.

Commission of the European Communities (1989a) 'Annual Economic Report, 1989–1990' in *European Economy*, November, no. 42, Luxembourg: Office for Official Publications of the European Communities.

Commission of the European Communities (1989b) *Report on economic and monetary union in the European Community* [Part 1 of the Delors Report], Luxembourg: Office for Official Publications of the European Communities.

Commission of the European Communities (1989c) *Collection of papers submitted to the Committee for the Study of Economic and Monetary Union* [Part 2 of the Delors Report], Luxembourg: Office for Official Publications of the European Communities.

Commission of the European Communities (1990a) *European Economy*, supplement A, March, Luxembourg: Office for Official Publications of the European Communities.

Commission of the European Communities (1990b) 'The impact of the internal market by industrial sector: the challenge for the Member States', *European Economy/Social Europe* (special edition), Luxembourg: Office for Official Publications of the European Communities.

Commission of the European Communities (1992) 'Removing legal obstacles to the use of the ECU', *White Paper* for the Council, 23 December, Brussels.

Commission of the European Communities (1993) *Data Banks on Companies Using the ECU*, Brussels: Directorate-General for Economic and Financial Affairs (DG II).

Commission of the European Communities (1994) 'Practical problems involved in introducing the ECU [Euro] as the European Union's single currency', *Memorandum*, April, Brussels.

Commission of the European Communities (1995a) 'Commission's recommendation for the broad guidelines of the economic policies of the Member States and the Community', *Document* COM(95) 228 final, 31 May, Luxembourg: Office for Official Publications of the European Communities.

Commission of the European Communities (1995b) 'One currency for Europe', *Green Paper* on the practical arrangements for the introduction of the single currency, 31 May, Luxembourg: Office for Official Publications of the European Communities.

Commission of the European Communities (1995c) *Vade-Mecum Budget 1995*, Luxembourg: Office for Official Publications of the European Communities.

Commission of the European Communities (1995d) *ECU Markets Review*, no. 9, June, Brussels: Directorate-General for Economic and Financial Affairs (DG II).

Commission of the European Communities (1996a) 'Economic forecasts of Spring 1996' in *The Economy of the Community in 1996–97*, Brussels: Directorate-General for Economic and Financial Affairs (DG II).

Commission of the European Communities (1996b) 'Commission's recommendation for the broad guidelines of the economic policies of the Member States and the Community', *Document* COM(96) 211 final, 15 May, Luxembourg: Office for the Official Publications of the European Communities.

Commission of the European Communities (1996c) 'Reinforcing political union and preparing for enlargement', *Opinion for the Intergovernmental Conference*, February, Luxembourg: Office for the Official Publications of the European Communities.

Commission of the European Communities (1996d) 'Secondary legislation for the introduction of the Euro and some provision relating to the introduction of the Euro: Proposal for a Council Regulation (EC)', *Communication* to the European Parliament, the Council and the European Monetary Institute, 16 October, Brussels, COM(96) 499 final.

Commission of the European Communities (1996e) 'Proposal for Council Regulations (EC) on the strengthening of the surveillance and coordination of budgetary positions and on speeding up and clarifying the implementation of the excessive deficit procedure', 16 October, Brussels, COM(96) 496 final.

Commission of the European Communities (1996f) 'Report on Convergence in the European Union in 1996', 6 November, Brussels, COM(96) 560 final.

Commission of the European Communities (1996g) 'The impact and effectiveness of the single market', *Communication* from the Commission to the European Parliament and the Council, 30 October, Brussels, COM(96) 520 final.

Commission of the European Communities (1997) 'Economic forecasts of spring 1997' in *The Economy of the Community in 1997–98*, Brussels: Directorate-General for Economic and Financial Affairs (DGII), April 23.

Committee of Governors of the Central Banks of the Member States of the EEC (1992a) 'Report of the Ad Hoc Working Group on EC payment systems', Basle.

Committee of Governors of the Central Banks of the Member States of the EEC (1992b) 'Recent developments in the use of the private ECU: a review of the issues', February, Basle.

Committee of Governors of the Central Banks of the Member States of the EEC (1993) 'The implications and lessons to be drawn from the recent exchange rate crisis', *Report* by the Committee of Governors, 21 April, Basle.

Connolly, B. (1995) *The Rotten Heart of Europe: The Dirty War for Europe's Money*, London: Faber & Faber.

Council-Commission of the European Communities (1970) 'Report to the Council and the Commission on the realisation by stages of Economic and Monetary Union in the Community [Werner Report]' (definitive text), October 1970 in *Bulletin of the European Communities*, Supplement, no. 11/1970, Luxembourg: Office for Official Publications of the European Communities.

Council of the European Union (1996a) 'Progress report by the Ecofin Council to the European Council on preparation for Stage 3 of EMU', 4 June, Brussels.

Council of the European Union (1996b) 'Conclusions of the informal Ecofin Council meeting of Dublin on 21 September', Brussels.

Davis, R.G. (1990) 'Intermediate targets and indicators for monetary policy: an introduction to the issues', *Quarterly Review*, Summer 1990: 71–82, New York: Federal Reserve Bank of New York.

De Grauwe, P. (1994) 'The need for real convergence in a monetary union', in C. Johnson and S. Collignon (eds) *The Monetary Economics of Europe: Causes of the EMS Crisis*, London: Pinter Publishers.

De Grauwe, P. (1995) 'Alternative strategies towards monetary union', *European Economic Review*, Vol. 39, no. 3–4: 483–491.

De Grauwe, P. and Vanhaverbeke, W. (1993) 'Is Europe an optimum currency area? Evidence from regional data', in P. Masson and M. Taylor (eds) *Policy Issues in the Operation of Currency Unions*, Cambridge: Cambridge University Press.

Deidda, M. (1993) 'Analysis of the behavior of the ECU: June 1992–April 1993', ref. II/416/93-EN, Brussels: EC Commission.

Denman, R. (1995) *Missed Chances*, London: Cassell.

De Pecunia. Review of the Center Ecu and European Monetary Integration Prospects (Acronym in French: CEPIME). Three issues a year. Brussels.

De Pecunia (1992) *Commercial Uses of the ECU: Transport and Communication Networks*, Vol. IV, no. 3, December.

De Pecunia (1994) *The ECU Revisited*, Vol. VI, no. 1, May.

Delors Report (1989). See Commission of the European Communities.

Deutsche Bundesbank [various years, t] *Annual Report [various years, t–1]*, Frankfurt am Main.

Deutschland (1994) 'Überlegungen zur europäischen Politik' [Reflections on European policy], *CDU/CSU-Fraktion* des Deutschen Bundestages, Position paper by K. Lamers and W. Schäuble, Bonn, 1 September. [This controversial paper was published in French in the *Revue des Affaires Européennes* (Paris), no. 1 (1995): 9–17.]

Deutschland (1995a) 'Die Europäische Union außen-und sicherheitspolitisch handlungsfähiger machen', Position paper by *CDU/CSU Fraktion* im Deutschen Bundestag, Berlin, 13 Juni.

Deutschland (1995b) 'Mehr europäische Rechtßtaatlichkeit' Position paper by *CDU/CSU Fraktion* im Deutschen Bundestag, Berlin, 13 Juni.

Dornbusch, R. (1976) 'Expectations and exchange rate dynamics', *Journal of Political Economy*, Vol. 84: 1161–1176.

Dornbusch, R. (1989) 'Europe 1992: macroeconomic implications', *Brookings Papers on Economic Activity*, Vol. 2: 341–362.

Droulers, F. (1990) *Histoire de l'Écu européen du Moyen Age à nos jours*, Lagny-sur-Marne: Éditeurs Aria Création et Rotopresse S. A.

Dumoulin, A. (1995) 'L'UEO [WEU] et la politique européenne de défense', *Problèmes Politiques et Sociaux*, no. 754, 8 septembre, Paris: La Documentation Française.

Ecu Banking Association (1995) *EBA Newsletter*, no. 3/95, July/September, Paris.
Ecu Newsletter [various years]. San Paolo Bank Holding SpA, Research and Strategy Unit, Galleria San Federico, Torino (Italy). Various issues.
Eichengreen, B. (1992) 'Is Europe an optimum currency area?', in S. Borner and H. Grubel (eds) *The European Community after 1992: Perspectives from the Outside*, London: Macmillan.
Eichengreen, B., von Hagen, J. and Harden, I. (1995) 'Hurdles too high', *Financial Times* (London), 28 November.
Emerson, E., Gros, D., Italianer, A., Pisani-Ferry, J., and Reichenbach, H. (1990) 'One market, one money: an evaluation of the potential benefits and costs of forming an economic and monetary union' in Commission of the European Communities, *European Economy*, no. 44, October, Luxembourg: Office for the Official Publications of the European Communities [also published as a book by Oxford University Press, 1992].
European Monetary Institute (1994) 'Recent developments in the use of the private ECU: statistical survey', *Foreign Exchange Policy Sub-Committee*, February, Frankfurt am Main.
European Monetary Institute (1995a) *Annual Report, 1994*, April, Frankfurt am Main.
European Monetary Institute (1995b) 'Developments in EU payment systems in 1994', *Report to the Council of the EMI*, Working Group on EU Payment Systems, February, Frankfurt am Main.
European Monetary Institute (1995c) 'The TARGET System (Trans-European Automated Real-Time Gross Settlement Express Transfer System, a payment system arrangement for Stage III of EMU)', *Report to the Council of the EMI*, Working Group on EU Payment Systems, May, Frankfurt am Main.
European Monetary Institute (1995d) 'The changeover to the single currency', November, Frankfurt am Main.
European Monetary Institute (1995e) 'Progress towards convergence', *Report* prepared in accordance with Article 7 of the EMI Statute, November, Frankfurt am Main.
European Monetary Institute (1996a) *Annual Report, 1995*, April, Frankfurt am Main.
European Monetary Institute (1996b) 'Recent developments in the use of the private ECU: statistical survey', *Foreign Exchange Policy Sub-Committee*, March, Frankfurt am Main.
European Monetary Institute (1996c) 'First progress report on the TARGET project', *Working Group on EU Payment Systems*, August, Frankfurt am Main.
European Monetary Institute (1996d) 'Progress towards convergence 1996', *Report*, November, Frankfurt am Main.
European Monetary Institute (1997a) *The Single Monetary Policy in Stage Three: Specification of the Operational Framework*, January, Frankfurt am Main.
European Monetary Institute (1997b) *Annual Report, 1996*, April, Frankfurt am Main.
Flam, H. (1992) 'Product markets and 1992: Full integration, large gains?', *Journal of Economic Perspectives*, Vol. 6 (4), Fall: 7–30.
France (1991) Sénat, *Rapport d'Information* sur 'l'état d'avancement de la conférence intergouvernementale sur l'Union économique et monétaire' submitted by Senator X. de Villepin on 4 avril, Paris: Palais du Luxembourg.
France (1996) Sénat, 'Rapport sur la Convention d'application de l'Accord de Schengen', *Report* requested by the Prime Minister and submitted by Senator P. Masson on 31 January, Paris: Palais du Luxembourg.
Fratianni, M. and von Hagen, J. (1990a) 'German dominance in the EMS: the empirical evidence', *Open Economies Review*, January.

Fratianni, M. and von Hagen, J. (1990b) 'The European Monetary System ten years after', *Carnegie Rochester Conference Series on Public Policy*, Spring.

Fratianni, M., von Hagen, J., and Waller, C. (1992) *The Maastricht Way to EMU*, Essays in International Finance no. 187, June, Princeton: International Finance Section, Princeton University Press.

Friedman, M. (1953) 'The case for flexible exchange rates', in M. Friedman (ed.), *Essays in Positive Economics*, Chicago: University of Chicago Press.

Genberg, H. (1989) 'Exchange rate management and macroeconomic policy: a national perspective', *Scandinavian Journal of Economics*, Vol. 91: 439–469.

Genscher, H.D. (1988) 'Memorandum für die Schaffung eines europäischen Währungsraumes und einer Europäischen Zentralbank', *Auszüge aus Presseartikeln*, Deutsche Bundesbank, 1 March.

German Banking Association (1996) *Guidelines for the Currency Changeover in Banks*, Köln. [This is a 600-page book ($660), addressed to German banks, containing a mass of details about getting ready for the Euro.]

Ghymers, C. (1995) 'La Coordination des politiques économiques dans la Communauté Européenne: Une évaluation en vue de la Conférence Intergouvernementale', *Revue du Marché commun et de l'Union européenne*, no. 385, février: 76–82.

Giavazzi, F. and Giovannini, A. (1989) *Limiting Exchange Rate Flexibility: The European Monetary System*, Cambridge, Mass. : MIT Press.

Giavazzi, F. and Pagano, M. (1988) 'The advantage of tying one's hands: EMS discipline and central bank credibility', *European Economic Review*, no. 32, June.

Giavazzi, F. and Pagano, M. (1995) 'Non-Keynesian effects of fiscal policy changes: international evidence and the Swedish experience', National Bureau of Economic Research Working Paper 5332, November, Cambridge, Mass.

Goldstein, M., Folkerts-Landau, D., Garber, P., Rojas-Suárez, L. and Spencer, M. (1993) 'International capital markets – Part I. Exchange rate management and international capital flows', *World Economic and Financial Surveys*, April, Washington, D.C.: International Monetary Fund.

Gros, D. and Thygesen, N. (1992) *European Monetary Integration: From the European Monetary System to European Monetary Union*, London: Longman.

Guilhaudis, J.F. (1993) *L'Europe en transition*, Paris: Montchrestien.

Hannoun, H. (1996) 'Passage à la monnaie unique', *Rapport* des Groupes de Travail de la Profession Bancaire, Paris: AFB diffusion, juillet.

International Monetary Fund (1984) 'Exchange rate volatility and world trade', *Occasional Paper*, no. 28, July, Washington, D.C.

International Monetary Fund (1996) *Annual Report, 1996*, Washington, D.C.

Issing, O. (1996) 'Europe: political union through common money?', *Occasional Paper* 98, London: The Institute of Economic Affairs.

Italianer, A. (1993) 'Mastering Maastricht: EMU issues and how they were settled', in K. Gretschmann (ed.) *Economic and Monetary Union: Implications for National Policy-Makers*, Amsterdam: European Institute of Public Administration.

Johnson, C. (1994) 'The UK and the Exchange Rate Mechanism', in C. Johnson and S. Collignon (eds) *The Monetary Economics of Europe: Causes of the EMS Crisis*, London: Pinter Publishers.

Jorion, P. (1986) 'The Ecu and efficient portfolio choice', in R. Levich and A. Sommariva (eds) *The Ecu Market: Current Developments and Future Prospects*, Lexington, Mass.: D.C. Heath.

Kant, I. (1795) *Zum ewigen Frieden* [Towards a Perpetual Peace], Stuggart: Philipp Reclam jun.

Kenen, P.B. (1969) 'The theory of optimum currency areas: an ecletic view' in R. A. Mundell and A.K. Swoboda (eds) *Monetary Problems of the International Economy*, Chicago: University of Chicago Press.

Kenen, P.B. (1992) 'EMU after Maastricht', *Occasional Paper*, no. 36, Washington, D.C.: Group of Thirty.

Kenen, P.B. (1995a) 'Capital controls, the EMS and EMU', *Economic Journal*, 105, January, 181–192.

Kenen, P.B. (1995b) *Economic and Monetary Union in Europe: Moving Beyond Maastricht*, Cambridge: Cambridge University Press.

Kremers, J.J.M. and Lane, T.D. (1990) 'Economic and monetary integration and the aggregate demand for money in the EMS', *IMF Staff Papers*, Vol. 37, no. 4, December [subsequent discussion in Vol. 39, no. 3, September 1992].

Krugman, P.R. (1991) *Geography and Trade*, Cambridge, Mass.: MIT Press.

Kydland, F.E. and Prescott, E.C. (1977) 'Rules rather than discretion: the inconsistency of optimal plans', *Journal of Political Economy*, Vol. 85, no. 3.

Lelart, M. (1988) 'L'ECU, monnaie de règlement', *Revue du Marché Commun*, no. 321, novembre: 526–531.

Lelart, M. (1994) *La Construction monétaire européenne*, Paris: Dunod.

Levich, R.M. (1987) 'The interbank Ecu market', in R.M. Levich (ed) *ECU: European Currency Unit*, London: Euromoney Publications PLC.

Levitt, M. (ed.) (1992) 'Preparation of business for a single European currency', *De Pecunia* (Brussels), June, Special Issue.

Maas, C. (1995a) 'The preparation of the changeover to the single European currency (interim report)', compiled by the *Expert Group* on the changeover to the single currency and submitted to the European Commission 20 January 1995. [The 'Progress Report' was submitted to the Commission on 10 May 1995.]

Maas, C. (1995b) 'L'introduction de la monnaie unique: analyse des aspects pratiques', *Revue des Affaires Européennes* (Paris), no. 4: 37–47.

Masera, R. (1986) 'An increasing role for the Ecu: a character in search of a script', in R. Levich and A. Sommariva (eds) *The Ecu Market: Current Developments and Future Prospects*, Lexington, Mass.: D. C. Heath.

Masson, P.R. and Symansky, S. (1992) 'Evaluating the EMS and EMU using stochastic simulations: some issues', in R. Barrel and J. Whitley (eds) *Macroeconomic Policy Coordination in Europe: The ERM and Monetary Union*, London: Sage Publications for the National Institute of Economic and Social Research.

Mastropasqua, C., Micossi, S., and Rinaldi, R. (1988) 'Interventions, sterilizations, and monetary policy', in F. Giavazzi, S. Micossi and M. Miller (eds) *The European Monetary System*, Cambridge: Cambridge University Press.

Mélitz, J. (1988) 'Monetary discipline, Germany and the European Monetary System', in F. Giavazzi, S. Micossi and M. Miller (eds) *The European Monetary System*, Cambridge: Cambridge University Press.

Micosi, S. (1985) 'The intervention and financing mechanism of the EMS and the role of the ECU', *Quarterly Review*, December: 327–345, Milano: Banca Nazionale del Lavoro.

Monetary Committee of the European Community (1989) *Compendium of Community Monetary Texts*, Luxembourg: Office for the Official Publications of the European Communities.

Moore, L. (1994) 'The economic analysis of preferential trading areas', in M.J. Artis and N. Lee (eds) *The Economics of the European Union, Policy and Analysis*, Oxford: Oxford University Press, Ch. 3.

Moulin, A.M. (1992) 'Le droit monétaire et les paiements en écus', *Bulletin trimestriel*, décembre, no. 84: 85–98, Paris: Banque de France.

Mundell, R.A. (1961) 'The theory of optimum currency area', *American Economic Review*, September: 657–665.

Nguyen, K. (1995) 'La phase de passage à la monnaie unique et les risques d'instabilité', *Lettre de conjoncture de la BNP*, octobre–novembre, Paris [reprinted in *Problèmes Économiques*, no. 2454, 10 janvier 1996, Paris: La Documentation Française].

Nithard (1926) *Histoire des Fils de Louis le Pieux*, Edited and translated by Lauer, Paris: Société d'Édition Les Belles Lettres. [Louis the Pious was the son of Charlemagne and the father of Charles II, Louis the German and Lothaire. Nithard was a historian of the Carolingian period. His mother, Berthe, was a daughter of Charlemagne.]

Nivollet, A.E. (1980) 'Le "Serpent" monétaire Européen', *Cahiers Français*, mai-juin, no. 196: 15–18. Paris: Documentation Française. [This article was originally published in the issue of mars-avril 1972, no. 153 and revised in the issue of juillet-août 1974.]

Nurske, R. (1944) *International Currency Experience*, Geneva: League of Nations.

Olszak, N. (1996) *Histoire des unions monétaires*, collection 'Que sais-je?', Paris: Presses Universitaires de France.

Organisation for Economic Cooperation and Development (1992) *Quarterly data disquettes*, Paris.

Padoa-Schioppa, T. (1988) 'The European Monetary System: a long-term view', in F. Giavazzi, S. Micossi and M. Miller (eds) *The European Monetary System*, Cambridge: Cambridge University Press.

Papadia, F. and Saccomanni, F. (1994) 'From the Werner Plan to the Maastricht Treaty: Europe's stubborn quest for monetary union', in A. Steinherr (ed.) *Thirty Years of European Monetary Integration from the Werner Plan to EMU*, Harlow, Essex: Longman Group Limited.

Patat, J. P. (1994) 'Le rôle des banques centrales dans le processus d'union monétaire', *Bulletin*, Supplément 'Études', 4e trimestre: 21–26, Paris: Banque de France.

Peck, M. (1989) 'Industrial organization and the gain from Europe 1992', *Brookings Papers on Economic Activity*, Vol. 2: 277–299.

Pisani-Ferry, J. (1994) 'Union monétaire et convergence: qu'avons-nous appris? *Document de travail* no. 94-14, décembre, Paris: Centre d'Études Prospectives et d'Informations Internationales.

Pisani-Ferry, J. (1995) 'L'Europe à géometrie variable: une analyse économique', *Politique étrangère*, été [summer].

Pöhl, K. O. (1990) Interview with *The Times*, London, 26 June [In answer to a speech given on 20 June by the then Chancellor of the Exchequer John Major, who addressed the German Industry Forum in London. This speech is a short version of the Treasury papers (United Kingdom 1990 and 1991).]

Pringle, R. (ed.) (1992) 'The currency crisis: a seven part special feature', *Central Banking*, Vol. 3, no. 2, autumn: 12–21.

Rambure, D. (1987) 'The ECU clearing and payments system' in R. M. Levich (ed.) *ECU: European Currency Unit*, pp. 35–36, London: Euromoney Publications.

Rey, J. J. (1982) 'Some comments on the merits and limits of the indicator of divergence of the European Monetary System', *Revue Banque*, no. 1: 3–15.

Rosenblatt, J. K. (1978) 'Separate agricultural units of account: an essential factor in EC farm policy', *Survey*, 20 November: 361–364, Washington, D.C.: International Monetary Fund.

Rosenblatt, J., Mayer, T., Bartholdy, K., Demekas, D., Gupta, S. and Lipschitz, L. (1988) 'The Commom Agricultural Policy of the European Community: principles and consequences', *Occasional Paper*, no. 62: November, Washington, D.C.: International Monetary Fund.

Saint-Simon, C.-H. de (1814) 'De la réorganisation de la société européenne' in *Oeuvres de Claude-Henri de Saint-Simon*, Tome I, Paris: Éditions Anthropos, 1966.

Salop, J. (1981) 'The divergence indicator: a technical note', *Staff Papers*, Vol. 28, December: 682–697, Washington, D.C.: International Monetary Fund.

Sardelis, C. (1993) 'Targeting a European Monetary aggregate: review of current issues', *Economic Papers*, July, no. 102, Brussels: Commission of the European Communities (DG II).

Schlesinger, H. (1997) 'The passage to the Euro', *Report*, Centre for European Policy Studies, Brussels.

Servais, D. (1991) 'The single financial market', *Document* of the Commission of the European Communities, Luxembourg: Office for Official Publications of the European Communities.

Spaventa, L. (1982) 'Algebraic properties and economic properties of the "Indicator of Divergence" in the European Monetary System', in R. Cooper et al. (eds) *The International Monetary System under Flexible Exchange Rates – Essays in Honor of Robert Triffin*, Cambridge, Mass.: Ballinger.

Steinherr, A. (1994) 'Excerpts from the judgement by the German constitutional court of 1993 regarding the Maastricht Treaty', in A. Steinherr (ed.) *Thirty Years of European Monetary Integration from the Werner Plan to EMU*, Harlow, Essex: Longman Group Limited.

Sweden (1994) Utrikesdepartmentet, *Sveriges Medlemskap I Den Europenska Unionen*, Ds 1994. 48, pp. 209–210, Stockholm.

Taylor, C. (1995) *EMU 2000? Prospects for European Monetary Union*, London: Royal Institute for International Affairs.

Thiveaud, J.M. (1989) 'L'Union latine: Europe, monnaie, et toile d'araignée', *Revue d'Économie financière*, 8/9, mars–juin: 19–26.

Thygesen, N. (1989) 'A European central banking system: some analytical and operational considerations (October 1988)' in Commission of the European Communities (1989c) op. cit., pp. 157–176.

Ungerer, H., Hauvonen, J. J., Lopez-Claros, A. and Mayer, T. (1990) 'The European Monetary System: developments and perspectives', *Occasional Paper*, no. 73, November, Washington, D. C.: International Monetary Fund.

United Kingdom (1989a) House of Commons, *Hansard*, Vol. 155, no. 32, 12 and 29 June, London: HMSO. [Remarks on the Delors Report by Nigel Lawson, Chancellor of the Exchequer.]

United Kingdom (1989b) Treasury, *An Evolutionary Approach to Economic and Monetary Union*, November, London: HMSO.

United Kingdom (1990) 'The UK proposals for a European Monetary Fund and a 'hard ECU': making progress towards economic and monetary union in Europe', HM Treasury *Bulletin*, 22 October, London: HMSO.

United Kingdom (1991) Treasury, *Economic and Monetary Union Beyond Stage I: Possible Treaty Provisions and Statute for a European Monetary Fund*, Proposals by the UK Government, January, London: HMSO.

United Kingdom (1996) Foreign and Commonwealth Office, *A Partnership of Nations: The British Approach to the European Union Intergovernmental Conference 1996*, March, London: HMSO.

Valéry, P. (1957) *Oeuvres complètes*, Paris: Gallimard.

Viner, J. (1950) *The Customs Union Issue*, New York: Carnegie Endownment for International Peace.

Vissol, T. (1989) 'La révision du panier de l'Ecu en juin–septembre 1989 et ses enseignements', *ECU*, no. 9: 8–16.

Vissol, T. (1994) 'L'ECU dans la phase de transition vers l'UEM', *Revue du Marché Commun et de L'Union Européenne*, no. 380, juillet–août: 425–436.

Werner Report (1970) See Council-Commission of the European Communities.

Westendorp, C. (1995) 'Progress Report' from the Chairman of the *Reflection Group* on the 1996 Intergovernmental Conference, Madrid: mimeo, 1 September.

Williamson, J. and Henning, C.R. (1994) 'Managing the monetary system', in
P. Kenen (ed.) *Managing the World Economy: Fifty Years after Bretton Woods*,
Washington, D.C.: Institute for International Economics.

World Trade Organization (1996) *WTO Focus*, Newsletter, May, Geneva.

Ypersele (van), J. and with the collaboration of Koeune, J. C. (1989) *Le système
monétaire européen: origines, fonctionnement et perspectives*, 3rd edition,
Luxembourg: Office for Official Publications of the European Communities.
[The second edition published in 1985 was translated into English.]

Index